CCNA™ For Dummies®

Cheat Sheet

OSI Reference Model layers

Layer	Name
7	Application
6	Presentation
5	Session
4	Transport
3	Network
2	Data Link
1	Physical

Protocols by OSI Layer

OSI Layer	Protocols, coding, conversions
Application	Telnet, FTP, SMTP
Presentation	ASCII, EBCDIC, JPEG, GIF, encryption
Session	RPC, ZIP, SCP, SQL, NFS
Transport	TCP, NBP, UDP
Network	IP, ICMP, BGP, OSPF, RIP
Data Link	MAC, LLC, Frame Relay, LAPB, PPP
Physical	Ethernet, Token Ring, HSSI, 802.3

Five steps of data encapsulation

1. User information is converted into data
2. Data is converted into segments
3. Segments are converted into packets (or datagrams)
4. Packets (or datagrams) are converted into frames
5. Frames are converted into bits

IP address classes

Class	Range	Default Subnet Mask
A	0 – 127	255.0.0.0
B	128 – 191	255.255.0.0
C	192 – 223	255.255.255.0

Switching types

- **Cut-through:** Reads only destination address before forwarding frame
- **Store and forward:** Reads entire frame before forwarding it on

ISDN terminal equipment types

Terminal equipment type	Description
TE1	ISDN standard terminal equipment
TE2	Before ISDN standards, requires terminal adapter (TA)

ISDN reference points

Reference point	Used between
R	Non-ISDN ports and TA (terminal adapter)
S	User terminals and NT2 devices
T	NT1 and NT2 devices
U	NT1 devices and terminators

Common well-known port assignments

Port Number	Assignment
20	FTP data transfer
25	SMTP (Simple Mail Transfer Protocol)
53	DNS (Domain Name System)
80	HTTP (Hypertext Transfer Protocol)
110	POP3 (Post Office Protocol)

ISDN Lines

ISDN each a (144Kb

ISDN P channe

D1119529

CCNA™ For Dummies®

Cheat Sheet

Common router commands

Command	Action
ipx routing	Turns on IPX routing
ipx network 1000 encapsulation novell-ether	Configures ipx network with ASN and frame type
conf t	Configure terminal
line vty 0 4	Configure virtual terminal lines beginning with 0 and ending with 4
enable password	Assign password
banner motd #	Create message of the day banner which shows during login
hostname Dummies	Assigns name to router
CTRL+A	Beginning of line
CTRL+P	Previous line
show history	Display console command history
startup-config	Configuration files stored in NVRAM
running-config	Configuration files stored in RAM
copy tftp run	Copies from TFTP server to RAM
router rip	Turns on RIP routing
access-list 15 permit 168.123.23.0 0..0.0.255	Permits actions from all hosts on this network
int e0	Ethernet interface 0
int s0.2	Subinterface 2 on serial interface 0

LAN Switching Basics

LAN Segmentation breaks up collision domains by creating more segments with fewer workstations in each segment. A LAN can be segmented with a bridge, switch, or router.

Bridges operate at the Data Link layer (Layer 2) and examine the MAC (Media Access Control) address of a frame and then forward the frame if it is not a local address. Bridges forward multicast messages.

Routers operate at the Network layer (Layer 3) and examine the network address of a packet and forward the packet using the best available route. Multiple active paths can exist to a destination.

VLAN (Virtual LAN) is a switch port that has been assigned to be of a different subnetwork.

Novell IPX Frame Types

Novell	Cisco
Ethernet_802.2	sap
Ethernet_802.3	novell-ether (default)
Ethernet_snap	snap
Ethernet_II	arpa

Hungry Minds™

For Dummies®: Bestselling Book Series for Beginners

TM

BESTSELLING BOOK SERIES

References for the Rest of Us! ®

Are you intimidated and confused by computers? Do you find that traditional manuals are overloaded with technical details you'll never use? Do your friends and family always call you to fix simple problems on their PCs? Then the For Dummies® computer book series from Hungry Minds, Inc. is for you.

For Dummies books are written for those frustrated computer users who know they aren't really dumb but find that PC hardware, software, and indeed the unique vocabulary of computing make them feel helpless. For Dummies books use a lighthearted approach, a down-to-earth style, and even cartoons and humorous icons to dispel computer novices' fears and build their confidence. Lighthearted but not lightweight, these books are a perfect survival guide for anyone forced to use a computer.

Already, millions of satisfied readers agree. They have made For Dummies books the #1 introductory level computer book series and have written asking for more. So, if you're looking for the most fun and easy way to learn about computers, look to For Dummies books to give you a helping hand.

Hungry Minds™

1/01

CCNA™
FOR
DUMMIES®

CCNA™ FOR DUMMIES®

by Ron Gilster,
Jeff Bienvenu,
and Kevin Ulstad

Hungry Minds™

Best-Selling Books • Digital Downloads • e-Books • Answer Networks • e-Newsletters • Branded Web Sites • e-Learning

New York, NY ◆ Cleveland, OH ◆ Indianapolis, IN

CCNA™ For Dummies®

Published by
Hungry Minds, Inc.
909 Third Avenue
New York, NY 10022
www.hungryminds.com
www.dummies.com

Library of Congress Catalog Card No.: 99-69383

ISBN: 0-7645-0690-0

Printed in the United States of America

10 9 8 7 6 5

1B/QU/QW/QR/IN

Distributed in the United States by Hungry Minds, Inc.

Distributed by CDG Books Canada Inc. for Canada; by Transworld Publishers Limited in the United Kingdom; by IDG Norge Books for Norway; by IDG Sweden Books for Sweden; by IDG Books Australia Publishing Corporation Pty. Ltd. for Australia and New Zealand; by TransQuest Publishers Pte Ltd. for Singapore, Malaysia, Thailand, Indonesia, and Hong Kong; by Gotop Information Inc. for Taiwan; by ICG Muse, Inc. for Japan; by Intersoft for South Africa; by Eyrolles for France; by International Thomson Publishing for Germany, Austria and Switzerland; by Distribuidora Cuspide for Argentina; by LR International for Brazil; by Galileo Libros for Chile; by Ediciones ZETA S.C.R. Ltda. for Peru; by WS Computer Publishing Corporation, Inc., for the Philippines; by Contemporanea de Ediciones for Venezuela; by Express Computer Distributors for the Caribbean and West Indies; by Micronesia Media Distributor, Inc. for Micronesia; by Chips Computadoras S.A. de C.V. for Mexico; by Editorial Norma de Panama S.A. for Panama; by American Bookshops for Finland.

For general information on Hungry Minds' products and services please contact our Customer Care Department within the U.S. at 800-762-2974, outside the U.S. at 317-572-3993 or fax 317-572-4002.

For sales inquiries and reseller information, including discounts, premium and bulk quantity sales, and foreign-language translations, please contact our Customer Care Department at 800-434-3422, fax 317-572-4002, or write to Hungry Minds, Inc., Attn: Customer Care Department, 10475 Crosspoint Boulevard, Indianapolis, IN 46256.

For information on licensing foreign or domestic rights, please contact our Sub-Rights Customer Care Department at 212-884-5000.

For information on using Hungry Minds' products and services in the classroom or for ordering examination copies, please contact our Educational Sales Department at 800-434-2086 or fax 317-572-4005.

For press review copies, author interviews, or other publicity information, please contact our Public Relations Department at 317-572-3168 or fax 317-572-4168.

For authorization to photocopy items for corporate, personal, or educational use, please contact Copyright Clearance Center, 222 Rosewood Drive, Danvers, MA 01923, or fax 978-750-4470.

Hungry Minds™ is a trademark of Hungry Minds, Inc.

About the Authors

Ron Gilster (i-Net+, Network+, A+, CCSE, MBA, and AAGG) has been involved with networking and internetworking since 1993 as a trainer, teacher, developer, merchant, and end user. He has more than 33 years of total computing experience, including more than 13 years involved with the networking of computers. Ron is employed by HighSpeed.Com, a leading LMDS, DSL, and broadband communications company and ISP, where he is responsible for the internal and external networking infrastructure of the corporation, including VPN, telephony, intranet, extranet, and Internet operations. He is the author of *A+ Certification For Dummies*, *Network+ Certification For Dummies,* and *i-Net+ Certification For Dummies,* plus several books on networking, the Internet, computer and information literacy, and programming.

Jeff Bienvenu (CCNA, Network+) has worked with Cisco networking hardware for more than three years, with experience managing the networks for a Cisco Regional Networking Academy and now as the Information Technology Administrator at HighSpeed.Com's corporate offices.

Kevin Ulstad (CCNA, Network+, A+) is currently a regional account executive for HighSpeed.Com. His recent experience includes stints as the LAN administrator for that company's local area networks.

Dedication

Ron Gilster: For Diane . . . and the hardworking, dedicated students, readers, and co-workers trying to better their lives, further their careers, or pursue their dreams through technical and career certification — may you achieve your goals. Best of luck!

Jeff Bienvenu: To Krisann, for her support, love and friendship. To Michaelle and Marcus, who have blossomed despite being burdened with me as their father. And to Dylan, for putting up with me though he would rather not.

Kevin Ulstad: I dedicate this book to Ron Gilster, for inviting me to be a member of the writing team and for his help and guidance; to Ciaran Bloomer, my first Cisco instructor, for turning me on to Cisco equipment; and to my wife, Linda, and children Heather, Megan, Ashlie, and Andrew, for providing me the support at home that allowed me to learn this field in the first place and to spend the time to help write this book. To all of you, my sincere thanks.

Authors' Acknowledgments

We would like to thank the wonderful folks at IDG Books who helped to get this book published, especially Joyce Pepple, Nate Holdread, Christine Berman, Carmen Krikorian, Megan Decraene, James Sample and the virtual cast of tens who work behind the scenes to shield us from the cold, cruel, technical part of the process. And to Brenda Cox and the Technical Support crew for their continued support to our valued readers.

Special thanks to Ciaran Bloomer for the superb technical editing job he provided.

Publisher's Acknowledgments

We're proud of this book; please send us your comments through our Online Registration Form located at www.dummies.com.

Some of the people who helped bring this book to market include the following:

Acquisitions, Editorial, and Media Development

Project Editor: Nate Holdread

Acquisitions Editor: Joyce Pepple

Copy Editor: Christine Berman

Proof Editor: Teresa Artman

Technical Editor: Ciaran Bloomer

Media Development Editors: Marita Ellixson, Megan Decraene

Associate Permissions Editor: Carmen Krikorian

Media Development Coordinator: Eddie Kominowski

Editorial Manager: Leah P. Cameron

Media Development Manager: Heather Heath Dismore

Editorial Assistant: Beth Parlon

Production

Project Coordinators: E. Shawn Aylsworth, Emily Perkins

Layout and Graphics: Karl Brandt, Beth Brooks, Joe Bucki, Matt Coleman Tracy K. Oliver, Jill Piscitelli, Brent Savage, Brian Torwelle, Erin Zeltner

Proofreaders: Laura Albert, Corey Bowen, Christine Sabooni, Charles Spencer

Indexer: Christine Spina Karpeles

Special Help
Amanda M. Foxworth, Production Services

General and Administrative

Hungry Minds, Inc.: John Kilcullen, CEO; Bill Barry, President and COO; John Ball, Executive VP, Operations & Administration; John Harris, CFO

Hungry Minds Technology Publishing Group: Richard Swadley, Senior Vice President and Publisher; Mary Bednarek, Vice President and Publisher, Networking and Certification; Walter R. Bruce III, Vice President and Publisher, General User and Design Professional; Joseph Wikert, Vice President and Publisher, Programming; Mary C. Corder, Editorial Director, Branded Technology Editorial; Andy Cummings, Publishing Director, General User and Design Professional; Barry Pruett, Publishing Director, Visual

Hungry Minds Manufacturing: Ivor Parker, Vice President, Manufacturing

Hungry Minds Marketing: John Helmus, Assistant Vice President, Director of Marketing

Hungry Minds Production for Branded Press: Debbie Stailey, Production Director

Hungry Minds Sales: Roland Elgey, Senior Vice President, Sales and Marketing; Michael Violano, Vice President, International Sales and Sub Rights

◆

The publisher would like to give special thanks to Patrick J. McGovern, without whom this book would not have been possible.

◆

Contents at a Glance

Cartoons at a Glance

By Rich Tennant

page 9

"If it works, it works. I've just never seen network cabling connected with Chinese handcuffs before."

page 185

page 33

page 263

page 305

page 319

page 111

Fax: 978-546-7747
E-mail: richtennant@the5thwave.com
World Wide Web: www.the5thwave.com

Table of Contents

Introduction

● ●

*I*f you have purchased or are considering purchasing this book, you most likely fit into one of the following categories:

- ✔ You know how valuable CCNA Certification is to a networking professional's career and advancement.
- ✔ You're wondering just what CCNA Certification is all about.
- ✔ You think that reading this book may be a fun, entertaining way to learn about the networking and internetworking with Cisco Systems, Inc. routers and switches.
- ✔ You love all *For Dummies* books and wait impatiently for each new one to come out.
- ✔ You're a big fan of anything Cisco and just can't get enough of it.

Well, if your situation fits any of these scenarios, this is the book for you!

If you're already aware of the CCNA Certification program and you're just looking for an excellent study aid, you can skip the next few sections of this introduction in which we do our best to convince you that this is the book you're looking for, mainly because it is (the book, that is). However, if you don't have the foggiest idea just what CCNA Certification is or how to prepare for it, read on!

Why Use This Book?

In what began as a way to ensure that its resellers could also properly support its products, Cisco Systems, Inc. developed what has become the most sought after and prestigious networking certification series available. To hold any Cisco certification indicates that you know your stuff regarding networking at a certain level. The exams developed to screen certification candidates are rigorous and downright hard. The result is that even the most knowledgeable and experienced Cisco networking professional needs at least a little help getting ready for the CCNA exam. The sole purpose of this book is to help you to shorten your preparation time for the CCNA exam.

As with all other *For Dummies* books, this book is a no-nonsense reference and study guide. It focuses on the areas that are likely to be on the exam, plus it provides a little background information here and there to help you understand some of the more complex concepts and technologies. This book presents the facts, concepts, processes, and applications included on the exams in step-by-step lists, tables, and figures without long explanations. The book focuses on preparing you for the CCNA exams, not on showing off our obviously extensive and impressive knowledge of networking and its related technologies (nor our modesty, I might add).

In developing this book, we made two groups of assumptions:

✔ You have an entry-level knowledge of networking, routers, bridges, switches, and other networking components, as well as a fundamental knowledge of electronics, computers, software, protocols, and troubleshooting procedures, and you only need a review and study guide for the exam.

✔ You have some experience with Cisco hardware and its integration into networking environments, but you need a refresher on the basics along with a review and study guide for the exam.

If our assumptions in either case suit your needs, then this is the book for you!

Using This Book

This book is organized so that you can study a specific area without wading through stuff you may already know. I recommend that you skim the whole book at least once, noting the points raised at the icons. For your last-minute cram before the exam, each part and chapter of the book is independent and can be studied in any order without confusing yourself.

Each chapter also includes a pre-test (Quick Assessment quiz) and post-test (Prep Test questions) to help you determine where your knowledge is weak and where you need to continue studying. The following sections tell you what we've included between the covers of this book:

Part I: The Basics

Part I provides some general information about taking the exam, an overview of the topic areas you should study, and a primer of the terms and concepts you must know for the CCNA exam. This includes an overview of the CCNA exam, its objectives and benefits, how to arrange to take the test, and some general tips on what to study and how to get ready for the test.

Part II: The OSI Reference Model

Part II provides you with a review of the OSI Reference model and the related fundamentals and background information you should know for the exam. This includes a look at the four layers of this model that are emphasized on the test.

Part III: Routers

Part III deals with the heart of the CCNA exam — routers. The exam concentrates on routers, their configuration, commands, and protocols. This may be the most important section of the book, not that the others are unimportant, but in the sense that the CCNA is actually the routing and switching exam, this part of the book represents at least half of what you should know.

Part IV: Network Protocols

Part IV has everything you need to know about the internetworking, including the infamous subnetting. Also included in this part are reviews on network (IP) addressing; the frames, protocols, and functions of TCP/IP; and security issues of the internetworked environment.

Part V: LANs and WANs

As its name implies, this part of the book covers the concepts and technologies used to organize networked resources into networks in local areas as well as wide areas. Although not obvious from the name, the use of switching systems is the focus in this part of the book. The CCNA exam focuses on routing and switching. This part covers the use of switches in a network and how they can be used to segment a LAN. The link types that can be used to create a WAN are also covered.

Part VI: The Part of Tens

This section provides additional motivation and study guides to help get you ready for the test, with advice about how to be sure that you're ready to take the test on Test Day and ten great Web sites where you can find study aids.

Part VII: Appendixes

This section gives you even more practice test questions, with ten sample test questions on each domain, as well as information about what's on the CD in the back of this book and how to use the CD.

What's on the CD

The CD-ROM included in this book contains a variety of study aids and practice tests to help you prepare for the CCNA exam. In addition, the QuickLearn game is on the CD-ROM to provide you with an easy, fun way to study. A few links to the Web sites of companies with training sites and sample copies of their wares are also on the CD.

Studying Chapters

CCNA For Dummies is a self-paced method of preparing for the exam. You don't have to guess what to study; every chapter that covers exam objectives guides you with

- ✓ Preview questions
- ✓ Detailed coverage
- ✓ Review questions

This step-by-step structure identifies what you need to study, gives you all the facts, and rechecks what you know. Here's how it works.

First page

Each chapter starts with a preview of what's to come, including

- ✓ Exam objectives
- ✓ Study subjects

Not sure that you know all about the objectives and the subjects in a chapter? Keep going.

Quick Assessment questions

At the beginning of each chapter, you find a brief self-assessment test that helps you gauge your current knowledge of the topics that chapter covers. Take this test to determine which areas you already understand as well as to determine the areas that you need to focus on most.

 ✔ If you're in a hurry, just study the sections for the questions you answered incorrectly.

 ✔ If you answered every question correctly, jump to the end of the chapter and try the practice exam questions to double-check your knowledge.

Study subjects

When you're studying a chapter, carefully read through it just like any book. Each subject is introduced — very briefly — and then you discover what you need to know for the exam.

As you study, special features show you how to apply everything in the chapter to the exam.

Labs

Labs are included throughout the book to step you through some of the processes you need to know for the exam, such as installation or configuration of a particular component. Here's an example of a lab included later in the book:

Lab 17-1   Configuring a Frame Relay Interface on a Cisco Router

1. Select the interface to be configured.

```
CCNA_for_Dummies(config)#int s0
```

   This command selects serial interface 0.

2. Enter the configuration mode for that interface.

3. Configure a network-layer address.

4. Select the encapsulation type cisco or ietf (cisco is the default).

```
Router(config-if)#encapsulation frame-relay [cisco|ietf]
```

5. Specify the LMI type (Cisco IOS 11.1 and earlier)

```
Router(config-if)#frame-relay lmi-type {ansi|cisco|q933i}
```

Tables

Sometimes, you need just the facts. In such cases, tables are a simple way to present everything at a glance.

Table 4-1	The IEEE 802 Standards	
Subcommittee	*Subject*	*Description*
802.1	Internetworking/	Defines routing, bridging, LAN Protocols and inter network communications
802.2	Logical Link Control (LLC)	Allows Network layer protocols to link to Physical layer and MAC sublayer protocols
802.3	Ethernet	*THE* Ethernet standard; defines CSMA/CD
802.5	Token Ring	Defines logical ring topology, media, and interfaces
802.12	High-speed networks	Defines 100 Mbps technologies

Prep Tests

The Prep Tests at the end of each chapter gauge your understanding of the entire chapter's content. These Prep Test questions are structured in the same manner as those you may see on your exam, so be sure to try your hand at these sample questions. If you have difficulties with any questions on the Prep Test, review the corresponding section within the chapter.

Icons Used in This Book

Time Shaver icons point out tips that can help you manage and save time while studying or taking the exam.

Instant Answer icons highlight information to help you recognize correct and incorrect exam answers.

Remember icons point out general information and subjects that you should know and understand for the test. While the information may not appear directly on the exam, it provides you with information you need to identify the correct response.

Tip icons flag information that can come in extra-handy during the testing process. You may want to take notes on these tidbits!

Feedback

We'd like to hear from you. If an area of the test isn't covered as well as it should be, or if we've provided more coverage than you think is warranted about a particular topic, please let us know. Your feedback is solicited and welcome. You can send e-mail to us at the following e-mail addresses:

Ron Gilster: rgilster@hscis.net

Jeff Bienvenu: bienvenu@innw.net

Kevin Ulstad: kulstad@highspeed.com

Part I
The Basics

The 5th Wave   By Rich Tennant

"BETTER CALL MIS AND TELL THEM ONE OF OUR NETWORKS HAS GONE BAD."

In this part . . .

You've decided you want to become CCNA certified and let the world know how much you know about local area networks, wide area networks, routing, switching, the OSI Model, TCP/IP, and internetworking. So where do you start? In this part of the book, we give you the particulars about the test, how to schedule the test, where to go, and what to do.

The CCNA exam covers just about everything you need to know about setting up, configuring, installing, administering, and maintaining a network using Cisco hardware and software. You won't find questions on general computing and technical basics, however; you know the bits and bytes and how data moves over wires and between computers. The CCNA exam makes the assumption that if you don't already know this stuff, you won't understand most of the questions on the test to begin with, so why bother? However, you had better know the ins and outs of configuring a router and connecting it into a network.

The CCNA exams are strictly pass-fail. If you get 755 of the total 1000 points possible, you pass. If you don't, well, you don't. It's that simple. Let us be your guide on what you should study for the test. And, oh yes — best of luck!

Chapter 1

The CCNA Examination

*R*egardless of the motives Cisco Systems, Inc. had in developing its Career Certifications, the certification exams included in this program have become desired, sought after, and required stepping stones in the career plans of many networking professionals. It matters not that Cisco may have had a built-in audience of technical professionals loyal to its particular line of hardware, because even without this army, Cisco has earned one of the largest market shares in internetworking hardware.

As you prepare yourself to join the ranks of professional networkers proudly wearing their Certified Cisco Networking Associate (CCNA) honors, as we have, you're most likely doing so to start your career, further your career, or re-engage your career. Where certifications like A+ concentrate on hardware issues, and Network+ and MCSE primarily focus on software issues, the CCNA exam deals with the software and functional issues of networking hardware in the focus of the internetwork. The CCNA certification is an earned honor that says to the world, and especially employers, that this person really knows his internetworking stuff, including routers, switches, bridges, and how they can be combined to provide the best possible networking environment for a given situation.

The CCNA exam transcends any particular operating system or computer manufacturer because Cisco hardware works with nearly every computing environment in use. If it can be networked, Cisco equipment will network it, and your CCNA certification says you are the person to build that network!

This book has one purpose and one purpose only — to prepare you for the CCNA exam. It is focused on what you need to know about taking the test, the testing experience, and the knowledge you need to pass the exam. After that has happened, and we know it will, we wish you all the success that comes with your CCNA certification.

A Little Background about the CCNA Exam

Cisco Systems, Inc. sponsors a complete hierarchy of career certifications that center on its routing, switching, LAN, and WAN products. Because Cisco Systems is the leading internetworking company in the world, it's only natural that certification on its equipment and software is a valuable credential for a networking professional.

What's included in CCNA certification?

The CCNA (Certified Cisco Networking Associate) exam fulfills only one step along the Cisco Network Support certification track, which is designed for professionals working directly with Cisco-based networks. This certification focuses on LAN and WAN routers and LAN switches.

Earning CCNA certification tells the world, and more importantly employers, that you're able to:

- Configure and implement networks to improve such operational areas as bandwidth, response times, reliability, and quality of service
- Configure and implement simple routed and switched networks
- Make improvements to networks that improve performance and provide for increased network security
- Configure and install an intranet locally or globally
- Analyze a variety of network performance issues and suggest appropriate application-oriented solutions

Who should get CCNA certification?

Cisco's target audience includes:

- The technical support staff of their resale channel partners
- Working networking professionals
- Graduates of the Cisco Regional and Local Networking Academy program
- Someone trying to break into the networking field

Is CCNA related to other certifications?

The CCNA certification is only one of several career certifications sponsored by Cisco Systems, Inc. Depending on the track, network support or network design, CCNA may be the first or second step on the certification track.

The ultimate goal of anyone getting Cisco certification should be the CCIE (Cisco Certified Internetworking Engineer) certification. This is the ultimate badge of honor in networking. But, because of the rigor of the CCIE exam, which draws equally on real-world, hands-on experience and the technical specifications of the gamut of Cisco Systems' hardware and software, you should work your way up to it.

Without getting too confusing, there are two tracks for Cisco certification: Routing and Switching and WAN Switching. As a matter of fact, there's a new CCNA exam just for WAN switching. It is called CCNA–WAN Switching.

This book is focused on the CCNA 2.0 (640-507) exam. The CCNA exam is strictly a routing and switching test, but it can be used for either the network support or the network design certification tracks.

In the network support specialization, the focus is on installation, configuration, and operation of routed and switched networks. These are networks that use LAN and WAN routing and switching. The test sequence used in this specialization starts with the CCNA exam, moves on to the CCNP (Cisco Certified Network Professional), and finally, the CCIE exam.

In the network design specialization, the focus shifts to the design of networks at the component level to perform simple and complex network routing and switching. The test sequence for the network design emphasis starts with the CCDA (Cisco Certified Design Associate), proceeds to the CCNA, and finally to the CCDP (Cisco Certified Design Professional).

So, depending on your ultimate goal, whether it be a designer of highly technical networks or as a builder of the same, the CCNA is a key step in either career path.

The Cisco Networking Academy program

The CNA (Cisco Networking Academy) program is a partnership developed by Cisco with high schools, community colleges, and colleges and universities around the world to provide a head start program to high school and college level students toward certifications.

The current academy program consists of four semesters that prepare students through a series of online and hands-on lessons and labs with the skills and knowledge they need to pass the CCNA exam. If you're new to Cisco networking, you may want to investigate whether this program is available in your area. If you're a graduate of a local networking academy, you know first-hand about the fine quality of this forward-looking program and its curriculum.

Why Get CCNA Certification?

That's a good question. And just where CCNA fits into the mix of certifications and resume alphabet soup is another good question. One thing for certain is that certification of any kind is fast becoming the minimum requirement for nearly all IT and Internet-related jobs, and it's not unusual for a network administration job to list the CCNA as a minimum requirement. Cisco Systems views CCNA as an excellent entry-level certification that should qualify the holder for a position as a networking technician on a routed or switched network.

Is CCNA better than Network+, or any of the MCSE certifications? It isn't necessarily better, and, in fact, it may be harder, but it's really just different. CCNA certification says something completely different about its holder than any of the other certifications, but then that's the point. The networking world is well aware of the CCNA exam and it's a widely recognized and respected certification.

What the CCNA Exam Covers

The CCNA exam consists of 78 to 81 questions, depending on which of the rotating test versions you're lucky enough to draw. The exam covers seven specific knowledge areas of internetworking technologies, as listed in Table 1-1. Some knowledge areas are emphasized more than others, as indicated by the percentage each represents of the whole test, and accordingly the number of questions also varies with the emphasis.

Table 1-1 describes the seven major knowledge areas of the CCNA exam, the topics included in each of the major areas, and the percentage of the total test each area represents.

Table 1-1	CCNA Exam Subject Areas	
Knowledge Area	*Approximate Percentage of Exam*	*Topic*
OSI Reference	30 %	The layers of the OSI model
Connection-oriented and connectionless network services		

Knowledge Area	Approximate Percentage of Exam	Topic
Data link and network addresses		
Reasons for a layered model		
The five steps of data encapsulation		
Flow control and three methods used in networking		
The OSI Network layer and how a router performs its functions		
WAN Protocols	10 %	Frame Relay, ISDN/LAPD, HDLC, and PPP
Frame Relay terms and features		
Configuring Frame Relay LMIs, maps, and subinterfaces		
Monitoring Frame Relay operations in a router		
PPP operations and WAN data encapsulation		
ISDN networking		
ISDN protocols, groups, reference points, and channels		
Cisco's implementation of ISDN BRI		
IOS	10 %	
User and privileged mode logins		
Context-sensitive help facilities		
The command history and editing		
Router elements (RAM, ROM, CDP, show)		
Managing configuration from the privileged exec mode		
Router passwords, identification, and banner		
Cisco IOS commands used for router startup		
Using the setup command to create an initial configuration		
Managing configuration files		
Loading software from: flash memory, TFTP server, or ROM		
Maintaining the Cisco IOS software image		
Preparing an initial router configuration and enabling IP		

(continued)

Table 1-1 *(continued)*

Knowledge Area	Approximate Percentage of Exam	Topic
Network Protocols	5 %	
Novell IPX operations		
Network addressing		
IP address classes and subnetting		
Configuring and verifying IP addresses		
IPX addresses and encapsulation types		
Enabling Novell IPX protocols and interfaces		
TCP/IP Transport- and Network-layer protocols		
ICMP operations		
IPX access lists and SAP filters		
Routing	20 %	
RIP routing protocol		
IGRP routing protocol		
Separate and integrated multiprotocol routing		
Issues from topology changes		
Segmenting a network with a router		
Network Security	5 %	
Standard and extended access lists		
Access list operations on a router		
LAN Switching	20 %	
LAN segmentation with bridges, routers, and switches		
Name and describe two switching methods		
Full- and half-duplex Ethernet operations		
Network congestion on Ethernet networks		
Fast Ethernet		
Cut-through and store-and-forward LAN switching		

Knowledge Area	Approximate Percentage of Exam	Topic
Spanning Tree Protocol		
Virtual LANs		
MAC addresses		

OSI Reference Model

A major part of the CCNA exam focuses on your knowledge of the OSI Reference Model and its seven-layer approach to network activities, functions, data formats, and communications. Of course, there is more emphasis in those layers of the model that deal with routing and routers, but every layer in the reference model is included on the exam. As you prepare for the exam, be sure this is an area you know and understand in detail.

WAN protocols

Routers are more often used to connect local area networks (LANs) to other networks than as an interior device on a single network. Because of this, the protocols used to carry data and control signals over wide area networks also have an emphasis on the CCNA exam. This part of the test focuses on Frame Relay, X.25, and point-to-point protocols, along with ISDN services.

Cisco IOS commands

The commands used to configure and monitor router activities play a key part in the everyday life of a CCNA. For that reason, the CCNA exam includes a number of questions on the configuration modes used for the various commands and the methods and sources used to load and back up the IOS software and the router's configuration.

Network protocols

Cisco routers must be able to interface with network protocols to properly interact with a network. On the CCNA exam, Ethernet and TCP/IP protocols are the primary focus reflecting the most popular network architectures in use in the real world. You need to know which network protocols are used on which layers of the OSI model and when and how the IP and IPX protocol suites are applied.

Routing

You must know the difference between a routed protocol and a routing protocol, including some examples and configuration methods. Internetworking issues are also included in this portion of the exam.

Network security

This section of the CCNA exam is concerned with passwords, encryption, and access lists implemented on the router, including how access lists are configured and operate under either IP or IPX protocol suites.

LAN switching

The other emphasis on the CCNA exam, beyond routing, is switching. One of the major emphasis areas of this section of the exam is LAN segmentation, including its benefits and how it is accomplished with routers, bridges, and switches.

Cisco career certification and survey

On the test you will be given a confidentiality statement that you must agree with to take the exam, some information on Cisco career certification, and a short survey about Cisco certifications. You will get a zero percent score for these items on the score sheet, but don't worry, they don't count against you.

Taking (And Passing) the Exam

The exam is online and interactive. It's well designed and provides you with every possible opportunity to pass. Questions are presented one at a time on the screen in an easy-to-read format with online help always available as you navigate the exam. Unfortunately, there is no subject-matter help available on the test. The exam doesn't exactly set out to trick you, but some questions include false information just to see if you really know your stuff. Contrary to what you may have heard or believe about this exam, Cisco wants you to pass the CCNA exam, but only if you have the knowledge required.

One new wrinkle on the CCNA that was implemented late in 1999 is that after you have answered a question, you cannot go back to review it. In fact, the questions aren't numbered, other than which number of the total 79 to 81 questions each one represents. So, answer each question carefully and don't click the Next button until you're sure of your answer(s).

To become CCNA certified, you need to get at least a 82.8% on the CCNA examination. Actually, the CCNA is scored on a point system, and you need to get 822 of the 1,000 points available, or you need to get roughly 53 of the 65 questions correct. Or, to look at it another way, you can miss, incorrectly interpret, misconstrue, or choke on no more than 20 questions if you want to pass.

You have 90 minutes to complete the test, which allows you plenty of time to work through the entire test as well as review your answers. However, you also must understand that when time is up, the test is over! Bam, zoom, no last-minute guesses — over; done; fini! So, watch the time carefully.

One other thing about taking the test. The physical setup of the testing facility varies from site to site. You find test centers in training companies, community colleges, universities, and the like. Regardless of how the testing center is organized, you are assigned to a single specific computer workstation to take the test. You're not allowed to take breaks, talk to anyone, or get up and move around. Many test centers have open microphones and video cameras in the room to monitor the test-takers. This is intended to prevent somebody from cheating or disturbing other test-takers. As strict as this sounds, your best bet is to forget about it and plan on sitting at your workstation for the duration, quietly taking your exam. Just watch how much coffee you drink right before the test!

Preparing for the Exam

You're already well on your way to CCNA success by reading this book. Use the Quick Assessment quizzes at the beginning of each chapter to identify the areas you need to study the most. In addition to this book (if you really think you need it), many excellent resources are available to help you prepare for the exam. I list some of the better World Wide Web and other resources at the end of this chapter, on the CD, and in the Part of Tens.

What's the best way to prepare for the CCNA exam? It all depends on you. Gilster's Law on Test Preparation is: You never can tell, and it all depends. You need to find the tools that work best for you. If you have a good deal of experience with networks and Cisco gear, you may only need to bone up in certain areas. If you're new to all of this, you should seek out as many sample tests as possible and keep taking them until you pass consistently. The sample test I include in Appendix A and those on the CD shouldn't be the only sample tests you use if you're fairly inexperienced, or even if you have loads of experience for that matter. A number of interactive study aids are available, some for purchase and some free to download. (See Chapter 18.)

Each chapter of this book contains tables and bulleted lists of the items you need to commit to memory for the test. Use these for general study as well as a last-minute review. Use the questions at the end of each chapter to test your general knowledge of the chapter contents and when necessary, review the section referenced in the answer for additional study. Sample test questions are also available in Appendix A and on the CD. In every case, we list where in the book you can find more information on an answer.

You really need to know the protocols, services, and functions that operate on each layer of the OSI model, physical and network addressing, network address subnetting, router configuration, and the basic commands of a router and their use. Use the test percentages shown in Table 1-1 as a gauge of how you should spend your time preparing for the test. Concentrate on the areas in which your knowledge is limited or where you don't have much experience. By all means, review everything you can, more than once, and take as many sample tests as possible.

Your chances of passing the exam and getting certified are better if you have experience with Cisco hardware and software implemented in a local area network. Your chances improve if your experience also includes wide area networks and diverse routing and switching situations. However, it's not required, only recommended.

Signing up to Take the Exam

The CCNA examination is conducted by Sylvan Prometric testing centers in more than 700 locations worldwide. To schedule an appointment to take the test in the United States or Canada, call Sylvan Prometric at 1-800-829-NETS (1-800-829-6387). You can also register online on the Sylvan Prometrics Web site at www.2test.com. For information on registering to take the CCNA exam in a country outside the United States or Canada, visit www.2test.com. Be sure to mention that you want to take the Cisco CCNA 1.0, exam #640-507.

Call at least two days before your desired test date, and the friendly and knowledgeable testing counselor will help you set a date, time, and location that's convenient for you. The test is not given at specific times or dates. You pick the date, time, and place. Some testing sites aren't available every day of the week, or even every month of the year, and some offer testing during only certain hours of the day. So the earlier you contact them, the better. I recommend calling Sylvan Prometric as soon as you think you're entering the final stages of your exam preparation.

Sylvan Prometric helps you find a testing center near your home or in the vacation spot you want to visit. When you schedule your test, you must either give them your credit card information or you can mail them a check or money order (not a great option if you're in a hurry), but they won't confirm your test date until after they receive the check.

How Much Does It Cost?

The cost of the CCNA exam is $100 (U.S. dollars) in the United States and Canada. The cost ranges from $150 (USD) to $300 (USD) in other countries. Sylvan Prometric accepts all generally accepted credit cards, but you can make other payment arrangements with them if needed, but before you can take the test, you must be paid in full.

World Wide Web Sites to Help You

Here are some URLs that have free information, sample tests, or products to help you prepare for the CCNA exam:

```
www.cramsession.com/cramsession/cisco/ccna/
http://welcome.to/ccna
www.mentorlabs.com/vlab/access
www.masontech.com
www.lilligren.com/cisco/leeccna.htm
www.henninger.net/ccna/
http://207.212.98.71/html/CCNA.htm
www.learntosubnet.com/
www.cisco-resellers.com/ccnaprep.htm
```

Where to Go from Here

If you're really committed to earning your CCNA certification, you are indeed certifiable. My advice is to use the study tool or tools that best suit your study habits and the time available. Don't be too cocky or overly confident about this test. Even if you've worked with networks, routers, switches, and the Internet most of your adult life, you probably haven't had the opportunity to work with every type of network in every situation. If you have, you can probably skip this test and go straight to the CCIE exams. But, some review can't hurt. Remember that the exam includes questions about commonly used terminology, practices, components, and protocols, along with questions about little-known facts on obscure services, devices or activities — an obvious attempt to separate the truly worthy from the pretenders.

When you request a test date from the nice helpers at Sylvan Prometric, give yourself time to study, if only for a couple of days. At the price of this test, you can probably afford the time much more than the cost of retaking the test or the humiliation that will surely be heaped on you by your coworkers and alleged friends should you not pass.

A Little Luck Never Hurts

I know I speak for the entire *For Dummies* team when I wish you the very best luck on the CCNA exam. And we'll be the first to congratulate you on earning your CCNA certification!

Chapter 2

The Language of the CCNA Exam

· ·

· ·

*N*etworking, especially the subset of networking that involves routing and switching using Cisco Systems, Inc. equipment and software, has a language all its own. In fact, most of this book is dedicated to teaching you first the language of the CCNA's world, along with the tools of the trade. However, in this chapter, we want to provide you with an overview of the terminology and concepts that are fundamental to all of networking, including Cisco networks.

Laying Out the Network Topology

Topology is the physical layout of the computer, other nodes and cabling of the network. For the exam, you're expected to know the most common types of network topologies.

Please accept our topologies

Local area networks are constructed in a physical layout form that best suits the network's location, the building, and where its nodes are located. Most LANs are laid out in a general shape and pattern that facilitates the connection of workstations and other devices to the network. This general shape and pattern is referred to as the network's topology.

There are four general network topologies:

▸ **Bus:** Nodes are connected to a central cable, called a backbone, which runs the length of the network. See Figure 2-1.

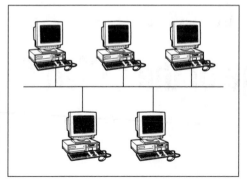

✔ **Ring:** The primary network cable is installed as a loop, or ring, and the workstations are attached to the primary cable at points on the ring. See Figure 2-2.

✔ **Star:** Each workstation connects directly to the central server with its own cable, creating a starburstlike pattern.

✔ **Mesh:** Each workstation connects directly to the server and all other workstations, creating a mess, I mean, mesh of network connections. This topology is not very common actually, but it is mentioned on the test.

Mixed topologies

The star topology is more commonly used today to cluster workstations on bus or ring networks. This creates hybrid or mixed topologies, such as the star-bus and the star-ring (also called the ringed-star):

✔ **Star-bus:** A very common implementation for Ethernet networks. A hub or switch is used as the central or clustering device that is then attached to the network backbone (see Figure 2-3). This is the most common topology of Ethernet networks.

✔ **Star-ring:** Used with ring (Token Ring) networks. A special type of hub, called a multistation access unit (MSAU), is used to cluster workstations and to connect to the next MSAU on the network to complete the ring. Instead of using a pure ring structure, the star-ring is the most common form of ring networks.

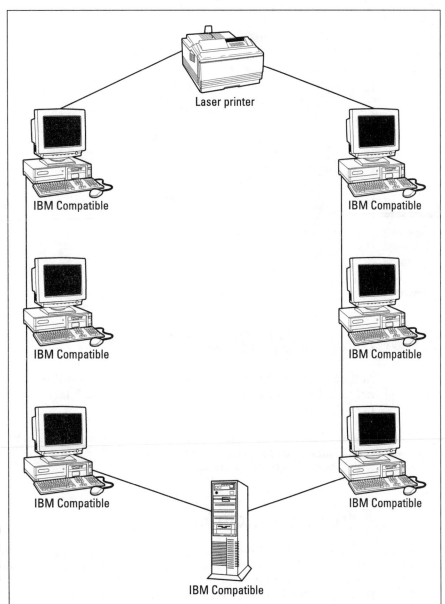

Figure 2-2:
A ring
network
topology.

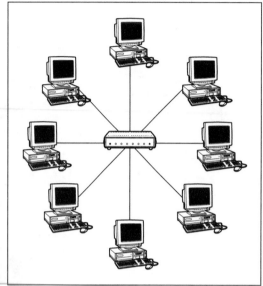

Figure 2-3:
A star-bus
network
topology.

Applying LAN Technologies

Although Chapter 4 provides a more detailed overview of specific LAN technologies, here's some background information on LAN technologies that you need to know for the test.

The three most common LAN technologies are Ethernet, Token Ring, and FDDI (Fiber Distributed Data Interface). The CCNA exam is heavily weighted with Ethernet technology questions.

Ethernet networks

Ethernet is by far the most popular networking technology in existence for LANs today. Ethernet networks are by definition built on a bus topology that operates on baseband rates of 10 Mbps, 100 Mbps, or 1,000 Mbps (1 Gbps). However, Ethernet usually is implemented on a star-bus topology with either 10 Mbps or 100 Mbps bandwidth.

Ethernet networks employ an access method called CSMA/CD (Carrier Sense Multiple Access/Collision Detection). Under CSMA/CD, when a station wants to send information over the network, it listens for other stations broadcasting. If the network isn't in use, it sends its message. On occasion, two stations may broadcast at the same time and a collision occurs. When this happens, each station retransmits its message using a back-off algorithm that specifies a random period of time each workstation should wait before retransmitting. Each network node examines all network traffic looking for messages addressed to it. If the message is addressed to a particular node, the node processes it accordingly, otherwise the message is ignored.

Token Ring networks

Token Ring networks usually operate at either 4 Mbps or 16 Mbps. Logically, Token Ring networks are laid out in a loop that starts and ends at the same node forming a ring (hence the name).

In contrast to the processes used on an Ethernet network, a token ring node receives messages only from its nearest upstream neighbor (NAUN) and sends signals to its downstream neighbor (which does not have an acronym). Like Ethernet though, Token Ring networks are implemented in a mixed star-ring topology in which each station is connected to an MSAU (multi-station access unit).

Token Ring networks use a token passing access method, in which only the workstation holding the token is allowed to transmit on the network. As the workstation completes its tasks, it places the token on the network for another node to use.

FDDI: The double-ring network

FDDI (Fiber Distributed Data Interface) is an ANSI (American National Standards Institute) standard that defines a dual ring technology that operates at 100 Mbps over fiber optic cabling. FDDI is not nearly as popular as Ethernet or Token Ring, but it is on the exam.

Because it's implemented on fiber optic media and its high data rates, FDDI is better suited for networks that operate over large geographic areas or in electronically hostile environments, or for networks that have large bandwidth demands. Because it employs two attached and interconnected rings that operate independently, an FDDI system has built-in media redundancy that can be applied when one or more ring segments fail.

Defining LANs, MANs, and WANs

There are essentially four general types of networks in the Cisco Systems world:

- **Local Area Network (LAN):** A LAN supports fast, low-error data transfer on a physical network infrastructure that covers a small, limited geographic area, such as within a single building or on a single floor of a building. A LAN connects and supports personal computers, peripherals, and other devices, as shown in Figure 2-4.

- **Metropolitan Area Network (MAN):** A MAN is a network that spans an area larger than a LAN but is less dispersed geographically than a WAN. A MAN network may connect several LANs on a single company's campus, or interconnect the LANs of several companies and businesses in one part of town, for example, the downtown area. So far, there is no Wide Organization Metropolitan Area Networks (WOMAN).

- **Wide Area Networks (WAN):** A WAN, as shown in Figure 2-5, is a network that interconnects LANs and MANs across a broad geographic area and uses some form of data transmission technology provided by a common carrier, including frame relay, SMDS (Switched Multimegabit Data Service), or X.25. See Chapter 17 for more information on WAN protocols.

- **Enterprise network:** There is no nifty acronym for an enterprise network, which is a network that incorporates a combination of LANs and WANs within a single company or organization.

You may run across the term *infrastructure* on the CCNA exam. When used to describe a network, it refers to all of a network's components, including its hardware, software, cabling, conceptual layout, and physical layout. This term is commonly used to describe the operating elements of a network to contrast from the data carried over the network. If fact, it's accurate to say that the network infrastructure carries the network's data.

Designing Networks: An Overview

We know that you're preparing for the CCNA exam and not the CCDA (Certified Cisco Design Associate) exam, but it's certainly a good idea for you to know some basic network design principles.

The following list contains major factors to consider when you design a network:

- **Connectivity:** The physical components of the network and how they relate to each other.

- **Control:** The tools used to monitor the network, correct its deficiencies, and the process of keeping the network secure.

- **Reliability:** The users must be able to depend on the network being available when they need to use it. Key concerns are software updates and timely backup of information.

- **Expandability:** A vital component to any network design is planning for the inevitable growth that occurs and having a plan to prepare for changes in technology.

After you consider these criteria carefully, use a three-step design approach to develop the network design. These steps are:

- **Analyze the requirements:** What are the objectives that the network must support and what accesses and restrictions need to be applied to protect the network's resources?

- **Develop the topology:** Which of the standard topologies (see the section, "Please accept our topologies," earlier in this chapter) best addresses the physical and organizational requirements of the network?

- **Configure the addressing and routing schemes:** This is one of the major topics of this book and the CCNA exam, but see Chapters 8, 9, and 10 for information on these activities.

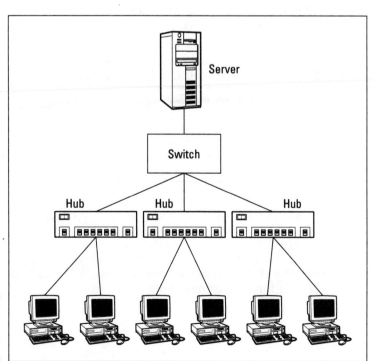

Figure 2-4:
A local area network.

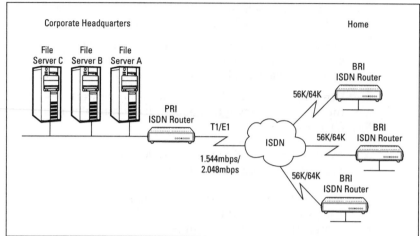

Figure 2-5:
A wide area
network.

Subnet Mask Review

There are three usable IP address classes: Class A, Class B, and Class C. Two other IP address classes do exist, but they're set aside for special purposes. Each IP address class (A, B, and C) has a finite number of bits assigned to hold each of the network and host IDs. Table 2-1 lists the number of bits designated for each of these identities in the 32-bit IP address.

Table 2-1	IP Address Class Bit Assignments	
Class	*Nbr of Network Bits*	*Nbr of Host Bits*
A	8	24
B	16	16
C	24	8

Whether or not a destination address is located on the local network must be decided without consideration to the IP address class of the network. For any subnetted network, a subnet mask can be applied to extract the network ID from the destination address. The network ID can then be compared to the local network ID and the message routed accordingly. To make this determination, every IP address must have a subnet mask.

Table 2-2 lists the default subnet masks for the IP address classes.

Table 2-2	Default Subnet Masks for the IP Address Classes	
Class	*Decimal Mask*	*Binary Mask*
A	255.0.0.0	11111111 00000000 00000000 00000000
B	255.255.0.0	11111111 11111111 00000000 00000000
C	255.255.255.0	11111111 11111111 11111111 00000000

Part II
The OSI Reference Model

IN A DISPLAY OF PERVERSE BRILLIANCE, CARL THE REPAIRMAN MISTAKES A ROOM HUMIDIFIER FOR A MID-RANGE COMPUTER BUT MANAGES TO TIE IT INTO THE NETWORK ANYWAY.

In this part . . .

The OSI Reference Model is the basis for communicating over a network, whether it be a local area network, a wide area network, or the internetwork. The OSI model, as it's called for short, defines the rules, mechanisms, formats, and protocols used to guide how data flows from one device to another.

For the CCNA exam, you need to know the functions, guidelines, and protocols of all seven layers of the OSI model, especially which functions, guidelines, and protocols are on which layer. In addition, you must know why a layered approach to network communications is used and why this approach is a good thing.

The largest single topic section on the CCNA exam is about the OSI model and its layers, especially the lower four layers. The five chapters in this part provide you with the information you need to know about the OSI model for the exam. They also provide you with the foundation knowledge you need to understand the routing and switching topics covered in the later parts of this book.

Chapter 3

Routing Through the OSI Model

● ●

Exam Objectives

▶ Identifying the layers of the OSI reference model

▶ Describing the OSI reference model's functions

▶ Defining the reasons for using a layered model

▶ Explaining the conversion steps of data encapsulation

▶ Understanding the OSI model's Physical layer

● ●

*T*he underlying foundation of all Cisco networking is the Open Systems Interconnection Reference Model. In fact, the OSI model is the foundation of all network communications — Cisco and the others. To succeed on the job, and especially on the test, you must know each layer of the OSI model, its scope of operations, and its relationships to the other layers.

When you understand the OSI model and its layers, you'll have good general knowledge of networking. One goes with the other. A thorough understanding of the OSI model is critical to passing the CCNA exam. It's simply not enough to know the names of the seven layers, although that's essential. You need to know what each layer does and understand why the communication industry uses a layered network model.

We also include in this chapter some background information on the OSI model's Physical layer, the first layer. Although you won't be asked anything specific about this layer on the test, its concepts are important to other areas on which you will be tested, such as designing and installing a network.

If you're new to the OSI model, begin your studies here. Approach the OSI model like you're building a brick wall and study each layer and the "mortar" that connects them, from the bottom (Physical layer) up. If you're an experienced network technician or administrator and can spell ISO OSI backwards, it's still better to review the OSI model bottom-up. Regardless, this is stuff you really must know for the exam.

Quick Assessment

Identifying the layers of the OSI reference model

1 The official name of the OSI model is _____.

2 Layer 3 of the OSI model is the _____ layer.

3 The Physical layer is Layer _____ of the OSI model.

Describing the OSI reference model's functions

4 The OSI model layer on which routing is defined is the _____ layer.

5 The _____ layer defines the Ethernet and Token Ring networking standards.

6 Layers 5 through 7 are also called the _____ layers.

Defining the reasons for using a layered model

7 One of the benefits of a layered internetworking model is that changes to one layer _____ impact the other layers.

Explaining the conversion steps of data encapsulation

8 The Network layer converts upper layer PDUs into _____.

9 PDU stands for _____.

Understanding the OSI model's Physical layer

10 _____ is the wire type most commonly used on Ethernet networks.

Answers

1 *The Open Systems Interconnection Reference Model.* See "The layers of the OSI model."

2 *Network.* Review "Moving down through the layers."

3 *1.* Take a look at "Moving down through the layers."

4 *Network or Layer 3.* Check out "Moving down through the layers."

5 *Data Link or Layer 2.* See "Moving down through the layers."

6 *Upper.* Review "Other interesting OSI layer stuff."

7 *Do not or has no effect.* Look over "Reasons why a layered model is used."

8 *Packets.* Check out "Packaging the data."

9 *Protocol data unit.* See "Packaging the data."

10 *UTP or unshielded twisted-pair.* Review "Choosing the network cable."

The OSI: A Model of Efficiency

The CCNA exam asks you to provide at least three reasons that the "industry" uses layered interconnection models. First, here are some basic definitions. A layered model is one that takes a task, such as data communications, and breaks it down into a series of tasks, activities, or components. Examples of layered networking models include the seven-layer OSI model (which you need to know inside and out) and the Department of Defense (DoD) five-layer model. These two models are contrasted in Figure 3-1.

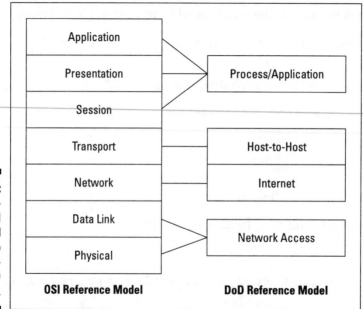

Figure 3-1:
The seven-layer OSI model contrasts to the five-layer DoD model.

Reasons why a layered-model is used

Expect to see a question on the exam that asks you to identify the reasons a layered model is used in internetworking. Actually, there are myriad reasons why a layered model is used, but we suggest that you memorize these possible responses:

  ✔ **Change:** When changes are made to one layer, the impact on the other layers is minimized. If the model consists of a single all-encompassing layer, any change affects the entire model.

- ✔ **Design:** A layered model defines each layer separately. As long as the interconnections between layers remain constant, protocol designers can specialize in one area (layer) without worrying about how any new implementations affect other layers.

- ✔ **Learning:** The layered approach reduces a very complex set of topics, activities, and actions into several smaller interrelated groupings. This makes learning and understanding the actions of each layer and the model on the whole much easier.

- ✔ **Troubleshooting:** The protocols, actions, and data contained in each layer of the model relates only to the purpose of that layer. This enables troubleshooting efforts to be pinpointed on the layer that carries out the suspected cause of the problem.

- ✔ **Standards:** Probably the most important reason for using a layered model is that it establishes a prescribed guideline for interoperability between the various vendors developing products that perform different data communications tasks. Remember, though, that layered models, including the OSI model, provide only a guideline and framework, not a rigid standard that manufacturers can use when creating their products.

The layers of the OSI model

Under its official name, the Open Systems Interconnection Reference Model, the OSI model was developed by the ISO (International Standards Organization) and released in 1984. Yes, it is the ISO OSI.

The OSI model is a layered model that describes how information moves from an application program running on one networked computer to an application program running on another networked computer. In essence, the OSI model prescribes the steps in the process of transferring data, in the form of ones and zeroes, over a transmission medium to another computer or device on a network.

Moving down through the layers

The OSI model breaks the network communications process into seven separate layers. From the top, or the layer closest to the user, down, these layers are:

- ✔ **Layer 7 — Application:** The Application layer provides services to the software through which the user requests network services. This layer is not nor does it contain any applications, and your computer application software is not on this layer. In other words, a program like Microsoft Word or Corel does not exist at this layer, but browsers, FTP clients, and mail clients do.

- **Layer 6 — Presentation:** This layer is concerned with data representation and code formatting.

- **Layer 5 — Session:** The Session layer establishes, maintains, and manages the communication session between computers.

- **Layer 4 — Transport:** The functions defined in this layer provide for the reliable transmission of data segments as well as the disassembly and assembly of the data before and after transmission.

- **Layer 3 — Network:** This is the layer on which routing takes place and, as a result, is perhaps the most important OSI layer to study for the CCNA test. The Network layer defines the processes used to route data across the network and the structure and use of logical addressing.

- **Layer 2 — Data Link:** As its name suggests, this layer is concerned with the linkages and mechanisms used to move data about the network, including the topology, such as Ethernet or Token Ring, and also deals with the ways in which data is reliably transmitted.

- **Layer 1 — Physical:** The Physical layer's name says it all. This layer defines the electrical and physical specifications for the networking media that carry the data bits across a network.

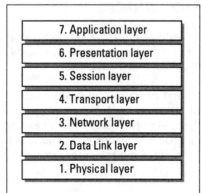

Figure 3-2:
The layers
of the OSI
model.

Other interesting OSI layer stuff

Layers 5 through 7 are generally referred to as the *upper layers*. Conversely, Layers 1 through 4 are collectively called the *lower layers*. Seems obvious, but you'll see this reference on the test.

You need to know the seven layers in sequence, either top-to-bottom or bottom-to-top. Here are some phrases to help you remember the layers of the OSI model:

- ✔ **"Please Do Not Throw Salami (or Sausage if you prefer) Pizza Away"** — this works for bottom-to-top. My personal favorite: both the phrase and the pizza.

- ✔ **"All People Seem To Need Data Processing"** — a top-to-bottom reminder.

- ✔ **"APS Transport Network Data Physically"** — APS refers to Application, Presentation, and Session. This one separates the upper and lower layer groups.

- ✔ **"Please Do Not Tell Secret Passwords Anytime"** — we know, these are getting lame!

Packaging the data

Each layer of the OSI model formats the data it receives to suit the functions to be performed on that layer. In general, the package of data that moves through the layers is called a Protocol Data Unit (PDU). However, as the data is reformatted and repackaged, it takes on unique names on certain layers. Table 3-1 lists the name each layer uses to refer to a message.

Table 3-1	PDU Names on the Layers of the OSI Model
OSI Layer	*PDU Name*
Application	PDU
Presentation	PDU
Session	PDU
Transport	Segment
Network	Packet
Data Link	Frame
Physical	Bits

Absolutely memorize the information in Table 3-1 to the point that you can recite the data unit name associated with each of the OSI model's layers.

Down one side and up the other

Keep in mind that the OSI model itself is never actually implemented, but the network hardware, protocols, and other software that form a network act in a layering and unlayering fashion that follows the guidelines of the OSI model. As shown in Figure 3-3, a packet is passed down through the OSI layers from the Application layer to the Physical layer, where it's physically transmitted to the Physical layer of the receiving network. At the receiving end, it's passed back up through the layers, from Physical layer to the Application layer.

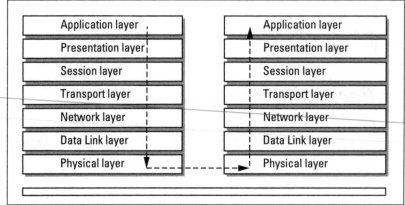

Figure 3-3:
The route data takes through the OSI model's layers.

Application layer	Application layer
Presentation layer	Presentation layer
Session layer	Session layer
Transport layer	Transport layer
Network layer	Network layer
Data Link layer	Data Link layer
Physical layer	Physical layer

As the data passes down through the OSI layers, each layer uses the services of the layers above or below it. A lower layer encapsulates the PDU from the upper layer, adding whatever header or trailer information needed at that layer, and sends it down to the next lower level. This process continues down to the Physical layer, which then takes the ones and zeroes and transmits them across the network's physical media. At the receiving end, the process is reversed and the data is passed back up until it reaches the Application layer.

As the PDU is passed down through the sending side layers, each layer performs its own brand of magic: formatting it, adding a CRC (Cyclic Redundancy Check) or another error-checking mechanism, breaking it into smaller pieces, and more. Each layer also adds its own header to the message. When transmitted by the Physical layer, the original message, if it is still in one piece, has three headers attached to it.

The header from each layer is intended to provide instructions to the counterpart layers at the other end. For example, the Transport layer of the sending side provides a header with instructions on sequence and reassembly for the receiving side Transport layer. As the packet passes up through the receiving side layers, the headers are stripped away until the original message is delivered to the destination application.

Getting Physical

For purposes of the CCNA exam, you should know what the Physical layer of the OSI model does, what devices operate on the Physical layer, some basic topologies (see Chapter 2), the distance limitations of the various network media, and how the media's distance limitations apply in wiring closets using horizontal and intermediate cross-connects. Gee, is that all? The point is that you should basically memorize the tables in this section.

Electrically speaking

The Physical layer of the OSI model defines the electrical and mechanical specifications used in networking, including transmission distances, the various types of media available, and electrical issues. The standards included in the Physical layer have been developed by various contributing organizations such as the EIA/TIA (the Electrical Industry Association/Telecommunications Industry Association), the IEEE (pronounced "eye triple-E" and meaning the Institute of Electrical and Electronics Engineers), UL (Underwriters Laboratories), and others.

Getting to know the wire

Although wireless LAN technologies are emerging, the CCNA exam only includes references to physical cable. So, don't waste your time researching wireless LAN systems.

What you need to know about physical network media, a.k.a. cable, centers around its physical properties and construction features. Here are some of the basic concepts you need to understand about all cable types:

- **Attenuation:** In nearly all cable there's a distance limit at which the signal on a wire weakens and no longer can be recognized.

- **Electromagnetic Interference (EMI):** Virtually all electrical devices emit electromagnetic waves that can cause interference and impair the signals of other devices.

- **Radio Frequency Interference (RFI):** Devices that broadcast wireless or radio signals can produce interference through radio wave transmissions picked up by other electrical devices, which is the cause of EMI.

- **Cancellation:** The electromagnetic fields of two wires placed in close proximity can cancel out each other. This is generally a good thing and helps control the signals being sent over the individual wires, but too much cancellation can destroy the integrity of the signal carried on either wire.

Choosing the network cable

There are three basic types of networking cable: twisted-pair, coaxial, and fiber optic. Each of these cables has different characteristics and capabilities. For the CCNA exam, focus your studies on unshielded twisted-pair wire. However, it won't hurt to review the characteristics of fiber-optic and coaxial cable just a bit as well.

The twisted-pair

Although its title sounds like the name of a low-budget horror movie, this section covers the most popular cabling used in networks — twisted-pair copper wire. This wire possesses all of the attributes of a truly popular cable: It's the lightest, most flexible, least expensive, and easiest to install of any of the popular network media. The bad news is that it's very vulnerable to interference and has attenuation problems as well. However, these problems are easily overcome with the right network design and implementation.

Twisted-pair wire comes in two types: unshielded (UTP) and shielded (STP), shown in Figure 3-4. Of the two types, unshielded is more commonly used. It's popular in Ethernet networks. Unshielded twisted-pair wire is just about what its name implies — two unshielded wires twisted together — but generally, network cable consists of four twisted pairs inside a single cable.

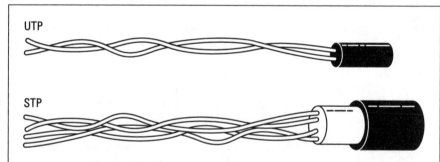

Figure 3-4: Twisted-pair wiring.

The unshielded truth

Unshielded twisted-pair (UTP) is the most common type of cabling used in networks. For all of the reasons discussed above, it provides the most installation flexibility and ease of maintenance of the big three cabling media. UTP is commonly referred to as 10BaseT Ethernet cable.

UTP cable is grouped into five categories, or "cats" as the real techies call them (as in Cat 3 or Cat 5):

> ✔ Category 1 and 2 — not used in networking. This isn't here and you didn't see it.
>
> ✔ Category 3 — a 4-pair cable supporting bandwidth up to 10 Mbps and is the minimum standard for 10BaseT networks.
>
> ✔ Category 4 — a 4-pair cable commonly used in 16 Mbps Token Ring networks.
>
> ✔ Category 5 — a 4-pair cable with bandwidth up to 100 Mbps, used for 100BaseTX and ATM (asynchronous transfer mode) networking.

The UTP references on the CCNA exam are usually to Cat 5 cabling, with a few Cat 3 references. Be sure you know which wire is involved and what the situation is on questions concerning cabling.

UTP uses an RJ-45 connector, which looks very much like the little clip connector on your telephone, only a little bigger. (See Figure 3-5.)

Figure 3-5:
UTP cable is
terminated
with an
RJ-45
connector.

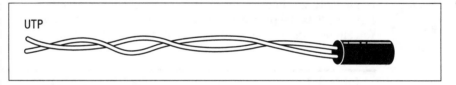

UTP

Shielding you from trouble

Shielded twisted-pair (STP), the other of the twisted-pair wire types, is common in Token Ring networks, but is not commonly used for Ethernet although it can be. STP has its wires wrapped in a copper or foil shield to help reduce EMI and RFI interference, which makes it more expensive than UTP wire.

What's this 10-Base stuff?

In the Ethernet world, cables are designated with a coding scheme that describes its characteristics. For example, thick coaxial cable is designated as 10Base5; thin coaxial cable is designated as 10Base2; and UTP is generally designated as 10BaseT.

The 10Base part indicates that the cable carries 10 Mbps bandwidths over baseband signals. In the case of coaxial cable, the 5 and 2 mean 500 meters and 200 meters, which are the approximate maximum segment lengths for these cables. The T in 10BaseT refers to twisted-pair cable.

Baseband is a network technology that sends its data over a single carrier frequency. Baseband networks require all nodes to participate in every message sent over the network. Typical baseband networks use UTP wiring, but can also use coaxial cable or fiber-optic cabling.

The other cable types

Fiber-optic cable is significantly more expensive than UTP and much more difficult to work with. Its advantages include its capability of carrying data over much greater distances and that it's resistant to both EMI and RFI, because it uses a light signal instead of an electrical impulse.

Coaxial cable comes in two types, generally referred to as thinnet and thicknet. Coaxial cable isn't generally used in new installations anymore, but you should know its characteristics for the exam.

Know the cable table

You'll likely see an exam question about cable types and their characteristics. Table 3-2 lists the primary characteristics for each of the major cable types. You should commit the contents of this table to memory.

Table 3-2	Network Media Characteristics		
Type	**Media**	**Maximum Speed**	**Segment Length**
10Base2	coaxial – 50 ohm thin	10 Mbps	185 Meters
10Base5	coaxial – 50 ohm thick	10 Mbps	500 Meters
10BaseT	UTP	10 to 1,000 Mbps	100 Meters
Fiber	multi-mode	10 to 1,000 Mbps	2000 Meters
Fiber	single-mode	10 to 1,000 Mbps	100,000 Meters

Working in the Wiring Closet

Questions and references to wiring closets and wiring practices are on the exam. If you have access to a wiring closet, equipment room, phone closet, or whatever you call the location where your network cabling interconnects, you should spend some time reviewing the connections and standards in use on your network.

Wiring standards

The EIA/TIA standards 568 and 568B are the most widely used wiring standards for network media. These two standards detail six elements of LAN cabling:

- Telecommunications Closets
- Equipment Rooms
- Entrance Facilities
- Work Areas
- Backbone Cabling
- Horizontal Cabling

The portion of the 568 standards that directly affects most networking situations is horizontal cabling. This part of the standards deals with the network media (wire, connectors, etc.) that run horizontally from the wiring closet to the workstation. Here's a summary of these standards:

- A minimum of two telecommunications outlets in each work area.
- A maximum distance for Cat 5 UTP cable in a horizontal cabling run is 90 meters. Remember this is not the maximum distance for Cat 5, which is 100 meters. It's the EIA/TIA standard for horizontal cabling runs using Cat 5 UTP.
- Patch cords at the horizontal cross-connect are not to exceed 6 meters.
- Patch cords from the wall to the workstation should not exceed 3 meters.
- Each floor should have a separate wiring closet.
- In cases where the square footage of the floor is more than 1,000 square meters or the horizontal cabling is longer than 90 meters, there should be another wiring closet added on the floor.

Cross-connecting the backbone

Visualize the horizontal cabling that runs into the wiring closet from a network workstation and then the cable that runs from the wiring closet to the network backbone. Okay, now that you have these two wires, how do you interconnect them? Why, with a cross-connect, of course.

The cross-connect is the connection that bridges the gap between the workstation cabling and the network cabling. A common method of creating network cross-connects is through a patch panel. Each cable is terminated into a patch panel and then a patch cord is used to interconnect each port on the patch panel.

As shown in Figure 3-6, backbone cabling connects the cross-connects that run from a main cross-connect to those located in an intermediate cross-connect and to its horizontal cross-connects and all of the termination points between them. An intermediate cross-connect is a cross-connect between a horizontal cross-connect and the main cross-connect. There are no workstations attached to an intermediate cross-connect. There can be no more than one cross-connect.

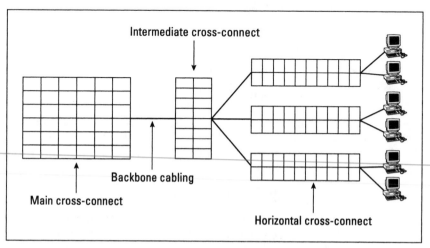

Figure 3-6:
Backbone cabling provides the interconnection to the cross-connects of a network.

There are some distance limitations defined under the 568 standards for backbone cabling. Table 3-3 highlights the distance requirements for backbone cabling. The values in this table may show up as criteria in one or more questions on the exam.

Table 3-3	Backbone Cabling Distance Requirements		
Media Type	*MCC to HCC*	*MCC to ICC*	*ICC to HCC*
Cat 5	90 Meters total	Running	Length
62.5u Fiber Optic	2000 M	500 M	1500 M
Single-mode Fiber	3000 M	500 M	2500 M

Physical Layer Hardware

The Physical layer contains all the physical hardware used to transport bits around the network. This includes network adapters, cabling, wall plugs, cross-connects, hubs, repeaters, and connectors. Even wireless network media are on the Physical layer.

Could you repeat that?

A repeater is a device you add to a network to solve attenuation problems in cable wire. A repeater cleans up the signal, gives it a boost, and sends it on its way. Although it sounds a lot like your mom, a repeater is a small device with usually one input and one output connector that can be added to the network where it's needed. A repeater is commonly used to overcome the 100-meter distance limitation of Cat 5 cabling.

Just a hub of activity

Hubs are either active or passive. A passive hub merely repeats any signals it receives from one of its ports to all other ports, without re-energizing the signal. Passive hubs don't help the attenuation distance of their networks.

Active hubs, in their most basic form, also include a repeater-type feature that re-energizes the signal before sending it on to its ports. Smart active hubs intelligently direct a signal to the port on which its destination exists.

Hubs are used in a star topology to provide mulitport connectivity to a network. Many workstations and peripherals can be clustered to a hub which is then connected to another hub, a switch, router, or directly to a cross-connect.

For the CCNA exam you need to remember that network adapters, the network cable media, repeaters, and hubs are all Layer 1 devices.

1 Which of the following is not a reason for using a layered model for internetworking?

A ○ Change

B ○ Troubleshooting

C ○ Standards

D ○ Cost

2 The layer of the OSI model that provides services to end-user software is

A ○ Application

B ○ Presentation

C ○ Session

D ○ Transport

E ○ Network

F ○ Data Link

G ○ Physical

3 The OSI layer that defines routing is

A ○ Application

B ○ Presentation

C ○ Session

D ○ Transport

E ○ Network

F ○ Data Link

G ○ Physical

4 The OSI layer that establishes and manages communications between computers is

A ○ Application

B ○ Presentation

C ○ Session

D ○ Transport

E ○ Network

F ○ Data Link

G ○ Physical

5 The OSI model layer that defines Ethernet and Token Ring networks is
A ○ Application
B ○ Presentation
C ○ Session
D ○ Transport
E ○ Network
F ○ Data Link
G ○ Physical

6 The Transport layer formats data into
A ○ Packets
B ○ Frames
C ○ PDUs
D ○ Segments

7 The distance limit in a wire at the point where the signal begins to fade is caused by
A ○ EMI
B ○ RFI
C ○ attenuation
D ○ cancellation

8 The T in 10BaseT represents
A ○ Twisted-pair
B ○ Tensile
C ○ Telecommunications
D ○ Telephony

9 Hubs, repeaters, and cable media operate on which OSI model layer?
A ○ Application
B ○ Presentation
C ○ Session
D ○ Transport
E ○ Network
F ○ Data Link
G ○ Physical

10 The most widely used wiring standards for network media are
A ○ RS-232
B ○ EIA/TIA
C ○ IEEE
D ○ U812

Answers

1 *D.* Cost is not a consideration in the OSI model as it would be dependent on too many factors. The OSI model and all other layered models, such as the DoD model, attempt to define related, yet independent networking activities. *See "Reasons why a layered model is used."*

2 *A.* We don't think we can say this enough — you really must know what each of the layers of the OSI model defines and the functions that operate on each. *Review "The layers of the OSI model."*

3 *E.* Most of the CCNA exam revolves around this question. Routing and switching is the focus of the CCNA with a heavy emphasis on routing and that is defined on the Network layer. *Look at "The layers of the OSI model."*

4 *C.* The Session layer builds (or in the words of the telecom folks, "nails up") and manages the communications session between two devices, hence its name. *Check out "Moving down through the layers."*

5 *F.* The Data Link layer also defines the MAC and LLC sublayers, but more on that in Chapter 4. *See" Moving down through the layers."*

6 *D.* Each of the OSI model's lower layers create specific PDU formats. The Transport layer creates segments, the Network layer creates packets, the Data Link layer creates frames, and the Physical layer, while not exactly a PDU, transmits data as bits. *Review "Packaging the data."*

7 *C.* Attenuation is when a signal transmitted over a wire begins to fade and lose its integrity. You should know the distance limits for UTP for the exam. *Look over "Getting to know the wire."*

8 *A.* You'll see quite a few references to 10BaseX references. The T does stand for twisted-pair wire, and you may also see F (fiber optic). *Check out "What's this 10-Base stuff?"*

9 *G.* Check this out: All of the wire and equipment used to move data bits across the network is on the Physical layer. Remember this. *See "Getting Physical."*

10 *B.* EIA/TIA 568a and 568b are the standards most commonly used for wiring and connector patterns. *Review "Wiring standards."*

Chapter 4

The Data Link Layer

• •

Exam Objectives

▶ Defining the functions of the Data Link layer

▶ Differentiating Data Link and network addresses

▶ Explaining the functions of a MAC address

▶ Listing the advantages of LAN segmentation

▶ Segmenting a LAN with a bridge

• •

Although the emphasis of the CCNA exam is clearly the Network layer of the OSI model, you really must know a number of Layer 2 (Data Link layer) concepts, technologies, and activities on the exam. As indicated in the exam objectives of this chapter, there is a wide range of Data Link layer functions you will need to review. You need to know the difference between Data Link layer addresses (especially the MAC [Media Access Control] address) and those used on other OSI layers; how the flow of data is controlled; and the whys and wherefores of segmenting a Local Area Network (LAN) using Layer 2 devices, namely bridges and switches. Yes, switches are also Layer 2 devices, but LAN switches are covered in Chapter 16.

The importance of the Data Link layer is that it provides the foundation upon which the addressing and data movement within the lower layer (Physical) and higher layers (Network through Application) of the OSI model is built. Understanding the other layers of the OSI model, especially what goes on in the Network and Transport layers, requires a solid understanding of Data Link principles, concepts, and technologies.

Our advice is that you review the information in this chapter carefully. When you're sure you understand it and how it relates to other networking components and activities, review it one more time. Then you'll be ready to move on to other OSI layers and especially routing and switching.

Quick Assessment

Defining the functions of the Data Link layer

1 The LLC sublayer of the Data Link layer is defined in the IEEE _____ standard.

2 The LLC sublayer transfers data in two ways: _____ and _____.

3 The access method defined in IEEE 802.3 is _____.

Differentiating Data Link and network addresses

4 The address associated with the physical device is its _____ address.

Explaining the functions of a MAC address

5 A MAC address is made up of two parts, the _____ and a(n) _____.

6 The MAC address is _____-bits in length.

Listing the advantages of LAN segmentation

7 _____ is the act of dividing up a network into smaller operating units.

8 The smaller operating units created when a network is divided up are _____, which are also called _____.

Segmenting a LAN with a bridge

9 A bridge is a _____ device.

10 Bridges operate on the _____ sublayer of the Data Link layer.

Answers

1 *802.2.* See "The sublayers of the Data Link layer."

2 *Connectionless, connection-oriented.* Review "Connecting on the LLC sublayer."

3 *CSMA/CD (Carrier Sense Multiple Access/Collision Detection).* Check out "Controlling access to the network."

4 *MAC (Media Access Control).* See "Communicating on the MAC sublayer."

5 *Manufacturer's ID number, unique serial number.* Look over "Communicating on the MAC sublayer."

6 *48.* Check out "Communicating on the MAC sublayer."

7 *Segmentation.* Review "Segmenting a Network for Fun and Profit."

8 *Segments, collision domains.* Take a look at "Segmenting a Network for Fun and Profit."

9 *Layer 2* or *Data Link.* Check out "Bridging the difference."

10 *MAC.* See "The MAC bridge."

Working on the Data Link Layer

We need to impress upon you the importance of the OSI model layers, and especially the Data Link layer. The Data Link layer is where data is packaged for transmission on the Physical layer as well as where data from the Physical layer is unpacked for use on the Network layer and above. This means that the Data Link layer must define both higher-level message formats and physical level formats, including two very important areas of network specifications: Media Access Control (MAC) addresses and the IEEE (Institute for Electric and Electronic Engineering) 802 specification.

Listing the functions of Layer 2

Remember that the OSI model is only a guideline and not a piece of software. On the CCNA exam, you find the items defined on a certain level described as being "on" that level or operating "at" that level. Don't let this language throw you. Try to envision the layers of the OSI model as stops on a two-way process that wraps and unwraps data bundles as they're shipped out or received.

The Data Link layer is the second layer of the OSI model. It directly supports the Network layer above it and interacts with and is supported by the Physical layer below it. It communicates with the Data Link layer on the opposite end of a transmission through the header and trailer it adds to the data frames it receives or passes on to the Physical layer.

Moving data across the Physical link is a primary role of the Data Link layer. It packages the data sent to it from the upper layers for transmission on the Physical layer. Another fundamental role of the Data Link layer is to reassemble data from the Physical layer for use in the upper layers.

However, there's a bit more involved than may appear. In completing these tasks, the Data Link layer performs a number of separate activities, including:

- Physical addressing
- Network topology
- Error notification
- Access to the physical medium (a.k.a. arbitration)
- Flow control

Each of these activities of the Data Link layer is discussed in this chapter. First, we review some underlying concepts to help you understand the separate activities of the Data Link layer, as well as some concepts you really need to know for the exam. See Chapters 2 and 3 for more information on network topologies.

Stacking up the IEEE 802 standards

Immediately after somebody invented networking by connecting two computers together to share files and send secret messages, it was apparent that it was a good thing. As local area networks (LANs) began to spread, it was obvious that if networks hoped to grow large or began to communicate with one another, some standards would be needed. To this end, the Institute for Electric and Electronic Engineering (IEEE), a well-known and highly respected organization, started a project in February, 1980, to create a set of standards for LAN architectures, cabling, and data transmission formats. The date that this project started is important because it formed the name of the project (the 802 project) and the resulting standards developed (IEEE 802) by it.

The 802 project's goal was to define the Data Link layer, including the logical link control (LLC) and media access control (MAC) sublayers (these are each discussed more fully later in this chapter) and beyond. To date, the 802 project and its 12-plus subcommittees have produced a variety of networking standards. Those defining the Data Link layer are listed in Table 4-1. The 802-dot number of each standard represents the number of the subcommittee assigned to develop and define each area. For example, the 802.3 standard is assigned to the 802.3 subcommittee.

The 802 Project defines 12-plus subcommittee standards groups. Don't waste time memorizing all of them. Concentrate only on those in Table 4-1.

Table 4-1	The IEEE 802 Standards	
Subcommittee	*Subject*	*Description*
802.1	Internetworking/ LAN Protocols	Defines routing, bridging, and internetwork communications
802.2	Logical Link Control (LLC)	Allows Network layer protocols to link to Physical layer and MAC sublayer protocols
802.3	Ethernet	*The* Ethernet standard; defines CSMA/CD
802.5	Token Ring	Defines logical ring topology, media, and interfaces
802.12	High-speed networks	Defines 100 Mbps technologies

Ethernet and the mighty 802.3

The IEEE 802.3 is the standard that defines the Ethernet, by far the networking standard of choice. The 802.3 standard defines the bus topology, the network media (10BaseX), and the functions of an Ethernet network, as well as defining the tools used on the MAC sublayer of the Data Link layer; primary of these in the Ethernet world is the CSMA/CD access method.

The sublayers of the Data Link layer

The Data Link layer is divided into two sublayers by the 802 standards: the Logical Link Control (LLC) and Media Access Control (MAC) sublayers. The LLC sublayer is defined in 802.1 and 802.2. The MAC sublayer is defined in the 802.1, 802.3, 802.5, and 802.12. Be sure you know the general subject of each of these standards for the exam.

Connecting on the LLC sublayer

The LLC (Logical Link Control) layer creates connections between networked devices. If you want to send data from your workstation client to a server on the same network segment, it's the LLC that creates and manages the connection required to transmit your data.

Conceptually, the LLC sublayer sits on top of the MAC sublayer. It's defined by the 802.2 standard to be topology independent. The LLC functions include:

- Managing frames to upper and lower layers
- Error control
- Flow control

The LLC works with the transport layer by providing connection-oriented and connectionless services. It manages and creates the communication link.

The LLC sublayer transfers data in two ways:

- **Connectionless services:** Messages are not acknowledged by the receiving device, which speeds up the processing. Although it sounds unreliable, this type of transfer is commonly used at this level because the upper OSI layers implement their own error-checking and control.
- **Connection-oriented services:** Because each message is acknowledged, this service is much slower than connectionless services, but it's much more reliable.

See Chapter 6 for more information on connectionless and connection-oriented services.

Going with the flow control

Another communications control defined on the LLC sublayer is *flow control*. Flow control meters the flow of data between network devices that may not be running at the same speeds. Please don't think that flow control *occurs* on the Data Link layer. The Transport layer of the OSI model actually manages the mechanisms used to control the flow of data between two hosts. The Data Link layer defines the data values used in the flow control signaling between two transmitting hosts. See Chapter 6 for more information on flow control.

In situations where one communicating device is sending information at either a faster or a slower rate than the other device, some form of control is necessary to meter the flow of data between the devices to avoid a loss of data. Flow control prevents the slower device from being swamped, and, more importantly, prevents data from being lost or garbled. It works by pausing the faster device to enable the slower device to catch up.

There are two types of flow control implemented in data communications — software and hardware. Software flow control, common to networking, involves a process called XON/XOFF, which roughly stands for transmission on/transmission off. This process involves the sending device continuing to send data until the receiving device signals (by sending a control character) that transmissions need to stop until the receiving device can catch up. When the receiving device is ready to go, it sends another control signal for the sending device to begin the data flow again.

Hardware flow control, also called RTS/CTS (Ready To Send/Clear to Send), uses two wires in a cable, one for RTS and one for CTS. The sending device uses the RTS signal to indicate when it's ready to send. The receiving device uses the CTS to indicate it's ready to receive. When either is turned off, the flow is interrupted.

Detecting errors in the flow

Another function of the Data Link layer is error detection. *Error detection* is the process of detecting whether errors occurred during the transmission of the bits across the wire. The Data Link layer uses a calculated value called the CRC (Cyclic Redundancy Check) that's placed into the Data Link trailer that's added to the message frame before it's sent to the Physical layer. The receiving computer recalculates the CRC and compares it to the one sent with the data. If the two values are equal, it's assumed that the data arrived without errors. Otherwise, the message frame may need to be retransmitted under control of an upper layer. Although the Data Link layer implements error detection, it does not include a function to perform error recovery. This is left for the upper layers to deal with, primarily on the Transport layer.

Communicating on the MAC sublayer

The MAC sublayer of the Data Link layer provides a range of network services, including controlling which network device has access to the network and providing for physical addressing.

The MAC sublayer carries the physical address of each device on the network. This address is more commonly called a device's MAC address. The MAC address is a 48-bit address that's encoded on each network device by its manufacturer. This works on the same principle that each domicile on your street has a unique address assigned to it by the Postal Service. It's the MAC address that the Physical layer uses to move data between nodes of the network.

A MAC address is made up of two parts: the manufacturer's ID number and a unique serialized number assigned to the device by its manufacturer. The 48-bits (6 bytes) of the MAC address are divided evenly between these two numbers. The first three bytes of the MAC address contain a hexadecimal manufacturer code that has been assigned by the IEEE. For example, Cisco's IEEE MAC ID is 00 00 0C (each byte holds two half-byte hexadecimal values), Intel's is 00 55 00, and IBM's is 08 00 5A. The remaining three bytes contain a hexadecimal number assigned by the manufacturer that's unique to each piece of equipment.

Just as you need to know someone's telephone number to call them, computers must know each other's addresses to communicate. Depending on the protocol in use, various addressing schemes are used. For the exam, you should be aware of TCP/IP and IPX addressing schemes (see Chapter 12 for more information).

In a workstation, the MAC address is usually burned into the NIC card. On a router, each port has its own MAC physical address. Theoretically, no two devices ever have the same MAC address. Although, we have heard of instances where this has occurred in a network with very unpleasant circumstances resulting.

I'm known as IP, but my friends call me MAC

Hardware (MAC) addresses are used to get data from one local device to another. However, not all network operating systems (NOS) use the physical address to reference network nodes. This sets up the conflict between the network (logical) address and the MAC (physical) addresses.

Network operating systems assign a logical network name to each networked device, such as ACCTG_SERVER, NT1, or FRED, to make it easy for its human users to reference its resources. On the other hand, references on the network itself, that is those on Layer 1 (Physical layer), use the physical addresses provided by the Data Link layer to reference the actual devices on the network. When you request services from the file server FRED, a service like DNS (Domain Naming System) or WINS (Windows Internet Name Service) is used to translate or resolve the node name FRED into its logical address, which is typically an IP address. In some cases, a HOSTS or LMHOSTS file may be used instead to resolve the node name to its logical address. The Data Link layer activities then resolve the logical address into its corresponding MAC address. To resolve between these two addresses involves a process called (what else?) address resolution, which associates logical network addresses to physical MAC addresses, and vice versa.

The protocol for this service is ARP (Address Resolution Protocol). ARP maintains a small database in memory, called the ARP cache, that cross-references physical and logical addresses. When a device wants to communicate with a local device, it checks its ARP cache to determine whether it has that device's MAC address. If it doesn't, it sends out an ARP broadcast request, as shown in Figure 4-1, to all devices on the local network. Each device examines the message to see whether the request is intended for it. If it is, the device responds with its MAC address, which is stored in the sending device's ARP cache. In the example shown in Figure 4-1, USER1 wants to communicate with FRED, a file server. However, USER1 doesn't have a MAC address in its ARP cache for FRED, so it sends out a broadcast message that asks FRED to respond with its MAC address, which FRED does.

When a workstation or server needs to communicate with a device remote to the local network, essentially the same process takes place with the exception that a router through which the remote device is accessed will likely respond with its MAC address and not that of the device itself.

Controlling access to the network

The primary media access control mechanism defined in 802.3 for use in the Data Link layer is CSMA/CD (Carrier Sense Multiple Access/Collision Detection) access method. CSMA/CD is the method used in Ethernet networks for controlling access to the physical media by network nodes. As its name infers, CSMA/CD (say it ten times fast to lock it away in your brain!) tries to keep network devices from interfering with each other's communications by detecting access attempts by multiple devices. When sneaky devices avoid detection, and they do, CSMA/CD detects and deals with the *collision* that undoubtedly occurs.

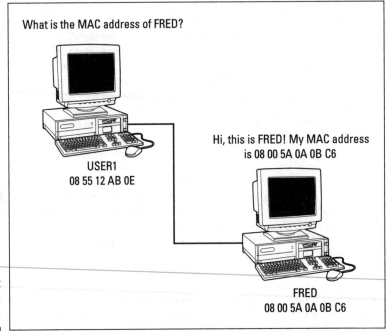

What is the MAC address of FRED?

USER1
08 55 12 AB 0E

Hi, this is FRED! My MAC address
is 08 00 5A 0A 0B C6

FRED
08 00 5A 0A 0B C6

Figure 4-1:
To resolve
an unknown
address on
the network,
a broadcast
request is
sent out.

Avoiding collisions

To avoid collisions, CSMA/CD devices "listen" or sense signals on the network backbone before sending a message over the network. If the network is
quiet, meaning it's not in use, the device can send a message. Otherwise, the
device waits until the network isn't in use. However, if between the time a
device decides the network is available and the time it actually transmits its
message, another device sends a message, the two messages may collide on
the network. When this happens, the device that detected the collision sends
out an alert to all network devices that a collision has occurred. All devices
quit transmitting for a random amount of time to clear the line.

The CSMA/CD process can be described as follows:

1. Listen to see whether the wire is being used.

2. If the wire is busy, wait.

3. If the wire is quiet, send.

4. If a collision occurs while sending, stop, wait a specific amount of time,
   and send again.

When a collision is detected by a sending device, it sends out a jamming signal that lasts long enough for all nodes to recognize it and stop broadcasting. Then each device waits a random amount of time to begin the CSMA/CD process again. This amount of time is determined by a back-off algorithm that calculates the amount of time the device should wait before resuming its attempts to transmit.

Working on a busy intersection

A collision domain is a network segment in which all devices share the same bandwidth. The more devices you have on a segment, the more likely that you'll experience collisions. With too many devices on a segment network, performance is considerably less than optimal. Increasing bandwidth is one way to deal with the problem, but a better way to deal with this problem is by using the available bandwidth more efficiently.

Segmenting a Network for Fun and Profit

Dividing a network into smaller parts, known as segments, decreases congestion and chances of message collision on each new segment. Yes, each new segment forms a new collision domain, but that doesn't mean it becomes a problem very quickly (not if the network is segmented properly). Devices within a segment share the same bandwidth. Data passed outside a segment contends with the next higher segment on the network or perhaps enters the network backbone, both of which are collision domains themselves.

Dividing up a LAN into smaller collision domains (segments) is called *segmentation.* Count on seeing this concept on the exam.When you segment a network, you increase the number of smaller collision domains.

Reaping the benefits of segmentation

For the exam, you need to recognize the following as the general benefits of LAN segmentation:

- ✔ Increased bandwidth per user
- ✔ Keeping local traffic local
- ✔ Reduced broadcasts (This benefit is associated with LAN segmentation with a router and not a Layer 2 device. Bridges and switches do not reduce broadcast traffic, which is a primary reason for using a router. We have included it here so that you have all of the benefits associated with LAN segmentation together.)
- ✔ Decreased collisions

Bridging the difference

A bridge, which is a Layer 2 device, is used to break larger network segments into smaller network segments. It works much like a repeater (see Chapter 3), but because a bridge works solely with Layer 2 protocols and Layer 2 MAC sublayer addresses, it operates at the Data Link layer.

The MAC bridge

No, McDonald's is not in the networking business now. Bridges are commonly referred to as MAC layer bridges because they operate on the MAC sublayer of the Data Link layer. As I discussed earlier in this chapter (see "Communicating on the MAC sublayer"), each network device has a unique identification number (MAC address) that identifies it on the MAC layer. A bridge uses the MAC address to perform its tasks, including:

- ✔ Monitoring network traffic

- ✔ Identifying the destination and source addresses of a message

- ✔ Creating a routing table that identifies MAC addresses to the network segment on which they're located

- ✔ Sending messages to only the network segment on which its destination MAC address is located

The bridge routing table

A bridge builds up its routing table by cataloging the network nodes that send out messages. A bridge examines the MAC address of a message's source or sending node. If this address is new to the bridge, it adds it to the routing table along with the network segment from which it originated. The bridge's routing table is stored in its RAM and just like a PC's RAM, it is dynamic — when the power goes off, it goes away. When the power is restored, the bridge rebuilds the table. Because most network nodes send and receive packets continuously, it doesn't take long to completely rebuild the routing table.

Bridging over troubled waters

The two devices you need to be concerned with for the exam are bridge and switch. Switches and LAN switching are a major portion of the exam. I cover them in depth in Chapter 16. Bridges, on the other hand, don't play as large a role on the exam, but they're important Layer 2 devices. It's important that you know that a bridge is the primary networking device used to create new segments on a LAN.

One problem that can arise on a bridged and switched network is caused by the lack of a time to live value (such as that used in Layer 3 protocols) assigned to Layer 2 messages. Because a Data Link frame can effectively live forever, it's possible that a packet addressed to an unknown MAC address may bounce around the network indefinitely. This condition can be avoided by allowing only a single path to be active between two segments at a time by using the Spanning Tree Protocol.

Spanning the tree protocols

The Spanning Tree protocol designates each interface on a bridge to be either in Forwarding or Blocking State. When an interface is in Blocking State, only special packets reporting the status of other bridges on the network are allowed through. All other packets are blocked. As you can probably guess, an interface in Forwarding State allows all packets to be received and forwarded. The state of a bridge's interfaces are affected whenever a path on the network goes down and the bridges negotiate a new path, changing interface states from Blocking to Forwarding, as needed.

The normal forwarding mode for a bridge is called store and forward. A store and forward bridge receives (stores) and examines an entire frame before forwarding it to the appropriate interface. The time it takes to examine each frame increases the latency (delay) in the network. Latency is the delay introduced by network devices, such as a bridge, switch, or router, as they process packets. Store and forward bridges create a variable amount of latency because they read in the entire frame, which are variable in length, before examining the frame and passing it on.

Bridging to the CCNA exam

You need to know the following key concepts concerning bridges (or bridging) for the CCNA exam:

- Bridges operate at Layer 2 and usually do not reduce broadcasts because a bridge forwards broadcast packets to all of its ports except the port on which the broadcast packet arrived. On the other hand, a router usually blocks broadcast packets.

- Bridges expand the distance of an Ethernet network because each segment can be built to the maximum distance.

- Bridges filter some traffic based upon MAC addresses.

- Bandwidth is used more efficiently.

- Local traffic is kept local.

Encapsulating Data

You can bet your last dollar that the CCNA exam includes questions about how data is transformed on its journey from the Application layer to the Physical layer. However, on the test, this transformation is referenced to the TCP/IP protocol stack (see Chapter 14) and not the OSI model. So, first learn the five steps of data encapsulation listed below and be sure you know the TCP/IP protocols that operate on each layer of the OSI model.

The five steps of encapsulation, as illustrated in Figure 4-2, are:

1. User information is converted into data.

2. Data is converted into segments for transport across the network.

3. Segments are converted into packets or datagrams and include the source and destination network addresses in the network header.

4. Packets and datagrams are converted into frames and the Data Link header is added.

5. The data in the frames is converted into bits for transmission over the physical media.

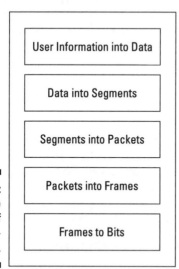

Figure 4-2:
The five steps of data encapsulation.

- User Information into Data
- Data into Segments
- Segments into Packets
- Packets into Frames
- Frames to Bits

You should absolutely be able to recite the five steps of data encapsulation. We suggest that you take five small pieces of paper and write one step of the encapsulation process on each piece. Then scramble them and organize them into the proper sequence. Do this until you can do it without fail.

Here's an example of the five steps of encapsulation that occur when a user uses a browser to open a Web page:

1. The user requests that the browser open a web page.

2. The Transport layer adds a header indicating that an HTTP process is requested.

3. The Network layer puts a source and destination address into its packet header that helps indicate the path across the network.

4. The Data Link layer frame puts in the hardware addresses of both the source node and the next directly connected network device (for example, a router).

5. The frame is converted into bits for transmission over the media.

As detailed in Chapter 14, the original message is encapsulated in the PDU of each layer, and a header (and perhaps a trailer) is added to the PDU. On each layer, the PDU takes on a new name, taking the data through encapsulation into segments, packets, frames, and finally converting the entire encapsulated message into bits for transmission over the physical media. Remember the words data, segments, packets, frames and bits, and the layers on which each PDU type is formed. On the Data Link layer, encapsulation takes the form of a frame. Table 4-2 lists the encapsulation forms by layer.

Table 4-2	Data Encapsulation by OSI Layer
OSI Layer	*Encapsulation*
Transport	Segment
Network	Packet
Data Link	Frame
Physical	Bits

Prep Test

1 Which of the following is not a Data Link layer activity? (Choose two.)

A ○ Physical addressing

B ○ Error notification

C ○ Routing

D ○ Flow control

2 The IEEE 802 subcommittee that defines Ethernet networking is

A ○ 802.1

B ○ 802.2

C ○ 802.3

D ○ 802.5

3 The Data Link layer is divided into two sublayers by the 802 standards

A ○ Logical Layering Control

B ○ Logical Link Control

C ○ Media Addressing Control

D ○ Media Access Control

E ○ A and C

F ○ B and D

G ○ B and C

4 Which of the following are provided by the LLC sublayer? (Choose two.)

A ○ SAP (Service Access Points)

B ○ Flow control

C ○ Physical addressing

D ○ Logical addressing

5 The calculated value used by the Data Link layer for error detection is

A ○ Checksum

B ○ Parity

C ○ CRC

D ○ The Data Link layer does not implement error detection.

6 The 48-bit physical device address defined on the Data Link layer is the

A ○ Network address
B ○ Media access control address
C ○ Logical address
D ○ Logical link control address

7 The protocol used to resolve logical addresses to physical addresses on a network is

A ○ ARP
B ○ DNS
C ○ HOSTS
D ○ CSMA/CD

8 Dividing a network into smaller collision domains is called

A ○ Bridging
B ○ Segmentation
C ○ Routing
D ○ Domaining

9 Which of the following networking devices is a Layer 2 device?

A ○ Router
B ○ Hub
C ○ Repeater
D ○ Bridge

10 Which of the following are steps in the encapsulation process?

A ○ Data is converted into segments.
B ○ Packets are converted into frames.
C ○ User information is converted into data.
D ○ Frames are converted into bits.
E ○ Segments are converted into packets.
F ○ All of the above.

Answers

1 *B, C.* Routing is defined on the Network layer (Layer 3) of the OSI model. Layer 2 does error detection, but it does not do error notification. This is done on the Transport layer. In addition to answers A and D, the Data Link layer also defines network topologies, and access to physical media. *See "Listing the functions of Layer 2."*

2 *C.* IEEE 802.1 defines routing, bridging, and internetwork communications. 802.2 defines the LLC sublayer and 802.5 defines Token Ring networks. *Review "Stacking up the IEEE 802 standards."*

3 *F.* The MAC (Media Access Control) and LLC (Logical Link Control) sublayers are defined on the Data Link layer. *Take a look at "The sublayers of the Data Link layer."*

4 *A, B.* The LLC sublayer of the Data Link layer defines flow control methods, timing mechanisms, and service access points (SAPs) which allow lower layers to communicate with Layer 3 protocols. *Check out "Connecting on the LLC sublayer."*

5 *C.* CRC (Cyclic Redundancy Check) is defined on the Data Link layer as the error-detection method. *See "Detecting errors in the flow."*

6 *B.* The MAC (Media Access Control) address is 48 bits long with 24 bits used for each of the manufacturer's ID number and the unique serial number assigned a device. *Review "Communicating on the MAC sublayer."*

7 *A.* The Address Resolution Protocol (ARP) maintains a small database in memory called the ARP cache that tracks MAC addresses to their associated network addresses. *Look over "How can we resolve this?"*

8 *B.* Segmenting a network decreases network congestion and decreases the chances of message collisions on the network. *Check out "Segmenting a Network for Fun and Profit."*

9 *D.* A router is a Layer 3 device and a hub and repeater are both Layer 1 devices. *See "Bridging the difference."*

10 *F.* If you understand this process and the sequence of its steps, you're beginning to get a pretty good understanding of what happens to data as it moves through the protocols that are defined on the layers of the OSI model. *Review "Encapsulating Data."*

Chapter 5

The Network Layer

∙∙∙

Exam Objectives

▶ Listing the functions of the Network layer
▶ Explaining Network layer router functions

∙∙∙

M ost of this book and the CCNA exam deal in one way or another with the Network layer. In fact, the CCNA exam could be renamed the Network Layer exam. When we were planning this book, we almost didn't include this chapter. But this chapter provides the string that binds together the whole CCNA package.

We give you the facts plain and simple: If you don't understand what happens on the Network layer, you won't pass the CCNA exam. If you weren't motivated to read this chapter before, you should be now.

Use this chapter to review the concepts of logical addressing and route selection. You may also want to peruse the section dedicated to Novell IPX (see "Routing IPX and other NetWare Stuff"), a primer that should help you on exam day.

The purpose of this chapter is to bring together any loose ends and provide you with a birds-eye view of routing. We think this is a good chapter to refer to as you prepare for the exam.

Quick Assessment

Listing the functions of the Network layer

1 There are two types of addressing used on a network: a _____ address and a _____ address.

2 A _____ address consists of two parts, a network portion and a host portion.

3 A Class A TCP/IP address uses _____ bits for the network portion and _____ bits for the host portion.

4 The Novell IPX addressing scheme uses a total of _____ bits in its address.

Explaining Network layer router functions

5 A _____ protocol is used to pass messages between routers to update and maintain routing tables.

6 A route that is manually configured in a router is a _____ route.

7 The type of routing in use when the router is able to make route determinations using metrics is _____ routing.

8 The three types of routing protocols are _____, _____, and _____.

9 _____ is a Novell proprietary protocol that operates on the Network layer.

10 On a NetWare network, the protocol used to advertise the services available on a network is _____.

Answers

1 *Physical, logical.* See "Addressing it logically."

2 *Logical.* Review "Addressing it logically."

3 *8, 24.* Take a look at "Addressing it logically."

4 *80.* Check out "Addressing it logically."

5 *Routing.* See "Comparing routed and routing protocols."

6 *Static.* Review "Choosing static or dynamic routes."

7 *Dynamic.* Look over "Choosing static or dynamic routes."

8 *Distance vector, link state, hybrid.* Check out "Routing or is that rooting?"\

9 *IPX.* See "Routing IPX and other NetWare Stuff."

10 *SAP (Service Advertisement Protocol).* Review "Broadcasting the SAP."

Reviewing Routing Foundations

The Network layer (Layer 3) of the OSI Reference Model basically defines logical addressing and the ways that packets are moved from source to destination on a network. In other words, the functions of the Network layer can be broken down as follows:

- ✔ Message addressing
- ✔ Path determination between source and destination nodes on different networks
- ✔ Routing messages between networks
- ✔ Controlling congestion on the subnet
- ✔ Translating logical addresses into physical addresses

In the following sections we take a closer look at these functions.

Addressing it logically

There are two different types of addresses on a network: a physical address (see Chapter 4) and a logical address. A logical address has a logical connection to all other addresses on its network. This contrasts to a Layer 2 MAC (physical) address, which while fixed to a specific network node, has no relationship to any other device on the network.

In order for a packet to be delivered from source to destination, its Layer 3 logical address must consist of two parts, a network and a host portion. The network portion of this address is used for routing on the internetwork level. The remaining parts of the logical address, which include the host portion, are used to send the packet to its final network and to its associated physical address.

This two-part (network, host) addressing scheme is incorporated into all protocols that are tested on the CCNA exam. Be sure you know the three schemes listed in Table 5-1 for the exam.

The following table lists the protocols and how this addressing scheme is implemented.

Table 5-1	Logical Address Construction		
Protocol	*Total Address Length*	*Bits in Network Portion*	*Bits in Host Portion*
TCP/IP	32	Class A – 8 Class B – 16 Class C – 24	Class A – 24 Class B – 16 Class C – 8
IPX	80	32 or less (only significant digits listed)	48 bits (MAC address)
AppleTalk	24	16 or less (indicates one or many in cable range)	8 bits or less (dynamically assigned)

Cisco routers can handle many other Layer 3 protocols such as Banyan Vines, DECnet, and X.25.

Moving a packet across the internetwork

Figure 5-1 shows how a packet travels from a PC on a local network through the internetwork (created by interconnecting routers) to a destination PC on a remote network.

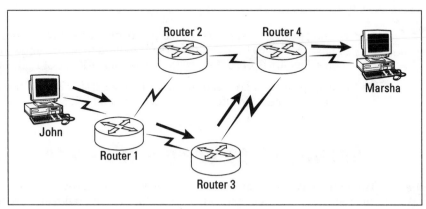

Figure 5-1:
A packet may take any number of paths when moving across the internet-work.

If John is sending an e-mail to his friend, Marsha, the packet (or packets) that carries his message is routed over the internetwork, moving from router to router until it reaches the destination network and finally Marsha's host computer. As it travels, the packet moves up and down the OSI layers at each point along the way.

When the message (which moves down through the seven OSI layers on John's computer before it's sent out on the local network in binary form) arrives at Router 1, it moves up from the Physical layer to the Data Link layer to the Network layer. At Layer 3, it's determined that the message is not on a network attached to Router 1 and the message is sent down through the Data Link layer to the Physical layer and on to Router 3.

This up and down movement continues until the message reaches Router 4. On Layer 3 it's determined that the message is addressed to a network attached to Router 4 and passed along to the destination network. Each router on the path between John and Marsha strips away the Data Link header, examines the destination network portion of the address and searches for the network ID in its routing table. The routing table indicates whether the network ID is the network attached to the router. If not, the message is re-encapsulated and sent on to the next router. Eventually, the message finds the destination network, or dies trying, and is stored in Marsha's mailbox.

Comparing routed and routing protocols

Cisco routers support multiple protocols that can be used for routing. These protocols do not interface with one another, nor do they interfere with each other. In fact, separate and independent routing tables are maintained for each protocol.

You absolutely must understand the difference between a routed and a routing protocol.

- ✔ Routing protocols support routed protocols. A routing protocol is used to pass messages between routers for maintaining and updating routing tables. Examples of routing protocols are RIP, IGRP, OSPF, EIGRP.

- ✔ Routed protocols are used to carry end-user traffic across the internetwork. Examples of routed protocols are IP and IPX.

Choosing static or dynamic routes

Two definite types of routes can be assigned inside a router for route determination: static or dynamic. Static routes are configured manually and by the network administrator for those network addresses for which a single route is desired. The good news is that static routes aren't shared with other routers. The bad news is that if the topology of the network changes, you may need to manually update any static routes used for it.

Dynamic routing enables the router to make route determinations by using routing metrics and efficiencies. Any changes to the topology of the network are updated to the routing table automatically. See Chapter 11 for more information on dynamic routing.

Routing, or is that rooting?

You need to know three different types of routing protocols for the CCNA exam: distance vector, link state, and hybrid. Table 5-2 provides the details about each one.

Table 5-2	Routing Protocol Types	
Protocol	*Characteristics*	*Examples*
Distance Vector	Uses hop count; views the network from its neighbors' perspective; frequent updates; copies its routing table to neighbors	RIP, IPX RIP, IGRP
Link State	Shortest path; common view of network; event-triggered updates; LSPs (Link State packets) sent to all network routers	NLSP, OSPF, IS-IS
Hybrid	Distance vector with more accurate metrics; no periodic updates; only event-triggered	IS-IS, EIGRP

Layer 3 devices and protocols

This may sound obvious, but routers are Network layer (Layer 3) devices. The TCP/IP protocol stack includes several Layer 3 protocols, including IP, ARP, and ICMP. Novell NetWare's IPX is also a Network layer protocol.

Routing IPX and other NetWare Stuff

Make no mistake about it, the CCNA exam emphasizes TCP/IP. However, you really should have some knowledge of Novell's NetWare IPX for the test.

IPX is a member of the IPX/SPX proprietary suite of protocols. IPX operates at the Network layer. It is connectionless and uses datagrams.

Some NetWare terms you really need to know are:

- **Service Advertisement Protocol (SAP):** The NetWare protocol used to advertise (update) the services available over the network.

- **Routing Information Protocol (RIP):** A distance vector routing protocol similar to RIP in TCP/IP that uses ticks, hop counts, and split horizon metrics.

- **NetWare Link Services Protocol (NLSP):** A link state routing protocol that is the default routing protocol on NetWare 4.11 and higher.

- **Novell Directory Service (NDS):** Novell's Directory Service protocol.

- **NetWare Core Protocol (NCP):** Providing client-to-server connections and applications.

Novell servers and routers announce their services using SAP broadcasts. Because of this, NetWare clients automatically discover available network services. A special type of SAP advertisement is the Get Nearest Server (GNS) which enables the client to locate the nearest server for login.

Broadcasting the SAP

Routers and servers keep lists of the services available in the network in server information tables, which have an aging device to delete expired entries. To let network servers and routers know about changes on the network, a SAP (Service Advertisement Protocol) broadcast is made every 60 seconds by default.

Routers do not forward SAP broadcasts. Instead, they use the information in the SAP broadcast to build their own SAP table, which is then forwarded to other network routers every 60 seconds. This amount of traffic can cause congestion on the network, so some networks use SAP filters to screen out redundant messages on input, output, or just those sent from a specific router.

Filtering the SAP

Each SAP broadcast message advertises a certain type of SAP service. Each SAP service is identified by a hexadecimal number. You can expect to see these SAP service ID numbers on the exam:

- 278 – Directory Server
- 7 – Print Server
- 4 – NetWare File Server

Getting to the nearest server

When a node powers up on a Novell network, it sends out a broadcast searching for the nearest server it can log into. This process is known as Get Nearest Server (GNS). If the nearest server is not on the local network segment, the Cisco router responds to the request using its SAP table to provide the address of the nearest server. GNS responses can also be filtered by using SAP filters.

Can I get your IPX address?

Earlier in the chapter we explained the structure of an IPX address (see the section, "Addressing it logically"), but when a Cisco router is a part of an IPX network, the network portion of the address must be determined. The easiest method is to ask the Novell network administrator. Other methods include:

✔ Inquire from a neighboring Cisco router by using the show CDP Neighbors Detail command

✔ Telnet into the neighboring router and get running configuration information

✔ If the neighboring router is non-Cisco (gasp!), log in and use NetWare Config utility

Each Cisco router on the network must use the same IPX network number as the rest of the existing network.

Do you have an IPX socket wrench?

An individual node may have multiple processes operating over IPX at the same time. In order to identify which process an incoming packet is destined for, each process is associated with a socket number.

An IPX socket is a 16-bit number that's added to the end of the network and node addresses in the IPX header. In the IPX addressing scheme, it looks like this

```
network.node.socket
```

where network is the 32-bit network ID, node is the 48-bit MAC address of the destination device, and socket is a 16-bit code that designates the service requested. For example, a socket value of a hexadecimal 451 means that NCP (NetWare Core Protocol) services are requested. Other examples are 452 for SAP and 453 for RIP.

Configuring the router for IPX

Configuring the router for use with the Novell NetWare IPX protocol is a two-step process:

1. Enabling IPX routing: This is done in global configuration mode. You may also enable load sharing if you want. See "Enabling IPX globally" later in this section.

2. Assigning networks to interfaces: This step in the process assigns network numbers to each interface. Remember that multiple network numbers can be assigned as long as each uses a different encapsulation (frame) type. To apply an encapsulation type, you need to use a Cisco keyword and not the Novell frame type's name. Table 5-3 lists the Novell IPX frame types and the corresponding Cisco keywords.

Table 5-3	Novell IPX Frame Types and Cisco Keywords	
Interface	*Novell Frame Type*	*Cisco Keyword*
Ethernet	Ethernet_802.3	novell-ether (default)
Ethernet_802.2		sap
Ethernet_II		arpa
Ethernet_SNAP		snap
Token Ring	Token-Ring	sap (default)
FDDI	Fddi_snap	snap (default)

Enabling IPX globally

The commands that can be used in Global configuration mode to enable IPX routing are:

✔ **IPX routing:** Enables IPX routing. A node address must be entered on serial interfaces. On other interfaces, a MAC address is used if none is specified. Here is an example of this command:

```
CCNA_For_Dummies#config t
Enter configuration commands, one per line. End with
        CNTL/Z.
CCNA_For_Dummies(config)#ipx routing
CCNA_For_Dummies(config)#^Z
CCNA_For_Dummies#sh prot
Global values:
    IPX routing is enabled
```

✔ **IPX network:** Enables IPX on individual interfaces and sets the encapsulation type. Here is an example of this command:

```
CCNA_For_Dummies(config-if)#ipx network 2100 encapsula-
        tion novell-ether
```

✔ **IPX maximum paths:** Enables load sharing. Default is 1, which means it's disabled by default.

✔ **IPX route destination-net next-hop:** Allows a static route to be overridden by a route learned dynamically.

Interfacing locally

IPX subinterfaces are generally used to enable multiple logical networks on a single hardware interface. Subinterfaces create virtual interfaces on the router and can be used to run secondary level IP, IPX, and other addresses on a single interface.

The IPX network command assigns network numbers to the interface. The first logical network configured is considered the primary network and others are considered secondary. Here's an example of the commands used to assign a subinterface (number 1001) for IPX with default encapsulation to Ethernet0 interface:

```
CCNA_For_Dummies(config)#int e0.1001
CCNA_For_Dummies(config)#ipx network 192 encap novell-
        ether
CCNA_For_Dummies(config)#^Z
CCNA_For_Dummies(config)#
```

If you have trouble understanding these commands, review Chapters 9 and 10 and then look at this example again. You'll definitely see code samples on the test.

1 Which of the following is not a function of the Network layer?

A ○ Message addressing

B ○ Path determination

C ○ Physical addressing

D ○ Routing

2 The type of address that has a connection to all other addresses on the network is

A ○ Logical

B ○ Physical

C ○ MAC

D ○ Internal

3 Which of the following lists the correct number of bits used for the network and host portions of a Class C IP address?

A ○ 24, 8

B ○ 16, 16

C ○ 8, 24

D ○ 32, 48

4 The protocol type used to carry end-user traffic across the internetwork is

A ○ Routing protocol

B ○ Routed protocol

C ○ Static routing

D ○ Dynamic routing

5 The protocol type used to pass messages between routers to maintain and update routing tables is

A ○ Routing protocol

B ○ Routed protocol

C ○ Static routing

D ○ Dynamic routing

6 The routing protocol type that uses hop count to determine routes is

A ○ Link state

B ○ Hybrid

C ○ Distance vector

D ○ None of the above

7 Which of the following is a distance vector routing protocol?

A ○ OSPF

B ○ IGRP

C ○ IS-IS

D ○ EIGRP

8 Which of the following SAP Service IDs advertises a Directory Server on the network?

A ○ 4

B ○ 7

C ○ 200

D ○ 278

9 The length in bits of the IPX network.node.socket address is

A ○ 32

B ○ 48

C ○ 80

D ○ 96

10 The Cisco router command used to enable IPX routing is

A ○ IPX maximum paths

B ○ IPX route destination-net next-hop

C ○ IPX network

D ○ IPX routing

Answers

1 C. Physical addressing is a function defined on the Data Link layer. Other functions of the network layer control congestion on the network and translate logical addresses into physical addresses. *See "Reviewing Routing Foundations."*

2 A. A logical address is related to and relative to all other logical addresses on a network and the internetwork. *Review "Addressing it logically."*

3 A. Before you tackle routing, IP addressing, and subnet masking, be sure you know the number of bits in the network and host portions of the three major IP address classes. *Look over "Addressing it logically."*

4 B. A routed protocol is capable of being forwarded or routed by a router. *Check out "Comparing routed and routing protocols."*

5 A. A routing protocol is used to support and maintain the information used by routers to perform routing. *See "Comparing routed and routing protocols."*

6 C. A distance vector protocol uses metrics, such as hop count, to determine routes for a packet. *Review "Routing, or is it rooting?"*

7 B. Other distance vector protocols are RIP and IPX RIP. *Take a look at "Routing, or is it rooting?"*

8 D. Each SAP broadcast advertises a certain type of network service. Several hexadecimal numbers are assigned to network service types. You should be familiar with a few. *Check out "Filtering the SAP."*

9 D. The elements of the address that includes the network address (32-bits), node address (48-bits), and IPX socket (16-bits) are a 96-bit address that's included in the IPX header of a frame. *See "Do you have an IPX socket wrench?"*

10 D. IPX routing must be configured in Global configuration mode, and the IPX routing command enables IPX routing on an interface. *Review "Enabling IPX globally."*

Chapter 6

The Transport Layer

Exam Objectives

▶ Differentiating connection-oriented and connectionless services

▶ Defining flow control

▶ Describing flow control methods

As part of our Top 7 countdown (or count up, depending on how you look at it), we now look at Layer 4 of the OSI model — the Transport layer. Although the Transport layer isn't as prominent on the CCNA exam as the Network layer (see Chapter 5), the Transport layer is where protocols are defined that make and manage the connection between two computers. It's also where the techniques that regulate the flow of data are defined. On the exam, the Transport layer is second in importance only to the Network layer and just a little behind the Data Link layer (see Chapter 4).

You need to understand two key concepts in this chapter. Unfortunately, each concept has two or more parts you really need to know.

You should know the differences between the protocols that are connection-oriented and those that are connectionless. We know that to somebody fairly new to the Transport layer (and aren't we all?), the concept of connectionless communications appears to be an oxymoron. Trust us, connectionless protocols are alive and well on the Internet. In fact, for the test, it's also a good idea to know which Transport layer protocols are connectionless and which are connection-oriented.

The other major concept is flow control. Data flows between two computers or devices in either measured, even bursts or in a flow that resembles a fire hose. It's within the context of the fire hose that you need to know how to turn the flow on and off so that your interface isn't flooded, causing data to be lost. As we said, this concept is called *flow control,* as in control the flow, and you need to know three different types of flow control, no less.

 We suggest that after you read this chapter, you may want to reread Chapter 5 and visualize the interactions between the Network and Transport layers. Visualizing interactions is a good way to understand the inter-layer interactions that take place moving a network message over the internetwork.

Quick Assessment

Differen-
tiating
connection-
oriented
and connec-
tionless
services

1 A protocol that establishes a virtual circuit and includes a process for error recovery is considered to be _____.

2 _____ protocols depend on protocols on other OSI layers to provide error recovery.

3 TCP and SPX are _____ protocols.

4 UDP and IPX are _____ protocols.

5 _____ delivery is a benefit of connection-oriented protocols.

Defining
flow
control

6 _____ is the technique used to stop and restart a transmission so that a receiving station's buffer is not overfilled and data is lost.

7 The primary reason for congestion between two communicating devices is _____.

Describing
flow control
methods

8 The three basic forms of flow control are _____, _____, and _____.

9 The _____ flow control method notifies the sending station before its buffers are full.

10 The flow control method that allows a certain number of packets to be transferred before an acknowledgment is required is _____.

Answers

1   *Connection-oriented.* See "The benefits of being connection-oriented."

2   *Connectionless.* Review "Using a connectionless protocol."

3   *Connection-oriented.* See "The benefits of being connection-oriented."

4   *Connectionless.* Review "Using a connectionless protocol."

5   *Reliable.* Take a look at "Making a positively reliable delivery."

6   *Flow control.* Check out "Going with the Flow and Staying in Control."

7   *The sending computer sends messages faster than the receiving computer can process the messages.* Look over "Going with the Flow and Staying in Control."

8   *Buffering, Congestion avoidance, Windowing.* See "Going with the Flow and Staying in Control."

9   *Congestion avoidance.* Review "Avoiding the congestion."

10 *Windowing.* Check out "Flowing through the windows."

Transporting Data Over the Network

The four main functions of the Transport layer are:

- ✔ Segment and assemble upper-layer applications
- ✔ Transport segments from one host to another host
- ✔ Establish and manage end-to-end operations
- ✔ Error recovery

In the networked production environment of the OSI model, the Transport layer is the shipping and receiving department. Its primary duties are to package data payloads for shipment between network nodes, ship the packages to their destinations using the best available carrier type, and then provide whatever services are needed to ensure that the data packages reach their destinations. In carrying out these duties, the Transport layer's shipping and receiving department allows incoming packets to arrive out of sequence and patiently repacks and arranges them so that they are passed on to the upper layers in proper size and order.

Supporting the transport services

In carrying out its duties, the Transport layer performs a range of support activities, including:

- ✔ Maintaining data integrity through flow control techniques
- ✔ Multiplexing the data from upper layer applications
- ✔ Setting up and tearing down any virtual circuits established to transport the data over the network
- ✔ Hiding any network-dependent information from the upper layers (which will only confuse them)
- ✔ Breaking down Session layer (Layer 5) datagrams into segments
- ✔ Monitoring the error-free delivery of the data to its destination
- ✔ Providing for general connection management and data transfer services
- ✔ Providing for the reliable (but, not guaranteed) delivery of data

And you thought the Network layer was busy!

Transporting protocols

Be sure you can recognize the Transport layer protocols from their three-letter abbreviations. The most common protocols associated with the Transport layer, and the protocols you should know for the exam, are the following:

- **TCP (Transmission Control Protocol):** The protocol primarily concerned with the reliable delivery of packets that requires an acknowledgment of a packet's arrival at its destination.

- **UDP (User Datagram Protocol):** The TCP/IP best-effort protocol that isn't concerned with the reliable delivery of packets and doesn't bother with overhead such as acknowledgments.

- **SPX (Sequence Package Exchange):** The Novell protocol most akin to TCP. It guarantees data delivery.

- **NWLink (NetWare Link):** Microsoft's version of Novell's IPX/SPX.

- **ATP/NBP (AppleTalk Transaction Protocol/Name Binding Protocol):** AppleTalk's data transport protocols.

- **NetBIOS/NetBEUI (Network Basic Input/Output System/NetBIOS extended User Interface):** Microsoft's network protocols that work together to manage communications and provide data transport services.

TCP, UDP, and SPX are Transport layer protocols. Network layer protocols include IP, ICMP, and IPX.

SPX is connection-oriented and its packets are tracked through the use of a sequence number associated with each packet. A positive acknowledgment must be received from the destination device for each packet before another packet is sent. A print server is an example of an application that implements SPX.

Getting Well Connected

The exam tests your knowledge of connection-oriented and connectionless protocols. You need to be able to list the characteristics of each type of protocol, as well as name some Transport layer protocols and indicate the type of connections they use.

The benefits of being connection-oriented

A protocol is considered connection-oriented if it meets one of two criteria:

- ✔ Data is transmitted over a negotiated, established path, a virtual circuit, between two nodes.
- ✔ The protocol includes a process for error-recovery.

Before data is exchanged over a connection-oriented protocol, the processes used to successfully establish an end-to-end connection must have all been completed successfully. In the negotiation phase of this process, the sending and receiving stations must agree on some synchronization parameters, confirm that a transfer of data is authorized, and indicate that they're ready to transfer data. For the exam, you should be familiar with the "three-way handshake" described in Chapter 14.

The common analogy for a connection-oriented protocol is the use of a registered letter. When you send a registered letter through the Postal Service, you take the letter to the post office, a carrier delivers it to its destination, the receiver signs for the letter, and the Postal Service sends you a notice that your letter was delivered. Similarly, a connection-oriented protocol requires that every packet must be acknowledged before it sends the next packet. In a way, each packet is a registered letter.

For the exam, you should know that the following protocols and link types are connection-oriented:

- ✔ Frame Relay
- ✔ TCP
- ✔ SPX
- ✔ X.25

Using a connectionless protocol

In contrast to the connection-oriented type of protocols, connectionless protocols are like open pipes. What you put into the pipe at one end should come out of the pipe at the other end. But there are no guarantees. A connectionless protocol does not use a virtual circuit, or connection-oriented conduit, and no error-recovery functions are included. Connectionless protocols depend on error-recovery to be provided by a higher OSI layer.

Connectionless protocols involve less processing overhead than do connection-oriented protocols, because they don't establish, maintain, or tear down virtual circuit connections. This also means that a connectionless protocol is much faster. The common analogy for a connectionless protocol is dropping a letter into the mailbox. You assume the letter will be transported and arrive at its destination, but you have no guarantee that it will happen for sure.

You can be sure to see these connectionless protocols on the test:

- ✔ IP
- ✔ IPX
- ✔ UDP

Remember that IP and IPX are Network layer protocols.

Making a positively reliable delivery

Reliable delivery is a benefit of connection-oriented protocols. This reliability is achieved through a technique called positive acknowledgment, which requires the receiver to remain in contact with the sender via a virtual circuit and send back an acknowledgment each time data is received and deemed to be error-free. The sending device must wait for the acknowledgment from the receiving device before it can send additional data.

If data is lost, the receiver requests a retransmission of the data. Just how much data is to be retransmitted depends on the protocol in use. Some protocols require an entire group of data segments be retransmitted including the missing or erroneous segment. Other protocols require that only the missing segment be re-sent.

In order to account for segments that may get totally lost en route, the sender uses a timer. If an acknowledgment for a message segment isn't received in the allotted time, meaning the timer reaches zero, the segment is presumed lost in space and retransmitted. This mechanism provides reliability to the protocol. For segments that do reach their destinations and for which acknowledgements are sent back to the sender, all is well.

Making a Fast Recovery

Error-recovery is a characteristic of connection-oriented protocols. It involves not only a system to detect errors, but also the steps necessary to recover the data detected as being in error. Usually, error-recovery merely requests retransmission of the bad packet.

Identifying an error recovery protocol

Layer 4 protocols that implement error recovery have the following characteristics:

- ✔ They are connection-oriented, which means they establish a connection prior to the transmission of data.

- ✔ Each PDU has header information used by the receiver to acknowledge the receipt of a packet and a system to check for errors in transmission.

- ✔ The sender requires notification of packets that have been successfully received.

Error-recovery should not be confused with error-detection. Error-detection involves the use of CRC (Cyclic Redundancy Check) and checksums that are included in segment headers. These mechanisms are used to detect whether a PDU was transmitted correctly. Chapter 3 includes a discussion on the Layer 2 error-detection activities. However, other layers, including Layers 3 and 4, also include some checksum mechanisms. Layer 4 includes both error-detection (error-checking) and error-recovery processes (see "Checking for errors" later in this chapter).

Checking for errors

The error-detection process used within an error-recovery protocol is called *error-checking*. Yes, that's three errors in one sentence, but be absolutely sure you know how each differs from the others. When you read a test question about errors, determine which is being discussed: checking, detecting, or recovery.

You use three primary methods for error-checking. They are parity bit, checksum, and CRC.

Checking for parity errors

Two types of parity can be used, odd-parity and even-parity. If odd parity is being used, the sending device counts the number of binary one bits and if the tally is an even number (say 1502 or 2216), a one parity bit is added to force the number of one bits to an odd value. The process works the same for even-parity. If the number of one bits is an odd number, a one parity bit is added so that the number of one bits will become even.

When the parity bit form of error-checking is used, the sending device counts the number of bits in the transmission and, if needed, adds a bit to ensure that the number of total bits is either an odd or even number, whichever method is in use. The receiving device also counts the bits (including the parity bit) and verifies that the correct number of bits arrived and that it was appropriately even or odd. If all is well, the packet is assumed to have arrived intact. Otherwise, if the wrong tally of bits arrives, a request is sent back to the sending device to retransmit the packet.

Counting heads

Another form of error-checking is the checksum. In this method, the one's complement is summed for all of the 16-bit words that make up the TCP segment or UDP datagram. If the segment has an odd number of bytes, a padding byte of zeroes is added to the end of the segment. This padding byte is not transmitted with the segment, it's only used for the calculation. The one's complement of the calculated sum becomes the checksum that is stored in the header and sent with the segment. At the receiving end, this same calculation is performed and compared to the checksum value in the segment header. If the totals are unequal, a request is sent back to the sending device to retransmit the segment.

Checking for math errors

Some protocols use the CRC number calculated on the Data Link layer (see Chapter 3) using a mathematical calculation to create a bit profile. If the CRC calculated on the sending end of the transmission is different from that calculated on the receiving end (using the exact same calculation), then a request is sent back asking for retransmission of the data.

It's 100 milliseconds, do you know where your data is?

In addition to the calculated error-checking methods, there's another method called time-out. This method is almost a no-brainer in that it's simple in its actions. After transmitting a packet, the sending device waits a reasonable amount of time for an acknowledgment. If it doesn't get an acknowledgment, the packet is considered lost and is retransmitted automatically. The amount of "wait time" is determined by the time-out mechanisms embedded into the protocol.

Going with the Flow and Staying in Control

Flow control is a technique used to prevent a receiving node from getting data so fast that its buffers overfill and data is lost. If the sending station is transmitting data faster than the receiving station can process it, a backlog begins to grow until the storage buffers fill up and overflow. This causes new incoming segments to be lost because there is nowhere to store them. This condition is called *congestion* and must be controlled to ensure the integrity of the message being transmitted.

To prevent congestion from happening, the receiving node sends a control message to the sending node when its buffers are almost full, telling the sending device to stop sending data. After the receiving device is able to clear its buffers by processing some of the data, it sends a control signal to the sending node that it can begin sending data again.

The three basic forms of flow control are:

- ✔ Buffering
- ✔ Congestion avoidance
- ✔ Windowing

Smoothing out the bumps

In the buffering method of flow control, the receiver allocates sufficient buffer (memory) space to store any occasional bursts of excess data until it can be processed. However, in this flow control method, no attempt is made to interrupt or slow down the data flow. If the buffers become full, any subsequent data has no place to be stored and is discarded, resulting in the loss of data. The buffering method expands and contracts much like a balloon, and just like the balloon, if too much is pumped in, it bursts.

Avoiding the congestion

The congestion avoidance flow control technique is similar to the buffering method, except that it uses a more precautionary approach to managing its buffers. Under a congestion avoidance method, the receiving device monitors its buffers to determine if they're about to fill up. When the receiver notices that its buffers are getting full, it sends a control message back to the sending device that tells it to stop sending information. After the receiving computer has emptied its buffers, it sends another control message telling the sender that it can start sending data again.

The advantage that the congestion avoidance technique has over the buffering method is that it prevents data from being lost. It also helps conserve memory space by requiring smaller buffer size. Of course, the smaller the buffers, the more often that flow will be interrupted.

Flowing through the windows

The windowing flow control method establishes a window, not like the Windows 98 kind, but a window that allows a certain number of packets to flow through it before the receiving device must reply with an acknowledgment. The sending device waits for acknowledgment from the receiving device after it sends out a certain number of packets.

The windowing method's window is actually a number that represents the maximum amount of data that can be sent until an acknowledgment is received from the destination node. The size of the window can directly affect throughput. If an acknowledgment is required after every packet, throughput suffers because of the amount of time used to send each acknowledgment. By increasing the size of the window, throughput is improved and reliability is still maintained.

Quenching the source

Another flow control method used in Cisco equipment is the source-quench message, which is a kind of hybrid technique. When the receiving node's buffer fills up and data is starting to be lost, the receiving node sends a source-quench request to the sending node for each packet that is lost. The sending node responds by slowing down its transmission rate until it no longer is receiving source-quench messages. The sending node then begins to slowly increase its transmission rate until it reaches its normal speed or another source-quench message is received.

The source-quench flow control method is much like what happens when you see a police car parked at the side of the road — you immediately slow down. You gradually speed up until you reach the speed limit or see another police car.

Prep Test

1 Which of the following is not a function of the Transport layer?

A ○ Segment and assemble upper-layer applications
B ○ Transport segments from one host to another
C ○ Routing
D ○ Error-recovery

2 Which of the following is not a Transport layer protocol?

A ○ TCP
B ○ ARP
C ○ UDP
D ○ SPX

3 SPX is a _____ protocol and its packets are tracked by a sequence number in each packet.

A ○ Connectionless
B ○ Best effort
C ○ Connection-oriented
D ○ Layer 3

4 A protocol that transmits data over a virtual circuit and has a process for error-recovery is

A ○ Connectionless
B ○ Connection-oriented
C ○ Congestionless
D ○ Fully recoverable
E ○ A and C
F ○ B and D

5 Which of the following protocols or standards is not connection-oriented?

A ○ TCP
B ○ SPX
C ○ IPX
D ○ X.25

6 Which of the following protocols is not connectionless?

A ○ SPX
B ○ UDP
C ○ IPX
D ○ IP

7 Only _____ protocols implement error recovery.

A ○ Connection-oriented
B ○ Connectionless
C ○ Ethernet
D ○ Frame relay

8 Which of the following is not an error checking method?

A ○ Parity bit
B ○ Hash total
C ○ Checksum
D ○ CRC

9 Which of the following is not a flow control method?

A ○ Buffering
B ○ Unbuffered
C ○ Windowing
D ○ Congestion avoidance

10 What are the two forms of parity bit error checking used to determine whether the correct number of bits in a transmission were received?

A ○ Even-parity
B ○ Odd-parity
C ○ Checksum
D ○ CRC

Answers

1 *C.* Routing is a Network layer (Layer 3) activity. The missing function for the Transport layer is that it establishes end-to-end operations. *See "Transporting Data Over the Network."*

2 *B.* ARP (Address Resolution Protocol) is a Data Link layer protocol. Other Transport layer protocols are NWLink, ATP/NBP, and NetBEUI. Review "Transporting protocols."

3 *C.* SPX is a Novell NetWare protocol that provides reliable delivery of packets. Look over "Transporting protocols."

4 *B.* Be on the lookout for questions like this one on the CCNA exam that give you way too many options and make you paranoid that you may not have included all possible options. Check out "The benefits of being connection-oriented."

5 *C.* IPX is a connectionless protocol. ATM and frame relay link types are also connection-oriented. *See "The benefits of being connection-oriented."*

6 *A.* SPX is a connection-oriented protocol. *Review "Using a connectionless protocol."*

7 *A.* Error recover protocols also require an acknowledgment be sent to the sender using information from the PDU header. *Take a look at "Identifying an error recovery protocol."*

8 *B.* A hash total is a method used to determine a checksum and CRC, but it is not an error checking method. *Check out "Checking for errors."*

9 *B.* We made this one up. The other three answers are the basic flow control methods you should know for the CCNA exam. *See "Going with the Flow and Staying in Control."*

10 *A, B.* Networking parity error checking can use either even- or odd-parity. *Review "Checking for parity errors."*

Chapter 7

The Upper Layers

• •

Exam Objectives

▶ Explaining half- and full-duplex Ethernet operations

▶ Defining the functions of the Session layer

▶ Identifying the functions of the Presentation and Application layers

• •

*J*ust in case you're wondering which upper layers the title of this chapter is referring to, it's the upper layers of the OSI Reference model. Can you name them? Of course you can! They are the layers above the Transport layer: Layers 5, 6, and 7, otherwise known as the Session, Presentation, and Application layers. Although these layers don't directly relate to routing, the CCNA exam covers what's defined on these layers and how they work. You can expect to see at least a question or two about these layers.

This chapter helps you understand the key concepts of the upper three layers of the OSI model, especially the concepts you need for the exam. This chapter, and the others in this part of the book, provides you with a good overview and review of the OSI model and the concepts, technologies, and applications it defines. This knowledge is essential to understanding the functions of the Cisco products you must know for the exam.

As an added bonus, at the end of this chapter you'll find a handy-dandy study guide that lists all of the OSI layers with a quick explanation of each and some examples of the hardware, software, and protocols that operate on each layer. We recommend that you earmark that page for use as you cram and for a quick pretest review on exam day.

Quick Assessment

Explaining half- and full-duplex Ethernet operations

1 When you use a _____-duplex transmission mode, you can transmit two ways, but only one way at a time.

2 Over a _____-duplex transmission mode, you can transmit two ways simultaneously.

3 The access method used with half-duplex networking is _____.

Defining the functions of the Session layer

4 A(n) _____ is a series of related connection-oriented transmissions between network nodes.

5 The Session layer is Layer _____ of the OSI model.

6 The Session layer coordinates requests and responses between _____ and _____.

Identifying the functions of the Presentation and Application layers

7 The four data services defined on the Presentation layer are: _____, _____, _____, and _____.

8 Three common Presentation layer data conversion standards are _____, _____, and _____.

9 The layer of the OSI model that is closest to the end-user is the _____ layer.

10 FTP (File Transfer Protocol) is a(n) _____ layer protocol.

Answers

1 *Half.* See "A half-duplex is not a housing unit."

2 *Full.* Review "Playing with a full duplex."

3 *CSMA/CD.* Look over "A half-duplex is not a housing unit."

4 *Session.* Check out "Communicating on the Session Layer."

5 *5.* See "Communicating on the Session Layer."

6 *Upper layer protocols, lower layer protocols.* Review "Communicating on the Session Layer."

7 *Data encryption, data compression, data formatting, data conversion.* Take a look at "Presenting the Presentation Layer."

8 *ASCII, EBCDIC, encryption.* Check out "Presenting the Presentation Layer."

9 *Application.* See "Applying the Application Layer."

10 *Application.* Review "Applying the Application Layer."

Communicating on the Session Layer

Layer 5 of the OSI model is the Session Layer, which establishes, manages, and terminates sessions between applications. So, what is a session?

A *session* is a series of related connection-oriented transmissions between network nodes. Another way to look at it is that a session is the interrelated communications between two or more presentation entities, which emphasizes that the Session layer provides services to the Presentation layer.

The Session layer coordinates transmitted data and directs it to the appropriate upper layer. The Session layer takes data from upper and lower layers and formats it for processing on lower or upper layers, as appropriate. It also lets the upper layers know whether further communications are expected from the current session. The Session layer coordinates the requests and responses between the upper layers and the lower layers for communication over the network. Any problems that occur on the Session layer or above are handled on this layer. However, this doesn't mean that the Session layer can correct the problem. It depends on other layers to help it out with most problems.

One of the more important functions of the Session layer is its role in deciding whether a communications session uses a simplex, half-duplex, or full-duplex transmission mode.

Communicating a la mode

The Session layer supports three different transmission or dialogue modes: simplex, half-duplex, or full-duplex mode, as shown in Figure 7-1.

Simplex, which you won't see on the exam, allows data to flow in one direction only. There's no facility for a response or acknowledgment to be carried back to the sender. A public address system at the ballpark is a simplex communications system.

A half-duplex isn't a housing unit

When you use a half-duplex transmission mode, you can transmit both ways (from sender to receiver and from receiver to sender), but only one way at a time. A citizens band (CB) radio is an example of a half-duplex system, along with many telephone speaker boxes. Only one party can speak at a time if you want to have a coherent conversation. Over.

For the CCNA exam, one of the Session Layer's transmission modes that you need to focus on is the Ethernet half-duplex and its design and operation. The key element to understanding half-duplex is that each of the two stations in a communications session can use only one circuit each at a time. The transmit circuit of one station is directly tied to the receive circuit of the other station. So, if one station is sending over its transmit circuit (accounting for its one in-use circuit), the other station is busy receiving on its active receive circuit. If the receiver wants to reply (thereby becoming the sender), it must wait until its circuits are idle to begin.

Avoiding whole collisions on the half-duplex

CSMA/CD (Carrier Sense Multiple Access/with Collision Detection) is used in half-duplex situations because the possibility for collisions exists. While each node waits until an entire transmission is received before taking any other actions (such as sending back an error notification), the other nodes on the network are also contending for the network.

Playing with a full-duplex

Full-duplex transmission mode allows communications to flow in both directions of a session simultaneously. The PSTN (Public Switched Telephone Network) is a full-duplex system that allows you to both speak and hear at the same time over the same circuit. While in full-duplex mode, two networked stations can both receive and transmit simultaneously. In effect, this doubles the effective bandwidth of the system because information can flow in both directions.

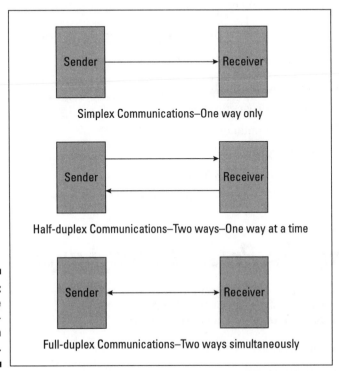

Figure 7-1:
The three basic transmission modes.

Simplex Communications–One way only

Half-duplex Communications–Two ways–One way at a time

Full-duplex Communications–Two ways simultaneously

Full-duplex mode is enabled by a combination of software and hardware but requires a network on which collisions cannot occur. Generally speaking, this requires a switched networking environment on which virtual circuits, like private pipes, are created between transmitting and receiving stations. Networked workstations must also have a NIC card capable of full-duplex operation.

Some facts and requirements you should know about full-duplex operations for the CCNA exam are:

- Requires full-duplex NIC cards
- Loopback and collision detection must be disabled in the NIC card, for reasons that are obvious to you, hopefully
- The NIC card's device driver must support simultaneous transmission and receiving
- Full-duplex circuits are capable of 10 Mbps, 100 Mbps, and Gigabit Ethernet data speeds

Testing your session skills

The CCNA exam is likely to list services and protocols asking you to identify the OSI model layer where each service or protocol is defined.

The following services and protocols are defined on the Session layer:

- ASP (AppleTalk Session Protocol)
- NFS (Network File Services)
- RPC (Remote Procedure Call)
- SCP (Serial Communications Protocol)
- SQL (Structured Query Language)
- X Window System and X Terminal
- ZIP (AppleTalk Zone Information Protocol)

Presenting the Presentation Layer

The main function of the presentation layer is to define the data formats used to provide a number of services to the Application layer. Included in these services, and the ones you need to know, are:

- Data encryption
- Data compression

✔ Data formatting

✔ Data conversion

Think of the Presentation layer like a United Nations translator: It translates the data it gets from the Application layer into a format that the receiving node's Application layer can interpret. The Presentation layer is also responsible for negotiating data transfer syntax between the application layers. This is the only layer that changes data. The other layers can put data in different encapsulation forms but the Presentation layer can change it. An example of this would be from changing the data from ASCII to EBCDIC. The Presentation layer not only formats and converts text but also audio, video, and graphic data.

On the exam, you may find references to some of the conversion standards defined on the Presentation layer for data conversion and formatting. Table 7-1 lists the Presentation layer standards by category. We recommend that you know which category each of the standards falls under.

Table 7-1	Presentation Layer Standards
Category	*Standards*
Data conversion	ASCII, EBCDIC, encryption
Audio/video conversion	MIDI, MPEG, QuickTime, AVI
Graphics conversion	GIF, JPEG, PICT, TIFF

Applying the Application Layer

The OSI model's Application layer is the layer closest to the user. Remember that the Application layer doesn't define the applications used by the end-user to perform tasks. Rather, it defines the communication services used by the user's applications to transmit data over the network. The Application layer provides access services to desktop (and notebook, and tower) computer applications.

The Application layer provides three basic services to applications. It makes sure the resources needed to carry out a session are present, it matches the application to the appropriate communication protocol or service, and it synchronizes the transmission of data between the application and its protocol.

The Application layer services and protocols you should know are:

✔ FTP (File Transfer Protocol)

✔ E-mail clients

> ✔ Web browsers
>
> ✔ Telnet
>
> ✔ SNMP (Simple Network Management Protocol)
>
> ✔ BBS (bulletin board system) servers
>
> ✔ EDI (Electronic Data Interchange) and other transaction services

A Quick Review of the OSI Model

Table 7-2 summarizes what you know about the layers of the OSI Reference Model, including a brief description of the functions defined on each layer and some examples of protocols or resources that operate on each layer. This is a very useful study aid for your last-minute review.

Table 7-2		OSI Reference Model Summary	
Number	*Layer*	*Activities*	*Protocols and Services*
7	Application	Identifies and establishes availability of communication partners. Determines whether resources are sufficient for the communication to occur.	FTP, SMTP, Telnet, Web Browsers, CMIP, and Virtual Terminal Protocol
6	Presentation	Defines data formats, including encryption, data conversion, audio/visual, and graphics.	MPEG, HTML, MIDI, ASCII, EBCDIC, TIFF, GIF, PICT
5	Session	Establishes, controls, and ends sessions. Full- and half-duplex communications.	NFS, SQL, NetBIOS, AppleTalk ASP, X Windows, RPC, DECNet SCP
4	Transport	Segments and reassembles data. Defines reliable and unreliable data transmission, and connection-oriented and connectionless protocols.	TCP, UDP, SPX

Number	Layer	Activities	Protocols and Services
3	Network	Concerned with end-to-end delivery of data, logical addressing, and routing and how routes are identified.	IP, IPX, and AppleTalk DDP
2	Data Link	Translates PDUs from higher layers into data frames. Defines the LLC and MAC sublayers.	Frame Relay, PPP, HDLC, IEEE 802.2, 802.3, 802.5, FDDI, ATM, SDLC, LAPB, ISDN
1	Physical	Defines the characteristics of the physical medium used to send and receive data bits.	EIA/TIA 232 and 449, RJ45, Ethernet, CAT 5, X.21, HSSI

Prep Test

1 A series of related connection-oriented transmissions between two network nodes is a

A ○ Socket

B ○ Session

C ○ Handshake

D ○ Virtual circuit

2 The transmission mode that's capable of transmitting in two directions but in only one direction at a time is

A ○ Full-duplex

B ○ Simplex

C ○ Half-duplex

D ○ Full-nelson

3 On half-duplex transmission networks, which access method is used to avoid collisions?

A ○ CSMA/CA

B ○ CSMA/CD

C ○ SDH (semi/demi/hemi)

D ○ Ethernet

4 The transmission mode that's capable of transmitting in two directions simultaneously is

A ○ Full-duplex

B ○ Simplex

C ○ Half-duplex

D ○ Half-nelson

5 Which of the following is not a bandwidth supported by full-duplex Ethernet networks?

A ○ 10 Mbps

B ○ 100 Mbps

C ○ Gigabit Ethernet

D ○ 1.54 Mbps

6 Which of the following is not a Session layer protocol or service?

A ○ NFS

B ○ SQL

C ○ FTP

D ○ RPC

7 Which of the following is not a Presentation layer data conversion standard or function?

A ○ ASCII

B ○ MPEG

C ○ EBCDIC

D ○ Encryption

8 Which of the following is not an Application layer protocol or service?

A ○ E-mail client

B ○ SNMP

C ○ FTP

D ○ TCP/IP

9 Which layer of the OSI model is concerned with end-to-end delivery of data?

A ○ Session

B ○ Transport

C ○ Network

D ○ Physical

10 Which of the following lists the layers of the OSI model in correct sequence, starting with Layer 1 and moving up?

A ○ Data Link, Physical, Network, Session, Transport, Application, Presentation

B ○ Physical, Network, Data Link, Transport, Session, Presentation, Application

C ○ Physical, Data Link, Network, Transport, Session, Presentation, Application

D ○ Application, Presentation, Session, Transport, Network, Data Link, Physical

Answers

1 *B.* The Session layer establishes, manages, and terminates sessions and provides services to the Presentation layer. You need to know what a session is so that you know what the Session layer does. *See "Communicating on the Session Layer."*

2 *C.* Think of it as two circuits (send and receive) making up a duplex. If you can transmit on only one circuit at a time, you're using only half of the duplex. *Review "A half-duplex is not a housing unit."*

3 *B.* Ethernet networks use CSMA/CD and that's what we're talking about here. *Take a look at "Avoiding whole collisions on the half-duplex."*

4 *A.* A duplex is made up of two (du) wires (plexes), so if you use both plexes at the same time, you're using the whole duplex, or a full-duplex. *Check out "Playing with a full duplex."*

5 *D.* Ethernet networks regardless of mode support 10 to 1,000 Mbps. *See "Playing with a full duplex."*

6 *C.* FTP (File Transfer Protocol) is an Application layer protocol. *Review "Testing your session skills."*

7 *B.* Okay, this may seem like a trick question, but if you read the question very carefully, you notice that the question asked about data conversion and not graphic conversions. Be sure you read the questions on the CCNA exam very carefully and answer them as they are posed. Don't supply more information than you're given or make assumptions about what the question means. It is what it is. *Look over "Presenting the Presentation Layer."*

8 *D.* You needed an easy one after the previous question. TCP/IP is a protocol suite and is most definitely not on the Application layer, although a few of the protocols in it are. *Check out "Applying the Application Layer."*

9 *C.* It's on the Network layer that routing, which is the mechanism that affects end-to-end delivery of data across the internetwork, is defined. *See "A Quick Review of the OSI Model."*

10 *C.* Just remember, "Please Do Not Throw Salami Pizza Away." *Review "A Quick Review of the OSI Model."*

Part III

Routers

By Rich Tennant

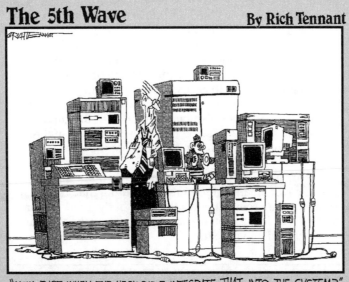

"NOW JUST WHEN THE HECK DID I INTEGRATE THAT INTO THE SYSTEM?"

In this part . . .

A very good, but very British, friend of mine pronounces routers as "rooters," claiming that what a "rooter" does is send packets over the best route (pronounced "root"). Regardless of how you pronounce it, he's absolutely right about what they do.

On a test focused on Cisco routing and switching, it's logical that a goodly portion of the test is about routers. Not only is it logical, it's a fact. In terms of the number of questions on the test, routers are only second to the OSI model. You must know about the makeup of a router and the commands used to access, configure, and manage a router. You must know how to work with the IOS software as well as how perform software updates or backups on the router. You must also be familiar with routed and routing protocols and be able to differentiate the two.

There are five chapters in this part of the book, all of which cover an area of routers and routing that you must know for the exam. Whether this part of the book is your first stop or last as you prepare for the exam, just be sure it is included on your study plan.

Chapter 8

Router Models

● ●

Exam Objectives

▶ Using a router to segment a LAN

▶ Describing the benefits of LAN segmentation

▶ Defining router elements

● ●

*F*or the CCNA exam, you need to be familiar with routers, especially how they think, how they relate to other networking devices, and where they fit into the networking world. There's quite a bit that you must know to pass the routers part of the test.

However, there are some things that you don't need to know for the exam. Just so you don't waste valuable time studying the wrong stuff, take these topics off your must-study list:

✔ You don't need to be able to field strip and reassemble a router either blindfolded or not.

✔ You don't need to memorize the processor speeds and specific memory amounts in particular Cisco router models, and you won't be asked to determine the proper memory or processor configuration for a router.

✔ There are no questions regarding the general anatomy of a router, and you won't be asked to list the main component parts of a router, with the exception of memory.

These are real-world topics that may be valuable to know on the job or to throw out casually in an interview, but they aren't on the test. Anyone who tells you to study this stuff for the exam is wasting your time.

This chapter also includes background information you must understand — without which some of the exam's questions may make no sense to you. Even with this background information, there's a chance that some questions may still be incomprehensible, but we think that may just be part of the Cisco game plan. We have no other explanation.

Quick Assessment

Using a router to segment a LAN

1 The three-tier hierarchical network design implemented by Cisco consists of the _____, _____, and _____.

Describing the benefits of LAN segmentation

2 Local traffic stays local and reduced collision domains are a result of _____.

3 A _____ can connect two or more _____ using two different routable protocols.

4 Logical addresses are used by a router to _____ LANs.

Defining router elements

5 There are _____ types of memory used in a Cisco router.

6 The Cisco IOS software resides in the _____ memory.

7 NVRAM stores the _____ file.

8 EPROM stores the _____ system image and _____.

9 _____ is a proprietary Cisco protocol that allows directly connected Cisco devices to learn about each other.

10 The default holdtime for CDP is _____.

Answers

1 *Core* (big, fast, and expensive), *Distribution* (campus backbone), *Access* (LAN segmentation). See "A Layered Approach to Networks."

2 *LAN segmentation.* Review "Why segment a network?"

3 *Router, LANs.* Take a look at "Segmenting a LAN with a router."

4 *Segment.* Check out "The specific benefits of segmenting with a router."

5 *Four* (RAM/DRAM, NVRAM, ROM, and EPROM). Look over "The Four Faces of Router Memory."

6 *RAM/DRAM.* See "RAM/DRAM a ding dong."

7 *Start-up configuration.* Review "The Four Faces of Router Memory."

8 *Operating, microcode.* Look over "Flashing the EPROM."

9 *CDP* (Cisco Discovery Protocol). Check out "Discovering CDP."

10 *180 seconds.* Take a look at "Stuff to memorize about CDP."

A Layered Approach to Networks

Cisco uses a three-tier hierarchical network model, like that illustrated in Figure 8-1, that consists of three layers: the Core layer, the Distribution layer, and the Access layer, which can be abbreviated as CDA. We recommend that you come up with an easily remembered phrase (a mnemonic) for CDA, such as Coeur d'Alene or the like. Using a mnemonic phrase may be too complicated, however, so just remembering core, distribution, and access may be a whole lot easier for you.

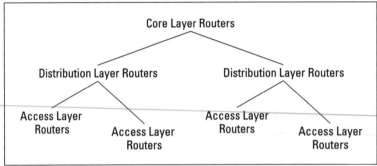

Figure 8-1:
The layers
of the Cisco
router
hierarchy.

Be prepared for questions on the exam that expect you to know the kinds and models of routers contained on each layer. You should be familiar with each of the layers, but don't lose any sleep over them. Save that for really intense topics, such as subnetting and wild card masking (see Chapters 13 and 15 to commence your sleeplessness).

Core layer routers

On the Core layer is where you find the biggest, fastest, and, not surprisingly, most expensive routers with the highest model numbers. Core layer routers are used to merge geographically separated networks. The focus of the core layer is on moving information as fast as possible, most often over dedicated or leased lines. Don't look for any hosts or workstations here; this is the land of servers.

Distribution layer routers

In the Cisco world, the famous campus backbone exists on the Distribution layer. Routers on this layer of the model are used to connect buildings or departments, such as accounting, production, and distribution — known in Cisco-speak as large functional groups.

Router layer specifics you really don't need to know

You really don't need to know the specific router model numbers within each layer for the CCNA exam, but if you have extra time on your hands and a few brain cells not otherwise occupied, it can't hurt to familiarize yourself with the following:

✔ Core layer routers are in the 7000 series or higher.

✔ Distribution layer routers are in the 3600 series.

✔ Access layer routers are in the 2500/2600 series.

To protect you from yourself, we won't go into any more detail than that. Now get back to studying the stuff you need to know.

Distribution routers represent the intermediate level of the Cisco model. On this layer, the packets of the network are filtered and forwarded up and down the router layers. The bulk of your routing policy decisions are made here. Mid-level network servers can also be found on the Distribution level.

Access layer routers

The Access layer is where the rubber meets the road. The Access layer is where host computers access a network and where most network traffic finds its destination. Access layer routers are used to segment LANs.

If you've been to or are enrolled in a CCNA training course, or you've completed a Cisco Networking Academy, it's very likely that the routers you used were Access layer routers.

Segmenting a Network with a Router

Segmenting a local area network with a router may not be the least expensive way to go, but it does have its benefits. You can expect to find questions on the benefits of segmenting a network with a router on the CCNA exam.

There are definitely less expensive ways to segment a network, such as with a bridge, and there are certainly faster, simpler ways, such as with a switch, but a router can provide benefits other devices cannot. We explain these benefits in the section, "The specific benefits of segmenting with a router."

Chapter 2 covers segmenting a network , broadcast domains, collision domains, and other terms and concepts you need to understand before tackling using a router to segment a network. Chapter 14 discusses segmenting a network using bridges and switches.

Why segment a network?

Here are some of the general benefits of segmenting a LAN, regardless of how that was accomplished:

- ✔ **Keeps local traffic local:** Breaking up a network into smaller segments reduces congestion on the network by reducing the overall traffic loads.

- ✔ **Increases the bandwidth available to each user:** Bandwidth is a shared entity, but each segment and its users have full use of the bandwidth available. For example, if there are 100 users on a 100 Mbps segment, each user has an average of 1 Mbps of available bandwidth. If this same segment were further segmented into 10 segments with 10 users on each segment, however, then every user would have an average of 10 Mbps of available bandwidth.

- ✔ **Fewer collisions:** In general, traffic tends to stay within a segment, and less traffic is routed beyond the segment to contend for access to the backbone.

- ✔ **Reduces Ethernet distance limitations:** There are inherent distance limitations on an Ethernet network (see Chapter 4). When a network is segmented with a router (and only a router; not a bridge, and not a switch), the beginning point from which the maximum distance for the cabling is determined is re-established.

Segmenting a LAN with a router

The CCNA exam focuses on why you would segment a LAN. As we said earlier in this chapter, there are several ways to segment a LAN — with a bridge, a switch, or a router. However, and only because this chapter is about routers, we focus on some facts and characteristics of LANs segmented with a router.

Just in case you're curious, *how* you segment a LAN with a router involves some knowledge of the network, its traffic, and topology. You could just pick a point in the LAN and plug the router in, but most likely, unless you are extremely lucky, you wouldn't see much improvement in the performance of the LAN.

Routers are used to segment fairly large, in terms of geography and number of nodes, or very high volume networks. In most cases, you are more likely to segment a LAN with a bridge or switch for the reasons discussed in Chapter 16.

Here are some things to consider before you segment a LAN with a router:

- ✔ A router can segment a LAN that includes different media types. For example, a LAN may have both Category 5 and Thinnet (coaxial) cable connecting to fiber optic cabling.

- ✔ A router can interconnect LANs that are using different protocols, provided they are all routable.

- ✔ A router does increase latency by adding the delay caused by the router examining each packet entirely before sending it on.

- ✔ A router can also provide more than one active link or route to a destination. On a larger LAN, this can provide route diversity and redundancy, which are always good things.

The specific benefits of segmenting with a router

So what are the benefits of using a router to segment a LAN and why would anyone want to do it? Excellent question, and one you're sure to find on the CCNA exam.

There are several reasons, including that you simply have money to burn. The real reasons, the ones you should know for the exam, can be summarized as:

- ✔ **Reduced size of broadcast domains:** Routers block broadcasts unless specifically instructed to forward them.

- ✔ **Smaller networks:** Routers create smaller networks, as opposed to dividing a large network into smaller pieces of itself.

- ✔ **Flexible addressing:** Routers segment a network by using logical, rather than physical, addresses. For example, a bridge uses the MAC (Media Access Control) or physical address to make its addressing decisions, whereas the router uses the logical or IP address.

- ✔ **Better administration:** A system administrator has more management tools available when using a router, thanks to the increased memory in a router and its ability to make routing decisions based on a multitude of factors.

The Four Faces of Router Memory

It's a no-brainer that the types of memory in a Cisco router are included on the CCNA exam. You should absolutely plan to see several questions about each type of memory in the router and the types of information stored in each.

Cisco routers have four basic types of memory: RAM/DRAM, NVRAM, ROM, and Flash (EPROM) memory.

Table 8-1 summarizes what you need to know about memory in a Cisco router for the test.

Table 8-1	Different Memory Types in a Cisco Router
Memory/Type	**Contents**
RAM/DRAM	Active program and operating system instructions, the running configuration file, routing tables
NVRAM	Startup configuration file
ROM	POST, bootstrap, and startup/power-up utilities (usually limited version of), Cisco IOS
Flash	Cisco IOS

You don't have to overload your brain with how much memory is in each router configuration, but you really need a good general understanding of the different types of memory and how each is used.

RAM/DRAM a ding dong

The primary working memory in a Cisco router is the RAM/DRAM (Random Access Memory/Dynamic Random Access Memory). Like your PC, the router uses RAM for storing its working files and data. The RAM in the router is specifically DRAM, the same type of RAM found in your PC. Like the RAM in your PC, if the power is lost or if you turn it off, all of the files and data stored in RAM are lost. That's what "dynamic" in the name means. DRAM is volatile, which means it must have a power source to do its thing.

For the exam, remember that the router's RAM is volatile DRAM that holds the working data and files of the router, and when the power is turned off, the contents of the RAM are lost.

In the Cisco router, RAM is used to hold:

- ✔ The working copy of the Cisco IOS software
- ✔ The command executive, also know as EXEC, which interprets the commands you enter from the router console
- ✔ The routing tables
- ✔ The active configuration file
- ✔ The ARP cache
- ✔ The packet buffers
- ✔ The packet hold queues

Did we mention that anything stored in RAM is lost when the router is powered off?

Good old stable, non-volatile RAM

Where DRAM is volatile and must have a power source to hold its contents, nonvolatile RAM (NVRAM) can hold its contents when the main power source is lost. You may even know this type of memory as static RAM (SRAM), but on the CCNA exam, remember it as NVRAM. The Cisco router uses NVRAM to store its startup configuration file.

ROM is not RAM

There's another type of memory, called ROM (Read-Only Memory), that's even more reliable than NVRAM. Like NVRAM, ROM does not lose its contents when the power is turned off. Information or programming stored in ROM is put there during the manufacture of a computer integrated circuit (IC), more or less permanently locked away forever.

On the Cisco router, ROM contains the program instructions for the power-on self-test (POST) diagnostics, the bootstrap program, which is the startup program for the router, and the router's operating system. Cisco routers contain two copies of IOS, a stripped down version that is stored in ROM and the full up-to-date version stored in Flash (see "Flashing the EPROM"). The IOS version in Flash memory is the one you should focus on for the exam.

Flashing the EPROM

There is a type of PROM that can be updated. An EPROM (Erasable Programmable Read-Only Memory) can be updated through a software update. This type of ROM is erasable and can be written to using a software-controlled operation called *flashing*. As volatile as this may sound, it isn't. EPROMs are non-volatile and retain their contents without a power source indefinitely, or at least until the next time they are flashed. And no, the software used to update an EPROM is not a flasher.

On the Cisco router, the Flash memory is an EPROM IC chip that holds the image and microcode of the router's operating system. Storing the operating system on Flash memory enables you to upgrade it without having to remove and replace ROM chips on the CPU board.

Discovering CDP

Two other internal elements of the Cisco router that you should know about for the CCNA exam are the Cisco Discovery Protocol (CDP) and the Show command. The CDP is explained in this section, but see Chapter 9 for information on the Show command.

CDP protocol facts

The Cisco Discovery Protocol (CDP) is a proprietary Cisco protocol that allows you to get (discover) information about directly connected Cisco routers, bridges, and switches. CDP, which is included in Cisco's entire product line, uses SNAP (Subnetwork Access Protocol), a Data Link layer protocol, and frames to communicate with routers and other network connectivity devices. CDP is supported by virtually all LAN media and transmission modes, including frame relay and ATM (Asynchronous Transfer Mode).

How CDP works

CDP automatically starts when a router is powered on and immediately goes to work by multicasting Data Link layer discovery messages looking for other Cisco devices. Any device wishing to be discovered sends back an SNMP (Simple Network Management Protocol) message containing configuration data on itself. This information in this message allows CDP to display information about the discovered devices, including information about different Network or higher layer protocols. CDP caches whatever it discovers in its router's RAM updating it periodically or whenever it changes.

Stuff to memorize about CDP

You can definitely expect questions about CDP on the CCNA exam. Here is what you should know about CDP for the test:

- ✔ CDP uses SNAP at the data link level, which makes it protocol independent.

- ✔ CDP detects attached devices regardless of what protocol they're running (for example, TCP/IP, IPX, or AppleTalk).

- ✔ CDP is enabled by default when the router is booted on all interfaces.

- ✔ CDP update requests are multicast by default every 60 seconds using Layer 2 multicast messages.

- ✔ CDP has a default holdtime. The amount of time a device holds a CDP update before discarding it is 180 seconds.

In Chapter 10, which covers router commands in more detail, we spend a little more time on CDP.

Prep Test

1 Which three-tier hierarchical network design is implemented by Cisco Certified Network Associates?

A ○ Center, Delivery, and Access

B ○ Crux, Dissemination, and Admittance

C ○ Core, Distribution, and Access

D ○ Transport, Network, and Data Link

2 The 3600 series router located at the "campus" backbone implementing access lists is an example of a router used at what design layer?

A ○ The Transport layer

B ○ The Distribution layer

C ○ The Network layer

D ○ The Data Link layer

3 Which of the following is not a resulting benefit of LAN segmentation?

A ○ Reduces collision domains

B ○ Reduces the inherent distance limitations of an Ethernet network

C ○ Keeps local traffic local

D ○ Increases bandwidth available on a per users basis

4 What do routers use to segment LANs?

A ○ SNAP

B ○ CDP

C ○ MAC Addresses

D ○ Logical Addresses

5 Where is the startup configuration file stored?

A ○ 000C8800 – 000CBFFF

B ○ 000B0000 – 000BFFFF

C ○ EPROM

D ○ NVRAM

6 What is not stored in the RAM/DRAM memory?

A ○ The working copy of the Cisco IOS software

B ○ The command executive

C ○ The routing tables

D ○ ARP cache

E ○ None of the above

7 Which statement is true about EPROM (Flash)?

A ○ You can upgrade the OS only by replacing the chips.

B ○ Flash memory is lost when the router is powered down.

C ○ The operating system and micro code are stored here.

D ○ The bootstrap program is stored here.

8 What characteristic of NVRAM is correct?

A ○ The working copy of the configuration file resides here.

B ○ Contains a backup copy of the configuration file.

C ○ Is not present on Cisco routers.

D ○ None of the above.

9 Which statement is not true about CDP?

A ○ Uses SNAP at the physical layer to detect attached devices.

B ○ Is enabled by default when the router is booted.

C ○ Updates are multicast every 60 seconds.

D ○ The default holdtime is 180 seconds.

10 Because CDP is media independent, it supports which upper-layer protocols?

A ○ TCP/IP

B ○ IPX

C ○ DDP

D ○ All of the above

Answers

1 *C.* Cisco implements a three-tiered router hierarchical routing model that includes core, distribution, and access layers. Know what each layer does, but really know the access layer of this model. *See "A Layered Approach to Networks."*

2 *B.* The key word in this question is backbone. In the Cisco router model, a campus backbone is on the Distribution layer. Routers on the Distribution layer are used to connect buildings or departments, and other large functional groups. *Review "Distribution layer routers."*

3 *A.* While reducing broadcast domains, reducing collision domains is not a benefit of segmenting a network. *Take a look at "The specific benefits of segmenting with a router."*

4 *D.* A router uses the logical address to segment a network. This is in contrast to a bridge that uses the physical address to segment a network. *Check out "The specific benefits of segmenting with a router."*

5 *D.* NVRAM (Non-volatile random access memory) stores the startup configuration and don't you forget it! *Look over "Good old stable, non-volatile RAM."*

6 *E.* All of these items are stored in RAM/DRAM on the Cisco router. Be prepared for these double negative types of questions and be on the lookout for questions that ask you to identify the incorrect item as well. *See "RAM/DRAM a ding dong."*

7 *C.* The EPROM, which can be updated through a process called flashing, holds the image and micro code for the operating system. *Review "Flashing the EPROM."*

8 *B.* This question is intended to make you think about the NVRAM in a slightly different way to prepare you for different wordings that may show up on the test. *Look over "Good old stable, non-volatile RAM."*

9 *A.* Be careful. CDP uses SNAP, but on the Data Link layer not the physical layer, to detect attached devices. This is the level at which you must know this stuff. *Check out "CDP protocol facts."*

10 *D.* CDP is supported by virtually all LAN media and transmission modes, including frame relay and ATM. *Take a look at "CDP protocol facts."*

Chapter 9

Router Basics

• •

Exam Objectives

▶ Logging into a router

▶ Using context-sensitive help

▶ Editing the command history

▶ Explaining passwords, hostname, and banner

• •

*M*ake no mistake, the CCNA exam tests you quite thoroughly on the objectives listed for this chapter. In fact, at this point in your preparations for the test, it's a good idea to sit down with a router and reinforce your understanding of router commands by actually typing in the commands and seeing the results.

Because this chapter covers only the most basic router commands and operations, nothing in it is especially mentally taxing. However, make sure you have a steel-trap grasp of these commands, concepts, and operations. On questions dealing with router commands, the CCNA exam questions include remarkably similar answers. Your ability to pick the correct answer will depend on how well you know the router commands, their results, and applications. We'll summarize this for you: Really know this stuff!

In this chapter, we guide you through the processes used to log into a router from a variety of different sources. Although there are more than 17 different operating modes you can use after you have logged in, you need to be familiar with only six of them for the CCNA exam. However, you need to know the five types of passwords used for security. You must know how to give your router a pet name, a hostname actually, and how to set up a command that displays messages to anyone logging into your router.

This may not be the most important chapter in the book, but it's certainly among the top 20. If you've had some good hands-on experience with Cisco routers, chances are you already know this stuff very well. However, if you're just getting started, this is very important foundation knowledge for the exam as well as on the job.

Quick Assessment

1 CLI stands for _____.

2 There can be up to _____ simultaneous telnet sessions active on one router.

3 The CLI prompt ">" represents the _____ Exec mode and the prompt "#" represents the _____ Exec mode.

4 The Global Configuration Mode is entered from the _____ Exec mode.

5 The prompt > or rommon> represents the _____ mode.

6 In a telnet session, the _____ key will auto-complete an unambiguous command.

7 Context sensitive help is available by using the _____ key.

8 To disable enhanced editing from the User Exec mode you would enter _____.

9 From the configuration mode, the last command you should enter is _____.

10 MOTD stands for _____.

Answers

1   *Command line interface.* See "Oh Phooey, There's No GUI."

2   *Five.* Review "Taking control."

3   *User, Enable* (Privileged). Take a look at "Working with the Exec command interpreter."

4   *Privileged or Enable.* Check out "Working with the Exec command interpreter."

5   *ROM Monitor.* Look over "ROM Monitor mode."

6   *Tab.* See "Help for the terminally lazy."

7   *Question mark* (?). Review "What is a four-letter word beginning with an 'h?'"

8   *Terminal no editing.* Look over "Editing History."

9   *Ctrl+Z or end.* Check out "Configuration mode."

10 *Message of the day.* Take a look at "Waving the Banner."

Oh Phooey, There's No GUI

The CCNA exam tests you on your ability to operate the router through its Command Line Interface (CLI). Those of you who remember the DOS command line, that paragon of user-friendliness, will have little or no problem with the CLI. However, if your technical life has been spent in the warm and safe cocoon of GUI (graphical user interface) screens and mouse clicks, then this may present a challenge for you.

Spelling and syntax: Getting it right

Without sounding too much like your high school English teacher, spelling and syntax are crucial elements of the CLI and its successful use. If you want a command to be successfully executed, you first must spell it correctly. Then you must get all of the command's parameters and components in their right places, and they must be spelled correctly as well.

One very important abbreviation is TLA, which stands for three-letter abbreviation. While most CCNA abbreviations are three letters, as in the abbreviations for protocols and technologies, there are also the more advanced FLA (Four-Letter Abbreviations) and the dreaded EFLAs (Extended Four-Letter Abbreviations) as well.

Depending on where you're coming from, the CLI can be like an old friend that you use every day, or it can be a cursed multiheaded monster that's constantly attempting to make your life sheer misery. If the latter is the case, remember that practice and perseverance are the virtues to conquer the monster and win the day. Feel better now?

Speaking of abbreviations, you should know for the test that Cisco IOS commands and parameters can be abbreviated to any length that still uniquely identifies the command or parameter. For example, the command configure terminal can be abbreviated to conf t, that contains enough of the original command to avoid being ambiguous. The shortest unique abbreviation for configure is conf. The abbreviation con wouldn't work because there's a connect command and it would be too ambiguous about which command you actually wanted. On the other hand, terminal is the only parameter of the configure command that begins with the letter t, so you only need its first initial. You can abbreviate it to one letter. You find other examples of abbreviated commands and parameters throughout this chapter.

Accessing the router

All Cisco routers have a console port, an asynchronous serial port, located on the back of the router and labeled CONSOLE. The console port lets you connect a computer to the router, and through a terminal emulator (such as Windows' HyperTerminal, SecureCRT from Van Dyke Technologies, or the like) create an interactive control console for the router.

Most Cisco routers also have an auxiliary port, labeled as AUX, located to the right of the console port. The auxiliary port allows a dialup modem to be attached, and asynchronous remote dialup access can be used along with a terminal emulator to configure or control the router.

In addition to using the console and auxiliary ports, you can also access the router via a virtual terminal connection, such as the TCP/IP Telnet protocol that is used to connect to remote devices, including routers, over a network. Cisco routers can support up to five Telnet sessions at one time.

Some other less popular, but available, ways that you can access a router for configuration are through a TFTP (Trivial File Transfer Protocol) server and through a network management station using the SNMP (Simple Network Management Protocol).

Logging into the router

To gain access to a Cisco router, you must know the password for the type of access you want to gain. There can be up to five different passwords on the router, with one for each type of access, but it's not uncommon for a router to have only one password set for all login types. However, Cisco recommends that the encrypted password created with the enable secret command should never be the same as any of the other passwords. The secret password should be the system administrator's edge in router security. It is encrypted when created and stored in the configuration files, so it can't be discovered. All other passwords are stored in clear text in the configuration data.

Figure 9-1 illustrates the action of logging into a router. In general, whether you log in from the console port, the auxiliary port, or over one of the other access methods, such as the Telnet protocol, you must know a password to gain access to the Exec command interpreter. Using the command interpreter, you may access User and Enable (also called Privileged) mode commands and actions, some of which may require an additional password.

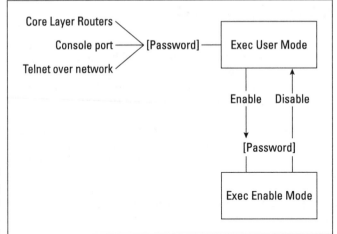

Figure 9-1:
Logging into
a router.

Working with the Exec command interpreter

Also known as the Command Line Interface, the Exec command interpreter has two Exec modes, or command groups, that can be used to perform a variety of functions.

The two Exec modes in the user interface are User Exec and Enable Exec (a.k.a. Privileged) modes.

A mode for the masses

After you successfully log into the router, you enter User Exec mode. In this mode, you can connect to other devices (such as another router), perform simple tests, and display system information. You know you're in User Exec mode if the prompt displayed on your screen looks like

```
RouterHostname>
```

where hostname represents the assigned name of the router. It's the greater than sign (>) that's significant here. This symbol on the prompt means that you're in User Exec mode.

A mode for the privileged

Enable Exec mode, which is also known as Privileged mode or Privileged Exec mode, is accessed from User Exec mode through the ENABLE command and a password. If an Enable Exec mode password has not been set, this mode can be accessed only from the router console port. From within Enable Exec mode, you can perform all User Exec mode functions. Plus, you have access to higher-level testing and debugging, detailed probing of the router functions, and updating or changing configuration files. The prompt that indicates this mode is:

```
RouterHostname#
```

where the pound or number sign (#) at the end of the prompt indicates Enable Exec mode.

Other command modes you may see on the test

The CCNA test focuses on the User Exec and Enable Exec modes, but you may encounter questions on other command modes. Here are other command modes that you may see on the test.

ROM Monitor mode

The ROM Monitor mode is displayed during the boot process if no operating system is loaded in the Flash memory. From this mode, the router's configuration can be completed. After configuring the router so that it may complete the startup process, the continue command moves you into User Exec mode. The prompt that indicates this mode is either just a greater than sign or the prompt

```
rommon>
```

However, the ROM Monitor mode can be avoided by booting the system from an alternative source, such as a TFTP (Trivial File Transfer Protocol) server.

Setup mode

When a router is first configured from the console port, Setup Mode is invoked. Setup mode can also be invoked from the Enable Exec mode prompt with the setup command, or by rebooting the router after deleting its startup-config file through the `erase startup-config` command.

The setup command is a prompted dialog that guides you through the setup process to configure the router. There's no special prompt for this action. For the exam, you should know that after the startup-config file (which is stored in the flash memory) is erased, the router will be in Setup Mode when it's restarted.

Another way to restart the router is to issue the `reload` command.

Configuration mode

You should expect to encounter a question on the test that deals with Configuration mode. Like the Setup mode, you enter this mode by using a command, in this case the `config` command. To move into what is called global configuration mode (remember this), enter the following config command at the Enable Exec prompt (the one with the # symbol):

```
CCNA_For_Dummies#config terminal
```

The parameter `terminal` or its abbreviation `t` is absolutely necessary. The config command can be used to configure the network settings and memory with the `config net` and `config mem` commands, respectively.

Configuration mode allows you to manually configure the router or make changes to the router's status. You may also descend to another mode within Configuration mode — the Configuration Interface mode — to make changes to individual interfaces.

The prompt for Configuration Mode is

```
RouterA#(config)
```

The prompt for Configuration Interface Mode is

```
RouterB#(config-if)
```

This should be fairly easy to remember. The word `config` without any other additions indicates good old plain Configuration Mode. The word `config-if` indicates you are in Configuration Interface Mode. The suffix `-if` means InterFace.

You should also know that there are two basic configurations stored in each router: the startup configuration and the running configuration. You can display these configurations by using the following commands:

```
show startup-config or sh star + TAB
show running-config or sh run + TAB
```

We want to be sure you understand the shortcut commands used in this example. The unique abbreviation for show is sh and in either form this command can be used to display the contents of a configuration file. The abbreviations star and run indicate the startup-configuration and the running-configuration, respectively. Don't worry about these abbreviations too much. In most instances on the exam, abbreviations are not used in favor of the full, spelled-out commands and parameters. However, you may see abbreviations in some examples or references, so it's a good idea to understand how to use them and what they mean. The Tab key is used to complete a shortcut command line.

To end or exit configuration mode, you press the Control (Ctrl) and Z keys together.

For now, don't worry about the commands and parameters used to create the router's configuration. The various commands used for this purpose are detailed in Chapter 10.

Mode alert

On the exam you'll find one or two questions that require you to match a command with the proper mode. After you understand the modes explained in this chapter, pay close attention to the mode in which a command is used. When taking the test, carefully read each question and answer and don't jump at what appears to be the first correct answer. Check the mode in use in all examples and be sure it's the correct mode for a particular command's usage. The CCNA exam is rift with misdirection commands aimed at testing your total understanding of when and how a command is used.

Getting By with a Little Help

Not all of the questions on the CCNA exam are killers. In what should be the easiest part of the test (at least it was for us because we use this facility exhaustingly), you can expect to see at least one question on context-sensitive help on the test.

There are two types of context-sensitive help available in both User Exec and Enable Exec modes: Word help and Command Syntax help.

What is a four-letter word beginning with an "h?"

Suppose, for example, that you know there's a specific command to perform a task, but you can't remember its command word. By typing its first letter (or as many letters as you feel are needed) and a question mark, without a space in between, the router displays a list of the available commands that begin with that letter. If there are multiple commands that meet your criteria, they will all be displayed. For example, entering "cl?" on the command line will list all of the commands that start with the letters "cl".

In this example, the name of the router, CCNA_For_Dummies, is displayed along with the #, indicating Enable Exec mode.

The location of the question mark in the command line entry is very important. If there's no space before the question mark, as in cl?, the command line interface lists all of the commands that begin with "cl." If there is a space before the question mark, as in cl ?, the command line interpreter attempts to display the next element of syntax for the command.

However, entering the letter C followed by a space and then a question mark (c ?) won't get you a list of all of the commands that begin with C. Instead, you get the response, "Ambiguous Command Request." Remember that the space in the command line indicates you want the CLI to complete the command line for you, if it can. Because it can't, it tells you that it doesn't have a clue as to what command you want.

Show me everything and let me pick

To see all the commands available for a command mode, simply enter a question mark at the command prompt. If the list being displayed requires more than one screen, only the first screen of information is displayed followed by the – – more – – prompt.

For you UNIX and Linux buffs, you probably know the more command very well. For those of you not of the UNIX/Linux persuasion, you can advance the display either by pressing the spacebar to advance to the next screen of information or by pressing the Enter key to move the display up one line at a time.

Help for the terminally lazy

Another gee-whiz feature built into the user interface is great for those who don't like to type. For example, suppose that late at night, you've just finished configuring a distant router through a Telnet session. You're so tired you can barely keep your eyes open, much less type. So, to end the telnet session you type **disc** and then press the Tab key. Lo and behold, the word "disconnect" is magically completed for you.

Expect to see a question that asks, "Which key do you press to complete a word or a shortcut command?" So open up a can of Tab and think about the correct answer.

Okay, show me the rest

Command syntax help displays the remaining syntax elements for partially entered command strings. By entering the command, or enough of the command to be recognized, followed by a space and a question mark, the command line interpreter displays the next parameter of the command. For example, Figure 9-2 illustrates a portion of what is displayed as a result of the string "show ?" being entered in Enable Exec mode.

```
CCNA_For_Dummies#show?
WORD                  Flash device information-format<dev:>[partition]
access-expression     List access expression
access-lists          List access lists
accounting            Accounting data for active sessions
aliases           Display alias commands
arp                   Arp Table
async                 Information on terminal lines used as router interfaces
.
.
.
```

Figure 9-2:
The results
of the
"show ?"
entry.

Editing History

Cisco routers include a user interface as a part of the IOS. This interface provides you with access to the command history, which is a history of the commands that have been entered on the router. This handy feature enables you to recall previously entered commands, especially long or complex commands, and access lists so that they can be edited, copied, or removed.

Life is good with enhanced editing

Enhanced editing mode is designed to make your life with routers easier. It provides you with such time savers as the ability to quickly enter one or more commands by repeating one or more entries.

Showing how truly enhanced it is, enhanced editing is automatically enabled in either Exec modes. To disable it, enter the command line **terminal no editing.** To turn it back on, enter **terminal editing.** Other important enhanced editing keyboard commands you should know are listed in Table 9-1.

Expect to see questions on the CCNA exam about the commands and features in Table 9-1 and the material right after it. We can't tell you exactly which ones are on the test. When you take the test, you too will be asked to sign Cisco's non-disclosure agreement. You don't have to sign it; that is, unless you want your certification.

Table 9-1	Enhanced Editing Keyboard Commands
Key(s)	*Action*
Ctrl+A	Move to the beginning of the current line
Ctrl+E	Move to the end of the current line
Ctrl+B (or left-arrow key)	Move back one character
Ctrl+F (or right-arrow key)	Move forward one character
Ctrl+N (or down-arrow key)	Recall most recent command
Ctrl+P (or up-arrow key)	Recall previous command
Esc+B	Move back to beginning of previous word (or beginning of current word)
Esc+F	Move forward one word
Tab	Complete the current word

Changing history

As listed in Table 9-1, the up-arrow key and the key combination Ctrl+P can be used to scroll back up through the recent history of commands and actions on the router. Be absolutely sure you remember these two keyboard commands, along with Ctrl+A (move to the beginning of the current line).

Other configuration commands used in editing the command history are:

- ✔ **Show history:** This command displays the contents of the command history.
- ✔ **Terminal history size:** This command is used to change the default value of how many lines of the command history are to be displayed by a show history command. The default is to show the last 10 commands.
- ✔ **Terminal no editing:** This command turns off the enhanced editing feature and is used to exit enhanced editing.

✔ **Terminal editing:** This command turns the enhanced editing feature back on. Enhanced editing is on by default and must be turned off with the terminal no editing command.

Your Router Needs a Name

If you want the generic name "Router" to display on every prompt line, and you don't plan to update or access your router from another router or other SNMP device, then you simply do nothing. To us, this would be like not giving a baby a name when it's born. This poor child would have to go through life as "Kid," "Boy," "Girl," or some other non-identifying indescript name. So, to avoid an identity crisis for your router, we believe that you will want to give your router its own unique name — its hostname. If fact, we highly recommend that you create a hostname for the router, and remember how to do it for the exam.

There are two simple rules to assigning what's called a hostname to your router:

✔ You must first enter Enable Exec (Privileged), the one that displays the number or pound sign prompt (#), and then enter Global Configuration mode, the one that adds the word "config" in parentheses.

✔ The command used to assign the hostname is hostname. When you're trying to remember all the details about configuring a router, it can seem that all configuration type actions are carried out under the configuration mode. That's why we're making such a big deal out of this. The prompt used to assign the hostname is very much like this sample:

```
Router(config)#hostname CCNA_For_Dummies
```

Let's Play Password

Earlier in this chapter, we talked about needing a password to log into the router (see the section "Logging into the router"). Passwords play an important role in the security of your router, protecting its configuration and access lists from evil-doers. In the same way that passwords are used to protect data networking elements by verifying that someone logging in has authorization to do so, passwords protect your network's routers as well. A Cisco router can have up to five different passwords, each on a different level. For the CCNA exam, you should know the processes used to manage and modify router passwords.

Don't be so sensitive

Cisco router passwords are case sensitive, which means that it really does matter whether an alphabetic character is uppercase or lowercase. In the ASCII (American Standard Code for Information Interchange) character set, every displayable character has a different hexadecimal and binary value. An uppercase A has a different value representation than a lowercase a. So, when you create a password, remember that it will be stored exactly how you enter it, for example, case SenSiTiVe. Also remember that when you use it to access the router, you must enter it exactly as it was stored, for example, case SenSiTiVe.

Getting into configuration mode

The first step in the procedure used to change a password on a Cisco router is to be in Terminal Configuration Mode, a.k.a. Global Configuration Mode. To gain Terminal Configuration Mode, use the following series of prompts and commands:

```
CCNA_For_Dummies#config t
Enter configuration commands, one per line. End with
     CNTL/Z.
```

After you're in configuration mode, the router name will be followed by the word config in parentheses (config), indicating the mode.

Changing the locks

There are five different passwords that you can set and use in a Cisco router: Enable Secret, Enable, Virtual Terminal, Console, and Auxiliary. The following sections show the commands used to set each one.

Setting the Enable Secret password

The Enable Secret password adds a level of security over and above the enable password. When enabled, this password, which is one-way encrypted, has precedence over the enable password.

The following statements show the commands used to set the Enable Secret password:

```
CNA_For_Dummies(config)#enable secret gilster
CCNA_For_Dummies(config)#^Z
```

The "^Z" entry is what's displayed when you press the Ctrl and Z keys at the same time. Do not enter a carat ("^") followed by a Z — the command line interpreter won't have a clue what you're trying to do.

Setting the Enable password

If no Enable Secret password is set, you should use the Enable password. It's also used for older router software versions. Remember that the Enable password is not encrypted, which is why the Enable Secret password is preferred. The router uses the Enable password only when no Enable Secret password has been created.

The following statements are used to set the Enable password:

```
CCNA_For_Dummies(config)#enable password gilster
The enable password you have chosen is the same as your
          enable secret.
This is not recommended. Re-enter the enable password.
CCNA_For_Dummies(config)#enable password jeff
CCNA_For_Dummies(config)#^Z
```

Setting the Virtual Terminal password

The Virtual Terminal (vty) password is used to gain access to the router using a Telnet session. Unless this password, also known as the vty password, is set, you cannot Telnet into the router.

The following statements show the commands used to set the Virtual Terminal password:

```
CCNA_For_Dummies(config)#line vty 0 4
CCNA_For_Dummies(config-line)#login
CCNA_For_Dummies(config-line)#password kevin
CCNA_For_Dummies(config-line)#^Z
```

The line command enters line configuration mode, which is used to configure physical access points, such as Telnet, and the console and aux ports. The vty 0 4 part of the command specifies that the password entered will apply to vty lines 0 through 4. It is possible to set a different password for different vty lines.

Remember that in order to carry out this action, setting the password on the vty lines, you must first indicate the lines to be affected. In this case, the command line vty 0 4 is the first line of the commands used to change the login password for all five virtual terminal lines.

Setting the Console password

The Console password is used to gain access to the router through the console port. Set it by using the following commands:

```
CCNA_For_Dummies(config)#line con 0
CCNA_For_Dummies(config-line)#login
CCNA_For_Dummies(config-line)#password nate
CCNA_For_Dummies(config-line)#^Z
```

Setting the Auxiliary password

The commands used to set the password on the auxiliary port are (they should look familiar):

```
CCNA_For_Dummies(config)#line aux 0
CCNA_For_Dummies(config-line)#login
CCNA_For_Dummies(config-line)#password linda
CCNA_For_Dummies(config-line)#^Z
```

Giving the Router an Identity

What's wrong with this prompt?

```
Router>
```

Every router must have a unique identifying name. Cisco calls this name a hostname. Router hostnames can't be duplicated within a LAN, otherwise why bother? Throughout this chapter, and the rest of the book, we have assigned our router the name "CCNA_For_Dummies." You may not want to use a name quite this descriptive, but whatever the naming scheme you choose, it should be somewhat meaningful. The hostnames you use should identify each specific router on the network uniquely. If your network has only one router, then the name is less important, of course. In which case, have some fun.

 You should definitely know how to set the router hostname for the CCNA exam. The key things to remember are: To accomplish this task the router must be in global configuration mode, and the command hostname is one word. Here's an example of how the hostname is set:

```
Router#config t
Enter configuration commands, one per line. End with
        CNTL/Z.
Router(config)#hostname CCNA_For_Dummies
```

Waving the Banner

Each router can be configured with a banner message to be displayed whenever someone logs into the router. The message part of the banner is called the *message of the day* (MOTD), a term borrowed from our UNIX friends. The MOTD banner is displayed at login and is a good way to get the word out about scheduled network downtime or any other endearments the administrator wants to share.

To create a MOTD banner, you must first be in global configuration mode. The command `banner motd` is followed by a delimiting character. The choice of the character you use to indicate the end of your message is totally up to you. When you enter the message, which cannot contain the delimiting character you've chosen, the command line interpreter knows the message is ended when you enter your delimiting character. For this reason, this character should normally be a special character not likely to be used in the motd message.

Here's a sample of the commands used to create or modify the motd banner:

```
CCNA_For_Dummies(config)#banner motd $
Enter TEXT message. End with the character '$'.
IOS upgrade scheduled for next Thursday.
$
CCNA_For_Dummies(config)#end
```

In this example, you need to press the Enter key after ending the message with the delimiting character ($). Actually, any character not included in the message can be used as a delimiter. Many administrators routinely use the pound sign character (#) as the delimiter.

The result of this would be that the next time anyone logs into the router, the following would be displayed:

```
IOS upgrade scheduled for next Thursday.

User Access Verification

Password:
```

The motd banner message is the first line displayed in the login display.

Inserting descriptions where you need them

You may also add descriptions to lines, interfaces, and other configured elements of your router. To do so, the command description is used to apply a name, circuit number, or other nomenclature to whatever element is currently being edited. The description command is very simple in that it contains only two elements: the command and the description. Here's an example:

```
CCNA_For_Dummies(config)#int e0
Enter configuration commands, one per line. End with
        CNTL/Z.
CCNA_For_Dummies(config)#description Ethernet link to Web
        Host
CCNA_For_Dummies(config)#^Z
```

These statements apply the description "Ethernet link to Web Host" to the Ethernet 0 interface.

Prep Test

1 In what mode can you connect to remote devices, perform simple tests, and examine system information?

A ○ Enable

B ○ Command Line Interface

C ○ User Exec

D ○ Privileged Exec

2 What command do you enter from the Enable Mode prompt to enter the setup mode?

A ○ Setup

B ○ Setup mode

C ○ Enable setup

D ○ Secret

3 In what mode can you access the configuration mode, perform higher level testing and debugging, and detailed probing of the router function?

A ○ Command Exec

B ○ Command Line Interface

C ○ User Exec

D ○ Privileged Exec

4 Given that a router has been named CCNA001WW001, which prompt would indicate that you are in the Privileged Exec mode?

A ○ ccna001ww001#

B ○ CCNA001WW001>

C ○ ccna001ww001>

D ○ CCNA001WW001#

5 What is the command to enter the privileged Exec mode?

A ○ Privilege

B ○ Exec

C ○ Enable

D ○ Secret

6 From within the Privileged Exec mode, what is the resulting prompt after entering the configuration mode?

A ○ RouterName>(config)

B ○ RouterName(config)#

C ○ RouterName>[config]

D ○ RouterName#(config-if)

7 What key stroke will enable the auto-completion of text from the CLI?

A ○ Tab

B ○ Alt+C

C ○ Alt+A

D ○ ?

8 What command do you enter from the Exec mode to disable editing capabilities from a terminal session?

A ○ Editing terminal no

B ○ No editing terminal

C ○ Terminal no editing

D ○ Terminal editing no

9 Which of the following is the correct prompt and command to assign the name CCNA001WW001 to a Cisco router?

A ○ router>hostname CCNA001WW001

B ○ router>set hostname CCNA001WW001

C ○ router#set hostname CCNA001WW001

D ○ router#hostname CCNA001WW001

10 In global configuration mode, what command is used to set the banner message that will be displayed when someone logs into a router?

A ○ banner motd $

B ○ set banner

C ○ set motd banner

D ○ set motd

Answers

1 *C.* After you successfully log into the router, you are in User Exec mode. In this mode, you can connect to other devices, perform simple tests, and display system information. *See "A mode for the masses."*

2 *A.* When a router is first configured from the console port, the router invokes setup mode. You can enter setup mode from the Enable Exec mode with the command setup. *Review "Setup mode."*

3 *D.* Also called Enable Exec, in Privileged Exec mode you can perform all User Exec mode functions, higher-level testing, debug router functions, and update the configuration files. *Take a look at "A mode for the privileged."*

4 *D.* The hostname assigned to the router appears before all prompts and the pound or number sign indicates Enable Exec or Privileged mode. Notice that the hostname is case sensitive. *Check out "A mode for the privileged."*

5 *C.* The command used to invoke Privileged mode is enable, which is why Privileged mode is also called Enable Exec mode. *Look over "A mode for the privileged."*

6 *B.* Expect to see this question on the test. Be wary of slightly different answers such as those shown in this question. Also remember that the keys used to end a config entry are Ctrl+Z. *See "Configuration mode."*

7 *A.* The question mark key is used to get help, but the Tab key requests auto-completion from the command line interpreter. *Review "Help for the terminally lazy."*

8 *C.* Remember that you're telling the terminal that you want no editing. Review the other command listed in this chapter as well. *Look over "Life is good with enhanced editing."*

9 *D.* Two things to remember on this: 1) you must be in Enable Exec mode (the "#" prompt), and 2) the command to set the hostname is hostname. *Check out "Giving the Router an Identity."*

10 *A.* The banner motd (message of the day) is displayed whenever someone logs into the router. The dollar sign character is used to delimit the text string. *Take a look at "Waving the Banner."*

Chapter 10

Router Commands

*J*udging from the exam, a CCNA spends all of his or her time working at the router. The result of this focus is that the CCNA exam expects you to know, in nitpicky detail, most of the major commands used to start up, configure, maintain, and manage the router's software.

One area of particular focus is command syntax. On the exam, expect to find at least one question, if not more, where the only difference between the correct answer and an incorrect one is some obscure syntax error. You should also concentrate on the procedures and commands used to create the initial setup of a router and enable it for Internet Protocol (IP).

This chapter focuses on only the router commands, configuration, and setup topics you'll see on the test. Keep yourself focused on these areas and don't waste too much time on unnecessary stuff. There's a lot of detail here. Work through each command and learn it completely before you move on.

The absolute best way to prepare for the test in this area is to practice. If you have access to a router, use it. If you don't, find one. We're flattered that you're reading our book, but all the reading and practice tests in the world won't get you ready like actually doing it.

We can't emphasize enough that you pay attention to command syntax and the mode used to execute each action. Someone in the past said that the devil is in the details. It's our guess that whoever said this did so immediately after taking whatever was the equivalent of the CCNA exam in his day.

Quick Assessment

Using the setup command

Identifying IOS commands used for router startup

Managing configuration files in privileged exec mode

Maintaining the IOS software image

Listing commands used to load IOS software

Copying and manipulating configuration files

1 When you power up a router for the very first time you'll enter the _____.

2 During setup you are prompted to accept three current passwords: _____, _____, and _____.

3 The five-step sequence of events during startup is _____, _____, _____, _____, and _____.

4 The _____ tells the router the location from which the IOS software is to be loaded.

5 The IOS may be loaded from _____, _____, or _____.

6 After having made changes to the running configuration file, you must type _____ to save it to the startup configuration.

7 The benefit of manually configuring a router is that you have _____ over the configuration.

8 The command Show _____ displays the software version, names of config files, and the configuration register.

9 To copy configuration files, you must be in the _____ mode.

10 The six commands for copying configuration files are _____, _____, _____, _____, _____, and _____.

Answers

1 *Setup mode.* See "Watch out, it's a setup!"

2 *Enable secret (if present), enable, and virtual terminal.* Review "What's the password?"

3 *POST, Locate the IOS, Load the IOS, Locate the Configuration File, Load the Configuration File.* Check out "If you start it up, it will never stop."

4 *Configuration register.* Take a look at "Are you registered?"

5 *Flash, TFTP Server, or ROM.* See "Are you registered?"

6 *Write mem (IOS versions 10.3 and earlier)* or *copy running-config startup-config.* Review "Command performance."

7 *Greater control.* Check out "The Manual Approach to Configuration."

8 *Version.* Look over "Command performance."

9 *Enable Exec* or *Privileged.* See "Making copies ... ."

10 *Copy start tftp, copy run tftp, copy run start, copy start run, copy tftp start, and copy tftp run.* Take a look at "Now that it's started, back it up!"

Setting up and Configuring a Router

Arguably, the thrill of being the first person to open the box and unpack a new router is one of the top thrills a person can experience in life. There is nothing quite like that new router smell to get your heart pumping. However, as joyful as this experience may be, it soon fades when you plug it in, fire it up for the first time, and realize that you're in the setup mode. If you hear the *Twilight Zone* theme about now, then you've experienced what we're describing.

Watch out, it's a setup!

The first time a router is powered up, it automatically enters the setup mode, and the router display should look something like this:

```
Router#setup
-- System Configuration Dialog --
At any point you may enter a question mark '?' for help.
Use ctrl-c to abort configuration dialog at any prompt.
Default settings are in square brackets '[]'.
Continue with configuration dialog? [yes]:
```

If you want to continue with the setup dialog (and you do!), setup displays its default answer in square brackets ([...]). All you need to do to accept the default value or response is press the Enter key.

Beyond the first time you power on the router, there are two other ways to access setup mode and both are entered in the Enable Exec (Privileged) mode:

- Enter the setup command at the # prompt to display the command sequence shown earlier in this chapter in the section, "Watch out, it's a setup."

- Enter the command erase startup-config (erase start and press the Tab key), with the administrator's permission of course, and then power the router off and back on to begin again just like when the router was brand new.

What's the password?

Setup shows an initial interface summary and then prompts you to accept the current values, if any, for the Hostname, Enable Secret, Enable, and Virtual Terminal passwords, or you can change them.

This sequence looks like this:

```
The enable secret is a one-way cryptographic secret used
    instead of the enable password when it exists.

Enter enable secret [<Use current secret>]:

The enable password is used when there is no enable
    secret and when using older software and some
    boot images.

Enter enable password [gilster]:
Enter virtual terminal password [ulstad]: bienvenu
```

As the first line indicates, when the Enable Secret password is used, you do not need an enable password on most of the newer Cisco routers. When in doubt, set it to a value you can remember, just in case. The Virtual Terminal password is used to gain access to the router through a telnet session from a remote host.

Setting up the interface

After you finish setting the passwords, the setup process continues by configuring the router's interfaces. Here's a sample of what should be displayed by setup at this point:

```
Configure IP? [yes]:
  Configure IGRP routing? [no]:
  Your IGRP autonomous system number [1]:

Configuring interface parameters:

Configuring interface Ethernet0:
  Is this interface in use? [yes]:
  Configure IP on this interface? [yes]:
  IP address for this interface [192.168.1.6]:
```

Notice that the setup process first asks whether you want to configure and enable the IP routing, and then this question repeats for each of the individual interfaces.

After you respond to all of setup's enable and configuration requests, the setup command displays a summary of the router's configuration as you just defined it and asks whether you want to accept the configuration shown. As a safety against a default value being accidentally entered, there is no default value and you must enter either yes or no. After you answer yes, the router's configuration as defined is then built and stored in NVRAM, and the router is ready to be put into service.

The configuration running in the router's RAM is the running-configuration, and the configuration saved in the router's NVRAM is the startup-configuration. Restarting the router loads the startup-configuration into RAM, where it becomes the running configuration. Copying the running-configuration to flash (NVRAM) overwrites the startup-configuration previously stored there.

If You Start It up, It Never Stops

After the router receives its initial configuration, the next time you power it on, the router goes through a five-step startup process:

1. A hardware check is performed by running the POST (Power On Self Test) and the bootstrap program is loaded to RAM from ROM.

2. The router uses the configuration register to locate the IOS software.

3. After the IOS is located, it's loaded to RAM and started.

4. The configuration file is located in NVRAM.

5. The configuration file is then copied into RAM from NVRAM.

We discuss each of these steps in more detail in the following sections.

POST it up

The POST on a Cisco router is similar to the POST that runs at startup on a personal computer. The router's POST checks its CPU, memory, and all of its interface ports to make sure they're present and operational, just as the PC's POST checks its CPU, memory, and peripheral devices.

If all is well, the bootstrap (also called the boot) program is read from ROM and begins the Locate and Load process.

Are you registered?

The primary purpose of the bootstrap program is to find a valid Cisco IOS image from a location specified by the router's configuration register. The configuration register contains the location from which the IOS software is to be loaded. The value representing the location of the IOS software can be changed using the config–register command from the global configuration mode. The hyphen or dash between config and register should be there.

Typically, the Cisco IOS is loaded from flash and that's the default value normally found in the configuration-register. The router looks for the IOS software to be in one of three places: flash memory, a TFTP server, or ROM.

The configuration-register holds a hexadecimal value that tells the router the location from which to load the IOS software. The hexadecimal value loaded to the configuration-register actually supplies a bit pattern that could also be provided through a hardware jumper block. Three settings determine where the router should look for the boot system:

- **0x02 through 0x0F:** When the configuration-register has the hexadecimal value 0x02 through 0x0F (which represents 0010 and 1111 in binary), the router looks for boot system commands in startup-configuration to tell it where to find IOS. If there are no boot system commands in the startup-configuration, the router then searches in the default places, then flash, then ROM, and then a tftp server.

- **0x00:** If the configuration-register value ends in 0x00 (binary 0000), the router enters Rom Monitor Mode. (See Chapter 8.)

- **0x01:** If the configuration register value ends in 0x01, the router boots from ROM.

Changing your boots

If you wish to change the source location from which you want the router to load the IOS system files, you can use the command boot system along with the parameter that directs the router to the source you wish to use. It is this command that the router will look for if the configuration-register tells it to look in the startup-configuration for boot system commands.

The following help command display shows the various parameters that can be used to tell the router where to look for the IOS.

```
CCNA_For_Dummies(config)#boot system ?
 WORD System image filename
 flash Boot from flash memory
 mop Boot from a Decnet MOP server
 rcp Boot from a server via rcp
 rom Boot from rom
 tftp Boot from a tftp server
```

The current setting of the configuration-register is displayed using the Show Version command.

It's not a trivial matter

Configuration files can also be stored outside the router itself. Using the Trivial File Transfer Protocol (TFTP), configuration files can be copied and stored on a TFTP server. In fact, after they're backed up to the TFTP server, these files can be used as the source of the configuration during the boot sequence. However, the primary reason to back up the configuration to an outside server is to ensure that the router has a source of its configuration if the configuration file on the router gets corrupted or accidentally (or possibly, intentionally) erased.

Backing up the flash

It's a good idea to have a backup copy of the router's flash memory on a TFTP server just in case the configuration file on the router gets corrupted or erased. Here's a sample of the command used and the results displayed by the router:

```
CCNA_For_Dummies(boot)#copy flash tftp
PCMCIA flash directory:
File Length Name/status
 1 3070408 c1600-y-1.111-12.AA
[3070472 bytes used, 1123832 available, 4194304 total]
Address or name of remote host [255.255.255.255]?
        192.168.1.2
Source file name? c1600-y-1.111-12.AA
Destination file name [c1600-y-1.111-12.AA]?
Verifying checksum for 'c1600-y-1.111-12.AA' (file #
        1)... OK
Copy 'c1600-y-1.111-12.AA' from Flash to server
 as 'c1600-y-1.111-12.AA'? [yes/no]yes
!!!!!!!!!!!!!!!!!!!!!!!!!!!!!!!!!!!!!!!!!!!!!!!!!!!!!!!!!!!!!!!!!!
        !!!!!!!!!!!!!!!!!!!!!!!!!
Upload to server done
Flash device copy took 00:00:52 [hh:mm:ss]
```

You can upgrade flash memory using the TFTP server. After you obtain an upgraded IOS image from Cisco, store it on the TFTP server and use the copy TFTP flash command to move it to the router's flash memory.

Now that it's started, back it up!

The two types of configuration files stored on a router are the startup configuration file and the running configuration file. These files can be copied to and from each other as well as to and from the TFTP server. The commands to copy these files are shown in the following list. (***Remember:*** To use these commands, you must be in Enable Privileged mode — the one with the # character prompt.)

```
CCNA_For_Dummies#copy start tftp
CCNA_For_Dummies#copy run tftp
CCNA_For_Dummies#copy tftp run
CCNA_For_Dummies#copy tftp start
```

These examples copy the startup configuration to the TFTP server; copy the running configuration to the TFTP server; copy the configuration stored on the TFTP server to the running configuration file on the router; and copy the configuration stored on the TFTP server to the startup configuration file on the router, respectively. Using the command completion help built into the command line interface, it's perfectly acceptable to type in only the word **start** or **run** to indicate the startup and the running configuration.

The other `copy` command that you may see on the exam is

```
CCNA_For_Dummies#copy run start
```

This command is used to save the running-configuration to flash.

Making copies...

Here's an example of the console output that results from the command to copy the startup configuration to a TFTP server:

```
CCNA_For_Dummies#copy star tftp
Remote host []? 192.168.1.5
Name of configuration file to write [ccna_for_dummies-
        confg]?
Write file ccna_for_dummies-confg on host 192.168.1.5?
        [confirm]
Writing ccna_for_dummies-confg !! [OK]
```

Remember that you must be in Exec Enable (Privileged) mode to copy configuration files.

Covering your tracks

It's a very good idea that after you update the running configuration that you make sure the startup configuration is also updated. Probably the best way to do this is to simply copy the running configuration to the startup configuration. The command to accomplish this is:

```
CNA_For_Dummies#copy run star
Building configuration...
```

If you forget to update the startup configuration, or decide not to, the next time you boot the router it will revert to its previous configuration, which could be actually what you planned all along.

A command performance

Table 10-1 includes a list of commands that not only should you know, but you should also know when to use them and why.

Table 10-1	Configuration Startup and Save Commands	
Command	**Action**	**When to Use**
Show version	Displays the current software version	Verifying the current software version and the name of the system image file
Show config	Displays the startup configuration which includes the current passwords assigned and information on the interfaces and routing protocols configured	Verifying the overall configuration
Show startup-config	Displays the startup configuration	Verifying the startup configuration
Show running-config	Displays the running configuration, which is the configuration in use	Verifying the running configuration
Setup	Begins the manual configuration prompting sequence	To enter or modify all or part of the router's configuration
Write mem	Used in IOS versions 10.3 and earlier to save changes made to the running configuration	Saves the running configuration to the startup-configuration. Performs the same action as copy running-config startup-config.
Reload	Copies the startup configuration into RAM	Resets the running configuration to the startup configuration
Erase startup-config	Deletes the startup configuration in NVRAM	Probably never. In effect, this resets the router back into its initial startup and configuration states

You can store multiple IOS versions in NVRAM (flash), and one way to free up space in NVRAM is to erase unused versions and buffers.

The Manual Approach to Configuration

An alternative approach to setting up the configuration on a router is to do it manually, which is Cisco's name for completing the setup one step at a time, as opposed to using the setup command. Although using the manual setup approach requires more time and attention to detail, it provides you with greater control over the resulting configuration and the amount of detail included. Using the setup command, as we did earlier in this chapter (see "Watch out, it's a setup!"), only a very basic configuration is enabled.

 To begin the process of building the router's configuration, you must first be in the global configuration mode. With that out of the way, you can begin entering each of the specific interfaces you wish to configure. Recall that by interface we mean the ports and connection points on the router. Depending on the router model in use, this may include an Ethernet port, one or more serial ports, and more. Ethernet ports are designated by either the word Ethernet or the letter "e," followed by its sequence number, beginning with zero. Serial ports follow a similar pattern: the word serial or the letter "s" and an integer port number. For example, to designate the first Ethernet port, the code e0 can be used and for two serial ports, s1 and s2 can be used.

Here's a sample of the commands used to manually configure an Ethernet port on a router:

```
CCNA_For_Dummies#config t
Enter configuration commands, one per line. End with
        CNTL/Z.
CCNA_For_Dummies(config)#int e0
CCNA_For_Dummies(config-if)#
CCNA_For_Dummies(config-if)#IP address ?
 A.B.C.D IP address
CCNA_For_Dummies(config-if)#IP address 192.168.1.6
% Incomplete command.
CCNA_For_Dummies(config-if)#IP address 192.168.1.6
        255.255.255.0
```

 Remember that to properly configure an Ethernet port, you must enter *both* the IP address and its subnet mask.

Prep Test

1 When a Cisco router is powered up for the first time, it is in which mode?

A ○ Global Configuration Mode

B ○ Setup Mode

C ○ Privileged Exec Mode

D ○ Ala Mode

2 The configuration running in the router's RAM is the

A ○ Startup configuration

B ○ Flash configuration

C ○ Setup configuration

D ○ Running configuration

3 Which of the following is not a step in the router's startup process?

A ○ POST

B ○ The configuration register is used to locate the IOS software

C ○ The configuration file is loaded to TFTP

D ○ The configuration file is copied into RAM

4 Which of the following configuration register values indicate that the instructions for loading the IOS software are in the startup-configuration file? (Choose two.)

A ❑ 0x0A

B ❑ 0x00

C ❑ 0x01

D ❑ 0x02

5 Which TCP/IP protocol is used to copy configuration files to the router from an outside host?

A ○ FTP

B ○ Telnet

C ○ TFTP

D ○ UUCP

6 What are the two types of configuration files stored in the router when it is powered on? (Choose two.)

A ❑ Setup configuration

B ❑ Startup configuration

C ❑ Running configuration

D ❑ Backup configuration

7 Which of the following commands is used to copy the current configuration of the router to the startup configuration?

A ○ copy run start

B ○ copy start run

C ○ copy flash run

D ○ copy run rom

8 Which of the following commands are used to remove the current startup configuration version?

A ○ write mem

B ○ erase startup-config

C ○ reload

D ○ copy start run

9 Which of the following is used to designate Ethernet interface 1?

A ○ Ethernet 1

B ○ eth0

C ○ int e1

D ○ ip ethernet1

10 The router can be booted from which of the following? (Choose three.)

A ❑ flash

B ❑ tftp server

C ❑ rom

D ❑ diskette

Answers

1 *B.* The first time a router is powered up, it automatically goes into the setup mode. Setup mode can also be entered with the setup command or by the erase startup-configuration command and turning off and back on the router's power. *See "Watch out, it's a setup!"*

2 *D.* The configuration stored in RAM, that is the configuration currently running on the router, is called the running configuration. *Review "And in conclusion: A configuration summary."*

3 *C.* Well, at least not automatically. You can boot the router's system from a TFTP server, but normally in the startup process the configuration file is located in NVRAM and copied into RAM. *Look over "If You Start It Up, It Never Stops."*

4 *A, D.* Any value between and including 0x02 and 0x0F in the configuration-register indicates that instructions have been included in the startup configuration for where to locate the IOS software. *Check out "Are you registered?"*

5 *C.* TFTP (Trivial File Transfer Protocol) can be used to copy IOS versions and configuration files from an outside host that is running a TFTP server. *See "It's not a trivial matter."*

6 *B, C.* The startup configuration is stored in NVRAM and the running configuration is "stored" in RAM. Remember that on the CCNA exam, you are to pick the best answers available and don't quibble over semantics. The test will win every time. *Review "And in conclusion: A configuration summary."*

7 *A.* The shortcut names for the running configuration and the startup configuration are run and start. Copying the running configuration over the startup configuration is how you save the current configuration of the router so it will be used the next time the router is booted. *Take a look at "Now that it's started, back it up!"*

8 *B.* Granted that the write mem command is used on IOS versions 10.3 and earlier, but it is still one way to remove the startup configuration. You can expect to see the erase start command on the exam. *Check out "A command performance."*

9 *C.* This command is used to designate that you wish to configure interface (int) Ethernet (e) one (1). *See "The Manual Approach to Configuration."*

10 *A, B, C.* In fact, depending on how complicated you wish to make your startup configuration instructions, you can include any number of valid boot system locations in the boot process. However, the router doesn't have a diskette or a CD-ROM drive, yet. *Review "Changing your boots."*

Chapter 11

RIP, IGRP, IPX, and Convergence

Exam Objectives

▶ Differentiating routed and routing protocols

▶ Configuring RIP and IGRP routing protocols

▶ Enabling Novell IPX and configuring interfaces

▶ Listing IPX encapsulation types

▶ Monitoring IPX operations

*T*here's nothing more certain than your finding questions about the IP and IPX protocols on the CCNA exam. This is one of several topics about which you must have a solid understanding to do well on the exam (as in *passing* the exam). Routed protocols are an important part of the exam. You should know how they're routed, as well as the processes and commands used to configure, enable, and troubleshoot them.

You must know that interior routing protocols, which are used inside a network with a common administration, and exterior protocols, which are used between networks, do not use common administration.

You should know how the interior protocols Routing Information Protocol (RIP) and Interior Gateway Routing Protocol (IGRP) are configured. As far as the external protocols go, we recommend that you be familiar with BGP (Border Gateway Protocol), EGP (Exterior Gateway Protocol), and IS-IS (Intermediate System-to-Intermediate System). In either case, remember that both interior and exterior protocols use an autonomous system number, which is a 16-bit number assigned by the IANA (Internet Assigned Numbers Authority), and how the ASN is assigned to the router.

We certainly don't mean to scare you at this point in your studies. If you calmly, yet pointedly, focus on RIP and IGRP, you'll cover most of the bases, but be sure to review the other topics we've mentioned, just to be sure.

Quick Assessment

1 A _____ protocol is used to transfer data and a _____ protocol is used to transfer route information.

2 Routing occurs at the _____ Layer of the OSI model.

3 The three primary types of routing are _____, _____, and _____.

4 The three algorithmic routing process classes available on Cisco routers are _____, _____, and _____.

5 A state of _____ occurs when all routers have the same knowledge of the network.

6 To add RIP routing to a router, the command _____ is used.

7 An IGRP router command requires a(n) _____ be included.

8 An IPX address consists of _____ bytes.

9 Ether, Sap, Snap, and Hdlc are the Cisco default _____ types.

10 The Cisco IOS command used to display IPX traffic statistics is _____.

Answers

1 *Routed, routing.* See "Inside versus outside."

2 *Network (Layer 3).* Review "A routing we will go."

3 *Static, dynamic, default.* Take a look at "Routing types you need to know for the exam."

4 *Distance-Vector, Link-State, and Balanced Hybrid.* Check out "Routing Algorithms."

5 *Convergence.* See "The blissful state of convergence."

6 *Router RIP.* Review "Adding a RIP route to the router."

7 *Autonomous system number.* Look over "IGRP routing."

8 *10.* Check out "Routing for the Novell riche."

9 *Encapsulation.* See "The biggest word in IPX networking."

10 *Show ipx.* Review "Monitor IPX routing."

Routed Versus Routing Protocols

When you review routers and their protocols, a good place to start is the difference between a routed protocol and a routing protocol. Knowing the difference between these two protocols is fundamental to understanding how routers route.

Inside versus outside

A routing protocol sends and receives routing information packets to and from other routers . A routed protocol can be routed by a router, which means that it can be forwarded from one router to another. Yes, protocols such as NetBIOS (Network Basic Input Output System) cannot be routed. That a routed protocol can be routed may seem obvious, but unless you know the distinction of it to a routing protocol, you may have trouble with the wording for some questions on the exam.

A *protocol* is a set of rules that defines how two devices communicate with one another. It also defines the format for the packets used to transmit data over communications lines. A *routed protocol* contains the data elements required for a packet to be sent outside of its host network or network segment. In other words, a routed protocol can be routed. Protocols used to communicate routing information between routers within an autonomous system are Interior Gateway Protocols (IGP), which are routing protocols, but not routed protocols.

Routing protocols gather and share the routing information used to maintain and update routing tables. That routing information is in turn used to route a routed protocol to its final destination. Routing Information Protocol (RIP), Interior Gateway Routing Protocol (IGRP) are the routing protocols you need to know for the exam. If you can remember what the abbreviations mean, you'll remember that they are routing protocols because they have routing in their names. Remember too, that they are not routed protocols.

In summary, routed protocols route your data and routing protocols send routing updates between routers about the status of the network so that your routed protocol data can be routed. Got that?

Examples of routed protocols are IP and IPX, and examples of routing protocols are RIP and IGRP.

A routing we will go

Routing is the process of moving data along a path from a source to a destination. The complexity of this process involves finding the most efficient route from a multitude of available routes. Routing occurs at the Network Layer of the OSI model. (See Chapter 5.)

To assist itself in making its routing decisions, the router builds routing tables to store information about routes to networks it has previously discovered. Most routers keep an entry, known as the default route, in their table to be used when the router doesn't have an explicit route for a frame. Figure 11-1 illustrates both what a routing table contains as well as where it fits into a network. Notice that it consists of network addresses and the interface to which each device, associated with an address, is connected.

Routers have the ability to route all routing and routed protocols.

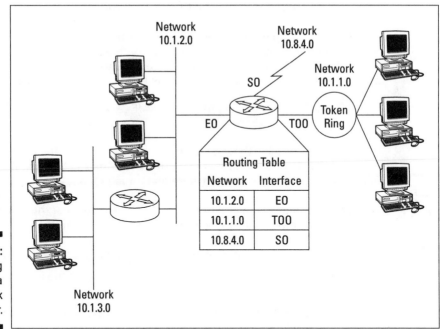

Figure 11-1:
The routing table in a network router.

Routing types you need to know for the exam

As far as the CCNA exam goes, there are three types of routing: static, dynamic, and default. We explain these routing types in the following sections.

One-lane roads

Static routes are fixed routes that are manually entered by the administrator into the router's configuration. If a static route is entered into the configuration, it must be manually updated should the network topology change. Not that the topology of the network is likely to change too frequently, but you may decide to change the segmenting structure or make other topology-level changes. When changes occur, the administrator must update the router configuration to include the changes, which is why static routing is not generally used in a large network. The time required to maintain the routing tables can become a burden.

Static routes are generally used if the internetwork, the part of the network that lies beyond the router, is accessible through only one path. A network with only a single path to the rest of the internetwork is known as a stub network. Static routes are also used for security reasons because they allow the administrator to restrict knowledge of the network from outside sources. A static route is configured on the router with a command like this:

```
CCNA_For_Dummies(config)#ip route 192.168.1.0
        255.255.255.0 192.168.1.1 3
```

This example contains the command (ip route) and the IP address of the destination network, the subnet mask, the IP address of the next hop router, and an administrative distance (more on that later).

Using the previous command example, the key elements of the static route configuration command are (memorize these for the exam):

- **ip route:** This is the command used to designate a static route.

- **destination address:** In this example, 192.168.1.0 is the IP address of the destination network.

- **subnet mask:** 192.169.1.0 is a Class C IP address and is using the default subnet mask for Class C addresses, 255.255.255.0.

- **next hop:** Following the subnet mask is the address of the next hop router, 192.168.1.1.

- **administrative distance:** This is a number between 0 and 255 that indicates how well the route can be trusted. The higher the number, the lower the trust. An administrative distance of 120 is about mid-range on the trustworthiness scale. So, as indicated by the 3 in the ip route command, this route is very trustworthy.

A dynamic personality

Dynamic routing is the process by which a network adapts automatically to the changes in topology or traffic as those changes occur. To be successful, dynamic routing requires timely maintenance of routing tables. The routing protocol used defines how this occurs and includes such information as when, what, and how the updates are sent.

When all else fails

A default route is very much like a static route. The administrator enters the default route, and it becomes the default path the router uses to forward packets for which it knows no other route to use. Without a default route, packets with unknown destinations are dropped.

When no specific next hop is listed in the routing table for a particular type of packet, the router uses its default route, a preassigned route that is generally available.

Plotting the Best Course

Routers use a series of calculations and metric-based decisions to determine the most efficient and economical route for a packet to use to reach its destination. In general, these calculations and decisions are embedded in an algorithm.

Moving to the algorithm

An *algorithm* is the process used to determine the solution to a problem. In routing, algorithms are used to determine the best route for traffic to take to get to its intended destination. The algorithm determines the metric (the number or numbers on which decisions are based) for routes through the network. The smaller a metric's value, the more likely the route is better than one with a higher metric. In the router's scheme of things, it uses smaller metric values to indicate better, faster, and more trustworthy routes. Conversely, higher metric values are awarded to routes that aren't always available or trustworthy. The routing algorithm is also used to update the routing table.

Determining a better route involves several metrics. Here are some of the metrics used to determine the better route. (Notice we have steadfastly avoided the word *best* here.)

- ✔ **Bandwidth:** Maximum throughput speed in bits-per-second.

- ✔ **Cost:** A arbitrary value assigned by the administrator for the crossing and intersection of networks.

- ✔ **Delay (also called latency):** A group of factors such as congestion or distance, for example.

- ✔ **Hop Count:** The number of routers a packet passes through to reach its destination.

- ✔ **Load:** The measure of traffic that flows through a router.

- ✔ **MTUs (Maximum transmission unit):** The largest message size allowed on all routes to the destination.

- ✔ **Reliability:** A value representing the amount of downtime for a network.

- ✔ **Ticks:** A measurement of delay, based on the clock in a personal computer, where one tick is $\frac{1}{18}$ of a second. It's used as part of the metric in IPX (Novell) RIP.

Routing Algorithms

There are three algorithmic routing process classes you need to be familiar with for the CCNA exam: the distance-vector algorithm, the link state (also called the shortest-path-first) algorithm, and the balanced hybrid approach, which is a combination of the distance-vector and link state algorithms.

Going the distance

A router using a distance-vector algorithm sends out all or part of its routing table to routers to which it is directly connected. In other words, it sends its routing table entries to those routers one hop away. These routers provide updated routing information which they have gathered from other routers, which in turn was gathered from other routers, and so on. This route information is updated at regularly scheduled intervals.

For the CCNA exam, you should remember that a distance-vector algorithm is concerned primarily with hop count, or the number of routers that a packet must pass through to reach its destination. Two of the protocols used in Cisco routers, and the two you need to focus on for the CCNA exam, RIP (Routing Information Protocol) and IGRP (Interior Gateway Routing Protocol) use distance-vector algorithms. In each of these routing protocols, the routing table lists a remote network and also the number of hops required to get to it.

Distance-vector routing protocols rely on secondhand information that is received from its nearby neighbors and do not themselves know the exact layout of the network.

RIP uses a maximum hop count of 15 and IGRP uses a maximum hop count of 255. Both are distance-vector routing protocols and interior routing protocols.

The blissful state of convergence

Delay problems can arise when distance-vector routers on a common network have different information on the topology of the network, especially when changes happen to the topology. When all routers on a network have the same knowledge of the network, the network is said to have convergence. The *time to convergence* is the time needed for all network routers to develop and store in their routing tables the same consistent and accurate picture of the network whenever changes occur.

Pulling out of a loop

Another common problem with distance-vector routing is routing loops. Routing loops are caused when routing tables are not updated accurately at the same time. Figure 11-2 illustrates a network with five routers. From all appearances, all is functioning fine. All of the routers have consistent knowledge and correct routing tables. The network has converged. All is well!

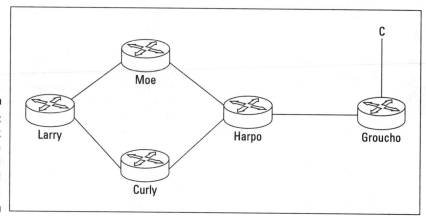

Figure 11-2:
A network with five routers and a potential problem.

That is, until network C crashed. Larry's assigned path to network C is by way of Moe, and Larry has a distance of 3 hops to network C in its routing table. Now that network C has failed, when Groucho sends an update to Harpo, Harpo stops routing packets to Groucho. However, routers Moe, Curly, and Larry continue to route packets to Groucho because they haven't yet been informed about the failure. When Harpo finally gets around to sending out its update, Moe and Curly stop routing to network C, but not poor Larry, who still believes that network C is a valid path because it has not learned of network C's failure.

In fact, Larry is inclined to prefer the route through Moe to network C because of its small 3 hop metric. Feeling very good about this efficient route, Larry sends an update to Curly, indicating the very good path to network C by way of Moe. Curly, who trusts Larry intrinsically like all good distance-vector routers, posts this routing information, including the hop count of 4, into its routing table reflecting the incorrect route information, and sends it on to Harpo, who stores the routing information, with a hop count of 5, into his routing table. In turn, Harpo sends the information to Moe and Groucho, and on and on it goes.

The result of the router version of the old party game, Rumors, is that any packet destined for network C will loop indefinitely between Larry, Moe, Harpo, Curly, and back to Larry. Each time the updated routing information is added to the routing tables, the hop count is increased, which creates a condition called counting to infinity, which is a key indicator that the network is slow reaching convergence.

Setting a loop limit

One solution to count to infinity routing loops (see previous section) is to set a maximum hop count variable on the router. This value sets the maximum number of hops that a possible route for a packet can have before it's discarded as a candidate route as being unreachable.

For the CCNA exam, you should know that RIP uses a maximum hop count of 15 and IGRP uses a maximum hop count of 255. What this means is that a packet caught in an infinite loop on the Stooge network shown in Figure 11-2 would, if RIP is in use, whip around the network until it reaches a router for the fifteenth time. This router drops the packet and sends a message back to the original sender stating why the packet was dropped.

Each packet has in its header a Time To Live (TTL) metric. This value indicates how many hops the packet has to reach its destination before expiring. It is the TTL value in the packet that defines "infinity." Counting to infinity simply means exceeding a packet's TTL value.

Scanning the split horizon

Another solution to counting-to-infinity routing loops is a technique called the split horizon. This technique prevents bad routing information from being sent back to its source. In simpler terms, routing information is not sent back in the direction from which it came, unless better information is available.

This means that RouterA does not inform RouterB about routes it (RouterA) received from RouterB in the first place. An exception to this rule is when RouterA has newer or better route information, such as a lower hop count, than it (RouterA) learned from RouterB to begin with.

So, in our stoogie example, any erroneous routing information updates Moe receives from Harpo would not be sent back to Harpo, opening the door for the truth in the form of a correct update from another source, Curly or Larry, to prevail.

Arsenic and old routes

A variation of the split horizon technique is route poisoning, which amounts to poison reverse routing. This evil-sounding technique assigns the maximum hop count plus one to the hop count metric of any route that is not available. If a router discovers a particular route to be unavailable, it sets its hop count to one more than the maximum of the protocol in use. In the case of RIP, setting the hop count metric to 16 (15 + 1) has the effect of closing the route. All RIP packets have a TTL value of 15 or less. Setting the hop count metric to 256 on an IGRP route has the same effect.

So, if network C goes down, Groucho assigns network C a hop count of 16 in its routing table (assuming RIP is in use), which removes network C as an available good route. Until network C notifies Groucho that it is once again available, the poison entry remains in the routing table. When a poisoned route is once again available and notifies its neighbors of its regained good health, the notification triggers updates to other routers.

Holding down the route

One more solution for counting-to-infinity loops that you should know for the exam is a *hold-down*. A hold-down works with route poisoning to make sure a poisoned route is not prematurely resurrected. In other words, it keeps the bad dead. The hold-down technique is intended to allow time for an unavailable network to return or to allow time for the network on the whole to stabilize itself so that the next best route can be chosen and put into use.

The triggering mechanism in a hold-down is a hold-down timer. When the route poisoning entry is made to the routing table, a hold-down timer is set, and neighboring routers are notified not to accept updates from the poisoned route until the hold-down expires and update messages are triggered. The timer's expiration triggers updates that notify neighboring routers that the hold-down has expired and they can begin accepting updates from the now resurrected route and resets the timer.

Three conditions affect the status of the hold-down timer:

- ✔ The first is when an update is received that indicates a network is no longer accessible. The network is marked as inaccessible and a timer is started. If before the timer expires it receives another update from the same router, saying the network is accessible, it stops the timer and puts the network back in the routing table.

- ✔ If an update from a router arrives that has a better metric for the down network than that stored, the router is marked accessible.

- ✔ Should an update arrive prior to the expiration of the hold-down timer from a different router that contains a metric worse than that currently stored, the update is ignored.

Three mechanisms used with distance-vector protocols to control routing (count to infinity) loops are split horizon, route poisoning, and hold-downs.

The state of the network

Although link-state routing is not covered extensively on the CCNA exam, you should at least understand what it is so that you can eliminate it as a possible wrong multiple-choice answer.

Link-state routing, which is also called shortest-path-first (SPF), is more complex and requires more processing and more memory than distance-vector routing. In this routing technique, each router keeps track of the state (the health) of its directly connected neighbors. It does this by broadcasting link-state packets (LSPs, also known as link-state advertisements [LSA], or simply "hello" packets) containing information about the networks to which the router is connected. The router uses the LSPs it receives from other routers to build a database about the network, and then uses the SPF algorithm to determine the shortest route to each network, which is stored in its routing table. When a change occurs in the topology, the use of LSPs results in faster network convergence than is possible with distance-vector routers.

There are several link-state routing algorithm schemes used on Cisco routers, including NLSP (NetWare Link Services Protocol), OSPF (Open Shortest Path First), and IS-IS (Intermediate System-to-Intermediate System).

Classful Routing

The CCNA exam expects you to be proficient at adding RIP and IGRP protocol statements to a router configuration. In an effort to live up to your expectations when you purchased this book, in this section we review the process used to add statements in both protocols.

You may encounter classful routing on the exam used to describe a routing protocol. Classful routing uses network identities to identify specific routes. RIP and IGRP, the routing protocols you should study the most, are classful routing protocols.

On the other hand, classless routing allows a block of IP addresses to be represented as a single route. CIDR (Classless Interdomain Routing) is the primary classless routing strategy. Protocols that use the classless routing strategy are also called prefix routing protocols.

Concentrate on classful router configurations. While you'll see CIDR addressing references on the exam, you probably won't see any configuration command statements involving CIDR classless notations.

Let 'er RIP

RIP (Routing Information Protocol) is a classful, distance-vector routing protocol. As such, it uses information provided to it by its neighboring routers to maintain information in a routing table about the cost, in terms of hops and other metrics, of a particular route.

Your focus on RIP when preparing for the CCNA exam should be adding RIP statements to the router. This is something you really should practice using a router, if at all possible. We don't mean that you absolutely cannot pass the test without using a router to study. What we mean is that it sure will be a lot easier to get ready using a router.

Showing your RIP

To display the current routing information on the router, including all types of existing routes, use the command

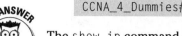

```
CCNA_4_Dummies#show ip route
```

The show ip command creates a display that contains the following:

```
CCNA_4_Dummies#show ip route

Codes: C - connected, S - static, I - IGRP, R - RIP, M -
       mobile, B - BGP, D - EIGRP, EX - EIGRP external,
       O - OSPF, IA - OSPF inter area, E1 - OSPF exter-
       nal type 1, E2 - OSPF external type 2, E - EGP, i
       - IS-IS, L1 - IS-IS level-1, L2 - IS-IS level-2,
       * - candidate default, U - per-user static route

Gateway of last resort is 210.93.105.0 to network 0.0.0.0
```

```
R 223.8.151.0/24 [120/2] via 210.93.105.1, 00:00:11,
        Ethernet0
R 201.100.11.0/24 [120/3] via 210.93.105.1, 00:00:11,
        Ethernet0
R 219.17.100.0/24 [120/3] via 210.93.105.1, 00:00:11,
        Ethernet0
R 192.5.5.0/24 [120/4] via 210.93.105.1, 00:00:11,
        Ethernet0
R 199.6.13.0/24 [120/2] via 210.93.105.1, 00:00:11,
        Ethernet0
R 205.7.5.0/24 [120/4] via 210.93.105.1, 00:00:11,
        Ethernet0
```

The Rs indicate routes placed in the routing table by RIP. It's very important that you understand that Cisco routers can support many different types of routes simultaneously. The Codes block at the beginning of the sh ip route display lists the various routing types that can be enabled. For example, a static route shows up with an S on the left side of its entry, and an IGRP entry has an I.

Adding a RIP route to the router

To begin entering RIP statements into the router, it must be in configuration mode. The command used to open RIP configuration mode is:

```
CCNA_4_Dummies#config t
Enter configuration commands, one per line. End with
        CNTL/Z.
CCNA_4_Dummies(config)#router rip
```

The prompt changes to include the mode identifier of config-router.

The primary RIP entry you would make would be to insert a RIP route into the router. The command to do this looks like the following:

```
CCNA_4_Dummies(config)#router rip
CCNA_4_Dummies(config-router)#network 210.93.105.0
CCNA_4_Dummies(config-router)#network 223.8.151.0
CCNA_4_Dummies(config-router)#^z
CCNA_4_Dummies#copy run star
```

In this sequence of commands, all the interfaces on the router that belong to the two networks specified in the network commands (210.93.105.0 and 223.8.151.0) will participate in the sending and receiving of RIP updates.

To verify that the commands were added to the running configuration correctly, run the show ip route command. (See "Showing your RIP," earlier in this chapter.) Remember that these entries are not added to the routing table. The routing table is updated when new routes are learned from RIP updates received from the routes now participating in RIP.

Be sure that you save your work and remember to copy the running configuration — the one you just changed — to the startup configuration so that it will be applied next time you start up the router.

IGRP routing

Adding an IGRP route to the running configuration uses essentially the same process as adding RIP routes (see "Adding a RIP route to the router," earlier in this chapter). One difference is that each IGRP entry must be identified to an autonomous system number (ASN), which is a network that operates under a single set of rules that may include one or more routing protocols. Routers may have several IGRP routing protocols existing between them. The autonomous system number, which can be in the range of 1 to 65535 (Gilster's lucky number), identifies which IGRP interface is to be used to update a particular route.

Remember that you can use contextual help from the CLI to show you the entries required for a command:

```
CCNA_4_Dummies(config)#router igrp ?
  <1-65535> Autonomous system number
```

The `IGRP router` command requires an autonomous system number to be assigned to the network entries included in the command. To enter IGRP networks, the command you use is something like this:

```
CCNA_4_Dummies(config)#router igrp 100
CCNA_4_Dummies(config-router)#network 210.93.105.0
CCNA_4_Dummies(config-router)#network 210.204.7.0
CCNA_4_Dummies(config-router)#^z
```

The `show ip route` command displays the contents of the routing table so that the newly added IGRP routing can be verified:

```
CCNA_4_Dummies#show ip route

Codes: C - connected, S - static, I - IGRP, R - RIP, M -
       mobile, B - BGP, D - EIGRP, EX - EIGRP external,
       O - OSPF, IA - OSPF inter area, E1 - OSPF exter-
       nal type 1, E2 - OSPF external type 2, E - EGP, i
       - IS-IS, L1 - IS-IS level-1, L2 - IS-IS level-2,
       * - candidate default, U - per-user static route
```

```
Gateway of last resort is 210.93.105.0 to network 0.0.0.0

R 223.8.151.0/24 [120/2] via 210.93.105.1, 00:00:11,
      Ethernet0
R 201.100.11.0/24 [120/3] via 210.93.105.1, 00:00:11,
      Ethernet0
R 223.8.151.0R 219.17.100.0/24 [120/3] via 210.93.105.1,
      00:00:11, Ethernet0
R 192.5.5.0/24 [120/4] via 210.93.105.1, 00:00:11,
      Ethernet0
R 199.6.13.0/24 [120/2] via 210.93.105.1, 00:00:11,
      Ethernet0
R 205.7.5.0/24 [120/4] via 210.93.105.1, 00:00:11,
      Ethernet0
I 204.204.7.0/24 [100/8576] via 210.93.105.1, 00:00:36,
      Ethernet0
```

In this example of the `show ip route` command, notice that most of the routing table entries are RIP entries as indicated by the R in the first position. The one new entry (marked with an I) is an IGRP entry.

To display only the IGRP entries, use the command `sh route igrp`.

Routing for the Novell riche

For the CCNA exam, you need to know the structure and commands used to configure a router for an IPX network. IPX is a proprietary protocol developed by Novell and used by its NetWare 4.*x* and earlier network operating systems.

An IPX address is a piece of cake compared to the intricacies of IP addressing, subnet masks, and the like. An IPX address has a simple and straightforward construction, consisting of a 10-byte hexadecimal number that is made up of a 4-byte network number and a 6-byte node number. The network number usually includes only the significant digits of the network ID. The node number is usually the MAC address of a NIC (Network Interface Card) adapter. An example of a Novell IPX address is:

Network	Node
3b2c.	0000.0b62.ed44

An IPX network address is an 80-bit number that is made up of a 32-bit network ID and the 48-bit MAC address. Because an IPX address includes the MAC address of a node, there's no need for ARP translations on an IPX network.

IPX basics

Netware servers use two protocols to communicate with a Cisco router: SAP (Service Advertising Protocol) and RIP (Routing Information Protocol). First of all, don't confuse this RIP with the RIP discussed up to this point in this chapter, because they are obviously very different. Don't worry about the inner-workings of NetWare RIP (which is actually very similar to TCP/IP RIP), because the CCNA exam emphasizes the latter. SAP is used to advertise services, which is why it's called that. Both of these NetWare protocols are used on IPX networks to update network servers regarding available services and routing information. A Cisco router must be able to interface with both SAP and RIP in order to function on the network.

The biggest word in IPX networking

A very key concept of IPX networking is encapsulation (which is also called framing), which involves how data is packaged for transmission across the network. NetWare is able to support many different types of upper-layer packet formats by encapsulating them inside of a standard layer 2 (Data Link Layer) frame and identifying it with a specific protocol header. However, Cisco's default encapsulation type doesn't necessarily match the one used by Novell. The router must be able to convert from Novell to Cisco for the routing protocol to work.

Table 11-1 lists the Cisco default encapsulation types and Table 11-2 lists the Novell encapsulations and their Cisco equivalents that you must know for the CCNA exam. Trust us on this one. Even if you don't quite understand it, memorize the contents of these two tables. Somewhere in the course of the 80 questions and 90 minutes, you'll need to know this stuff.

Table 11-1	Cisco Encapsulation Types
Interface	*Cisco Command Word*
Ethernet	novell-ether
Token Ring	sap
FDDI	snap
Serial	hdlc

Table 11-2 lists the Novell frame types and the corresponding Cisco frame type for each. Yes, memorize this, too.

Table 11-2	Novell Frame Types and Their Cisco Equivalents
Novell	*Cisco*
Ethernet_802.2	sap
Ethernet_802.3	novell-ether (default)
Ethernet_snap	snap
Ethernet_II	arpa
FDDI_snap	snap (default)
FDDI_raw	novell-fddi
FDDI_802.2	sap
Token-Ring	sap (default)
Token-Ring_snap	snap

Doing the IPX two-step

Configuring IPX on a Cisco router is a two-step process. The first step is to enable IPX routing from the global configuration mode:

```
CCNA_4_Dummies#config t
Enter configuration commands, one per line. End with
      CNTL/Z.
CCNA_4_Dummies(config)#ipx routing
CCNA_4_Dummies(config)#^Z
```

The second step is to configure IPX on each of the individual interfaces (e0, s1, etc.) you want to use.

You need the IPX network address and the frame type to activate IPX on an individual interface. If you omit them from the command, the default route is enabled using the default encapsulation for that interface. Also remember to use the Cisco keyword for the interface encapsulation type (see Tables 11-2 and 11-3) and not the Novell name for the interface encapsulation type.

Assuming you're still in configuration mode, here are sample commands that enable IPX routing on an Ethernet interface:

```
CCNA_4_Dummies(config)#int e0
CCNA_4_Dummies(config-if)#ipx network 5500
CCNA_4_Dummies(config-if)#^Z
```

This command series enabled IPX routing on a router using the default for encapsulation (see Table 11-2).

Monitoring IPX routing

After enabling IPX routing, you'll want to monitor its operation. Table 11-3 lists the Cisco IOS commands that can be used to display the status and operation of the router. You should become familiar with these commands, should you encounter them on the exam.

Table 11-3 Cisco Commands Used to Monitor Router Operations

Command	Action
Privileged Exec Mode	You must be in this mode to use the remaining commands in this table.
ping	Verifies that a network connection is reachable.
show ipx traffic	Displays IPX traffic statistics.
show ipx route [network]	Displays all IPX entries in the routing table or just one entry if the network value is entered.
show ipx interface	Displays a detailed view of an interface's IPX settings.
show ipx servers	Lists the IPX servers discovered through SAP advertisements.
debug ipx sap [activity | events]	Displays messages regarding SAP updates.
debug ipx routing [activity | events]	Displays messages about each routing update.

Prep Test

1 Which protocol is not a routed protocol?

- A ○ IPX
- B ○ IP
- C ○ EIGRP
- D ○ None of the above

2 Which protocol is not a routing protocol?

- A ○ RIP
- B ○ IGRP
- C ○ EIGRP
- D ○ IP

3 When there is no specific entry in the routing table a router will send packets out what gateway?

- A ○ serial0
- B ○ ethernet0
- C ○ default
- D ○ WAN

4 When might static routes be used most commonly in an internetwork?

- A ○ When there is only one path to access a network
- B ○ When there is no default route enabled
- C ○ When convergence occurs on the network
- D ○ When there is a bridge between Ethernet and Token Ring networks

5 When configuring a static route from the configuration mode, what are the required parts of static ip route configuration?

- A ○ destination router, subnet mask, destination network, metric
- B ○ destination network, subnet mask, next hop router, administrative distance
- C ○ source network, subnet mask, destination network, metric
- D ○ destination network, subnet mask, source network, metric

6 Which of the following is not a metric used in a routing algorithm?

A ○ Cost

B ○ Sap

C ○ Ticks

D ○ MTU

7 What are distance-vector algorithms, such as IGRP, concerned about? (Choose two.)

A ❏ Ticks

B ❏ Cost

C ❏ Load

D ❏ Hop Count

8 What enables a router using a link-state algorithm to know the exact topology of the network?

A ○ It uses LSP's to construct a database about the network.

B ○ It uses Snap packets to verify convergence.

C ○ It uses Sap to perform Split Horizon and Poison reverse.

D ○ None of the above.

9 What does an IPX address consist of?

A ○ A four-bit network number and a six-bit node number

B ○ A four-byte network number and an eight-byte node number

C ○ A six-byte network number and a four-byte node number

D ○ A four-byte network number and a six-byte node number

10 Which combination of Novell to Cisco frame types is incorrect? (Novell :: Cisco)

A ○ Ethernet 802.3 :: novell-ether

B ○ FDDI Raw :: snap

C ○ Token Ring :: sap

D ○ Ethernet II :: arpa

Answers

1 *C.* EIGRP (Enhanced IGRP) is an Internal Gateway Protocol (IGP) and as such is not a routed protocol. IPX and TCP/IP are both routed protocols and are not routing protocols. *See "Inside versus outside."*

2 *D.* Routing protocols are used to pass around information about the status of devices on a network and the best available routes for packets. TCP/IP is a routed protocol that is the primary protocol used on the Internet as well as many intranets. The other answers are all routing protocols. *Review "Inside versus outside."*

3 *C.* When there is no specific interface or port assignment, the router will route packets to the default gateway as the default route. *Check out "When all else fails."*

4 *A.* Static routes are used when there is one and only one route to a destination network. When multiple routes exist, dynamic routes can be used. *Take a look at "One-lane roads."*

5 *B.* The parts of the ip route command are the IP address of the destination network, the subnet mask, the IP address of the destination router, and a routing metric. *Look over "One-lane roads."*

6 *B.* SAP (Service Advertisement Protocol) is a Novell routing protocol used on IPX networks. SAP (service access point) is an addressing field in the 802.2 Ethernet specification. Neither is metrics used in routing. *See "Plotting the Best Course."*

7 *C, D.* Distance-vector algorithms are primarily concerned with how far networks are in terms of hops. However, IGRP is also concerned with the load on the network. *Review "Going the distance"*

8 *A.* Link-state algorithms broadcast link-state packets (LSPs) and use the LSPs they received directly from other routers to maintain a database about the network which is then used by the shortest-path-first (SPF) algorithm to determine the least cost (shortest) route to a network. *Look over "The state of the network."*

9 *D.* An IPX address is a 10-byte address that consists of a 4-byte network number and a 6-byte node identity (usually the MAC identity). Because IPX addresses use the MAC identity of a node, ARP (Address Resolution Protocol) is not needed. *Check out "Routing for the Novell riche."*

10 *B.* Be absolutely sure you memorize Tables 11-2 and 11-3 and understand the relationship of these two tables. That way you are ready for questions like this one on the exam. *Take a look at "The biggest word in IPX networking."*

Part IV
Network Protocols

The 5th Wave   By Rich Tennant

"If it works, it works. I've just never seen network cabling connected with Chinese handcuffs before."

In this part . . .

*F*orget the claims made in other parts of this book
about how important they are to the test, because
this is the most important part of the book when preparing for the CCNA exam. Based on our survey of CCNAs
who have successfully passed the CCNA exam, this is the
part of the test that gave more than 60% of the survey
respondents trouble. The remaining respondents claimed
that the topics in Part V was the troublesome area, but
what do they know?!

The topic of network protocols includes logical, physical,
and network addressing; TCP/IP protocols; router security; and, the really big and nasty, subnetting. Just the
mere mention of the word, subnetting, sends grown adults
screaming into the hills.

We have tried to tame this topic for you. We have
attempted to boil down this wild area of internetworking
to just the essential points you need for the CCNA exam.
Subnetting can be fun. Many of our very best network segments are subnets. Use this part of the book to make
subnets your friends.

Chapter 12

Network Addressing

- -

Exam Objectives

▶ Explaining the components of network addresses

▶ Defining IP address classes and subnetting

▶ Configuring IP addresses

▶ Verifying IP addresses

- -

*A*ddressing over a network is a lot like delivering pizza. It doesn't matter how fast the delivery service is — if the delivery person can't find the destination because he or she doesn't have the correct address, the payload, whether pizza or data, is wasted. The point is that if you want your pizza delivered on time and hot, you must provide the delivery person with your complete street address, including any apartment numbers or other identifying markings. If you want messages to be delivered across a network, you must use good network addressing techniques so that the destination network and host can be easily identified and the message delivered. In this chapter, we look at networking addresses from all angles. Well, at least as it relates to the CCNA exam that is. So, call for that pizza and settle back.

Networking addresses are as easy as A-B-C. IP address classes A, B, and C, that is. You need to know the range and scope of the IP address classes, including the special purpose addresses set aside from the class ranges.

You can expect to see questions about what is a correct TCP/IP address, IPX address, MAC address, and what type of class IP address a specific address is. As such, this certainly is a good chapter to review so that you can refresh those neurons that are holding this information already stored in your brain.

While we're on the subject of addressing, this is a good time to touch on a few other related subjects that might pop up on the test. These subjects include well known port numbers, autonomous systems numbers, and . . . well, I never give away the ending of a chapter at the beginning.

Quick Assessment

1 The two parts of an IP address are the _____ and the _____.

2 The _____ address is designated by a 48-bit or 6-byte hexadecimal number.

3 In IPX addressing the total address is _____ bytes long, _____ bytes for the network number, and _____ bytes for the node number.

4 The 32 bits of an IP address are broken into four _____.

5 Class A addresses use _____ bits, Class B addresses use _____ bits, and Class C addresses use _____ bits for the network portion of the address.

6 The default subnet masks for Class A, Class B, and Class C addresses are _____, _____, and _____, respectively.

7 When using anding (Boolean algebra), one and one equals _____ and one and zero equals _____ .

8 A subnet mask is displayed in either _____ or in _____ form.

9 A host number of all zeros is the _____ address and the host address of all ones is the _____ address.

10 The commands _____, _____, and _____ are used to verify IP addresses.

Answers

1 *Host, network.* See "Getting the Address Right."

2 *MAC.* Review "MAC addresses."

3 *10, 4, 6.* Take a look at "A Novell idea."

4 *Octets.* Check out "Octets and quartets."

5 *8, 16, 24.* See "IP address classes."

6 *255.0.0.0, 255.255.0.0 and 255.255.255.0.* Review "Classy masks."

7 *1, 0 (zero).* Look over "Boolean nightmares."

8 *Dotted decimal, bit-count.* Check out "Configuring an IP address."

9 *Network, broadcast.* See "Special addresses."

10 *Ping, trace (traceroute), telnet.* Review "Verifying an IP address."

Getting the Address Right

Just as the Postal Service expects you to have a single mailing address that uniquely identifies you for mail delivery, each node on a network must also be uniquely identified, and for just about the same reason. As a person, you have a number of different ways of being identified, including by your Social Security number, your phone number, your Wal-Mart frequent shopper's card number, and, of course, the address of your house or apartment. Although network nodes don't have the variety you do, a networked computer can be identified in several ways, including by a MAC (Media Access Control) address, an IP (Internet Protocol) address, an IPX (Novell Netware) address, or perhaps a URL (Uniform Resource Locator).

One thing all network nodes have in common is that in order for their addresses to be considered proper network addresses, they must have two parts present: a host address and a network address. The host address portion identifies the individual node. The network address portion identifies the network or network segment on which the host address can be found.

There are many network addressing schemes in use. For the CCNA exam, concentrate on the IP addressing scheme. You also want to familiarize yourself with Novell Netware IPX addressing, and be absolutely sure you understand MAC addresses in detail as well.

MAC addresses

In essence, a Media Access Control (MAC) address is the unique address of a network interface card (NIC). This address is burned into the NIC circuit during manufacturing and is a unique number that solely identifies each NIC. Every so often the system breaks down and NICs with duplicate MAC addresses are produced and installed in the same network. The network addressing situation that could never happen does, with predictably bad results. A MAC address is also referred to as a physical address or a burned-in address.

MAC addresses, which are Data Link layer addresses, differ from Network layer addresses. MAC addresses are flat addresses in that they identify only the node with which they are associated and have no relationship to any other network elements. In many ways, Mac addresses are like a Social Security number for NICs, identifying only one NIC at a time.

A MAC hex on you

A MAC address consists of a 48-bit or 6-byte hexadecimal number. It's represented in the form of six two-digit numbers separated by dashes. The first 24 bits (3 bytes) of the MAC address contain a code assigned by the IEEE (The Institute of Electrical and Electronics Engineers) to uniquely identify the manufacturer of the card, and the 24 bits (3 bytes) are a number uniquely assigned by the manufacturer. Figure 12-1 illustrates the MAC address and its parts.

On the test, you're not asked to convert hex to decimal or vice versa. So, don't waste your time studying that mystery of the ages.

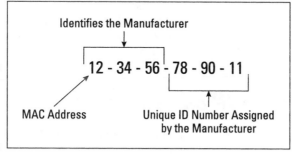

Identifies the Manufacturer

12 - 34 - 56 - 78 - 90 - 11

MAC Address

Unique ID Number Assigned by the Manufacturer

Figure 12-1: The MAC address and its parts.

Here are two points relating to MAC addresses that you're likely to see on the test:

- ✔ **ARP (Address Resolution Protocol):** Uses broadcast messages to learn the MAC or Ethernet address of a known IP address. The node with the broadcasted IP address responds with its MAC address, completing the set.

- ✔ **Reverse ARP (RARP):** Broadcasts messages to learn the IP address corresponding to a known MAC address. This requires the presence of a RARP (pronounced "rarp," what else?) server on the network. An example of where this procedure is used is booting a diskless workstation.

A Novell idea

Until Netware version 5, IPX was the default protocol for a Novell Netware network. You need to know IPX networking fairly well for the CCNA exam, but you especially need to know about IPX and MAC addresses.

An IPX address is 10 bytes (80 bits) long. Four bytes (32 bits) is the network number and 6 bytes (48 bits) is the node number. If 48 bits sounds familiar, it should. The node number is normally the MAC address of the node. Take our advice and memorize these numbers. Here's an example to help you visualize this better:

```
Network address:4b2c
Node address:0000.06d2.ef67
```

In this example, the value 4b2c represents the network address. It could have been shown as 0000.4b2c, but the leading zeros are usually left off. The remainder of the number is the node address. Its zeros are shown because they occur in the middle of the IPX address.

Remember that when you store a number in hexadecimal form, each byte (8 bits) holds two hex values. For example, the hexadecimal value "FF" is stored in a single byte. Just for the sake of trivia, each half-byte is called a *nibble*.

Unlike IP addresses (see "Working with IP addresses" later in this section), IPX addresses are not structured into classes. It's not uncommon for the net-work number not to use the entire 6 bytes. Any zeros at the beginning of the network address are dropped.

Working with IP addresses

You can probably work with decimal numbers much easier than with the binary numbers needed by the computer. It would be very awkward, not to mention time-consuming and error-prone, if humans had to write out network addresses in binary representation. To avoid the inherent problems of humans and binary numbers, the powers that be have devised a system to designate network numbers in decimal. Bless them!

Octets and quartets

The 32-bit IP (Internet Protocol) address is broken up into four octets, which are arranged into a dotted-decimal notation scheme. An octet is a set of 8 bits and not a musical instrument. We're sure you've seen an IP address some-where in the past, but just in case, here's an example of an IP address with its four octets arranged into its dotted-decimal scheme:

```
172.64.126.52
```

This example is the type of addressing used in the current and predominant IP version 4. You won't see IP version 6 on the CCNA exam.

Thinking in binary

The binary system uses only two values (0 and 1) to represent numbers in positions representing increasing powers of 2. We humans are accustomed to thinking and working in the decimal system, which is based on the number 10. To most humans, the number 124 represents $100 + 20 + 4$. To the com-puter, this number is 1111100, which is $64 (2^6) + 32 (2^5) + 16 (2^4) + 8 (2^3) + 4 (2^2) + 0 + 0$.

Each position in a binary number represents, right to left, a power of two beginning with 2^0 and increasing by one power as it moves left: 2^0, 2^1, 2^2, 2^4, etc.

Converting to decimal

You'll need to convert binary to decimal and vice versa on the CCNA exam to compute subnets and hosts. So, it's time for a quick lesson in binary-to-decimal conversion. There are 8 bits in an octet, and each bit can only be a 1 or a 0. What then do you suppose is the largest decimal number that can be expressed in an octet? Final answer? That's right, eight 1s (1111 1111). Okay, now for double the money, what is its equivalent decimal value? Need a lifeline?

The positions of the binary number represent powers of two:

2^7	2^6	2^5	2^4	2^3	2^2	2^1	2^0

Placing a 1 in one of the binary positions turns on that value and adds it into the decimal number representation. A zero in any position turns off the value in that position and it doesn't add into the number representation. For converting a binary octet that has all 1s, here's a handy conversion guide that shows the values assigned to each position in the octet to help you:

2^7	2^6	2^5	2^4	2^3	2^2	2^1	2^0
1	1	1	1	1	1	1	1
128	64	32	16	8	4	2	1

The binary number 1111 1111 converts into the decimal number

$$128 + 64 + 32 + 16 + 8 + 4 + 2 + 1 = 255$$

Therefore, the largest decimal number that can be stored in an IP address octet is 255. The significance of this should become evident later in this chapter and in Chapter 13.

IP address classes

Before we continue discussing other fun facts and stupid IP address tricks, we need to interject just a little bit about the IP address class system. Don't skip over this section! You need to know each class and the IP addresses included in each for the CCNA exam.

IP addresses are divided into five classes, each of which is designated with the alphabetic letters A to E. For the exam, forget about Classes D and E. Class D addresses are used for multicasting, and Class E addresses are reserved for testing and some mysterious future use.

Table 12-1 shows how the classes are split up based on the value in the first octet:

Table 12-1	IP Address Class Assignments
Class	*First Octet Value*
Class A	0–127
Class B	128–191
Class C	192–223

Using the ranges in Table 12-1, you can determine the class of an address from its first octet value. An address beginning with 120 is a Class A address, 155 is a Class B address, and 220 is a Class C address. Remember that you don't need to worry about Classes D and E for the exam.

Memorize Table 12-1 for the ranges of Classes A, B, and C. Knowing the address classes is very important for getting to the underlying data in some CCNA exam questions.

Are you the host or the network?

The 32 bits of the IP address are divided into network and host portions, with the octets assigned as a part of one or the other. Table 12-2 shows how each IP address class designates the network and host portions of the address.

Table 12-2	Network and Host Representation by IP Address Class		
Class	*Octet1*	*Octet2*	*Octet3*	*Octet4*
Class A	Network	Host	Host	Host
Class B	Network	Network	Host	Host
Class C	Network	Network	Network	Host

Each network is assigned a network address and every device or interface (such as a router port) on the network is assigned a host address. There are only two specific rules that govern the value of the address (beyond the IP address class, that is). A host address cannot be designated by all zeros or all ones. These are special addresses that are reserved for special purposes (see "Special addresses" later in this chapter).

Class A addresses

Class A IP addresses use the first 8 bits (first octet) to designate the network address. Actually, the first bit, which is always a 0, is used to indicate the address as a Class A address, and the remaining 7 bits are used to designate the network. The other three octets contain the host address. As shown in Table 12-3, there are 128 Class A network addresses, but because addresses with all zeros aren't used, and address 127 is a special purpose address, 126 Class A networks are available.

There are 16,777,214 host addresses available in a Class A address. Rather than remember this number exactly, you can use the following formula to compute the number of hosts available in any of the class addresses, where "n" represents the number of bits in the host portion:

$$(2^n - 2) = \# \text{ of available hosts}$$

Two addresses (all ones and all zeros) are not usable (see "Special addresses" later in this chapter).

For a Class A network, there are $2^{24}-2$ or 16,777,214 hosts. Half of all IP addresses are Class A addresses. You can use this same formula to determine the number of networks in an address class. For example, a Class A address uses 7 bits to designate the network, so $(2^7-2) = 126$, or there can be 126 Class A networks.

Class B IP addresses

Class B addresses use the first 16 bits (two octets) for the network address. The last two octets are used for the host address. The first 2 bits, which are always 1 0, designate the address as a Class B address, and 14 bits are used to designate the network. This leaves 16 bits (two octets) to designate the hosts.

So how many Class B networks can there be? Using our formula, $(2^{14}-2)$, there can be 16,382 Class B networks and each network can have $(2^{16}-2)$ hosts, or, 65,534 hosts.

Class C IP addresses

Class C addresses use the first 24 bits (three octets) for the network address, and only the last octet for host addresses. The first 3 bits of all class C addresses are set to 1 1 0, leaving 21 bits for the network address, which means there can be 2,097,150 ($2^{21}-2$) Class C networks, but only 254 (2^8-2) hosts per network.

Memorize the information in Table 12-3, especially the address ranges for each IP address class and the relative number of networks and hosts for each class. We don't recommend relying on the formula for the exam, but it may come in handy as a backup tool that you can use to check your answers.

Table 12-3		Characteristics of the IP Address Classes				
Class	Address Range	Identity Bits (binary value)	Bits in Network ID	Number of Networks	Bits in Host ID	Number of Hosts/ Network
A	0–127	1 (0)	7	126	24	16,777,214
B	128–191	2 (10)	14	16,382	16	65,534
C	192–223	3 (110)	21	2,097,150	8	254

Special addresses

A few addresses are set aside for specific purposes. Network addresses that are all binary zeros, all binary ones, and network addresses beginning with 127 are special network addresses. Table 12-4 lists the addresses that are set aside for special purposes.

Table 12-4		Special IP Addresses	
Network Address	Host Address	Description	Example
0's	0's	Default Cisco route	0.0.0.0
0's	Host address	Local network hosts	0.0.0.115
1's	1's	Broadcast to local network	255.255. 255.255
Network address	1's	Broadcast to network address	192.21. 12.255
127	anything	Loopback testing	127.0.0.1

Within each address class is a set of addresses that are set aside for use in local networks sitting behind a firewall or NAT (Network Address Translation) device or networks not connected to the Internet. Table 12-5 lists these addresses for each IP address class.

Table 12-5	Special Local Network Addresses
IP Class	Address Range
Class A	10.0. 0.0–10.255.255.255
Class B	172.16.0.0–172.31.255.255
Class C	192.168.0.0–192.168.255.255

Your best bet is just to memorize the addresses in Tables 12-1 through, and including, 12-5. There really is no simple shortcut to remembering these values.

The Curse of the Subnet Mask

Although it may sound like the subject of a very bad B movie, the topic of the subnet mask is one you need to prepare for. In Chapter 13, we get into the nuts and bolts of subnet masking, but we really can't finish the discussion on network addressing and configuring and verifying IP addresses without at least introducing subnet masking.

An IP address has two parts: the network identification and the host identification. Frequently, the network and host portions of the address need to be separately extracted. In most cases, if you know the address class, it's easy to separate the two portions. However, with the rapid growth of the Internet and the ever-increasing demand for new addresses, the standard address class structure has been expanded by borrowing bits from the host portion to allow for more networks. Under this addressing scheme, called subnetting, separating the network and host requires a special process called *subnet masking*. This process was developed to identify and extract the network part of the address. A subnet mask, which contains a binary bit pattern of ones and zeros, is applied to an address to determine whether the address is on the local network. If it isn't, the process of routing it to an outside network begins.

The function of a subnet mask is to determine whether an IP address exists on the local network or whether it must be routed outside the local network. The subnet mask is applied to a message's destination address to extract the network address. If the extracted network address matches the local network ID, the destination is located on the local network. However, if they don't match, the message must be routed outside the local network. The process used to apply the subnet mask involves Boolean algebra to filter out non-matching bits to identify the network address. See the next section, "Boolean nightmares," to find out what you need to know about Boolean algebra.

Boolean nightmares

Don't worry, you don't need to relive your algebra nightmares to pass the CCNA exam. *Boolean algebra* is a process that applies binary logic to yield binary results. What a relief, huh?

Working with subnet masks, you need only four basic principles of Boolean algebra:

✔ 1 and 1 = 1

✔ 1 and 0 = 0

✔ 0 and 1 = 0

✔ 0 and 0 = 0

Or in other words, the only way you can get a result of a 1 is to combine 1 and 1. Everything else will end up as a 0.

The process of combining binary values with Boolean algebra is called *anding*.

Classy masks

There are default standard subnet masks for Class A, B, and C addresses. Table 12-6 lists the commonly used subnet masks for each IP address class.

Table 12-6	Default Subnet Masks
Address Class	*Subnet Mask*
Class A	255.0.0.0
Class B	255.255.0.0
Class C	255.255.255.0

It's only a trial separation

Subnet masks apply only to Class A, B, or C IP addresses.

The subnet mask is like a strainer or filter that is applied to a message's destination IP address. Its objective is to determine if the local network is the destination network. It goes like this:

1. If a destination IP address is 206.175.162.21, we know that it is a Class C address and that its binary equivalent is 11001110 10101111 10100010 00010101 (see "Converting to decimal" earlier in the chapter).

2. We also know that the default standard Class C subnet mask is 255.255.255.0 (see "Classy masks" earlier in this chapter) and that its binary equivalent is 11111111 11111111 11111111 00000000.

3. When these two binary numbers (the IP address and the subnet mask) are combined using Boolean algebra, the network ID of the destination network is the result:

```
206.175.162.21  11001110 10101111 10100010 00010101
and
255.255.255.0   11111111 11111111 11111111 00000000
yields
                11001110 10101111 10100010 00000000
```

4. The result is the IP address of the network which in this case is the same as the local network and means that the message is for a node on the local network.

Chapter 13 covers subnet masking in much more detail, but this process should be enough to cover how IP addresses are configured at the router.

Routing IP Addresses

When you build a network, you need to figure out how many network IDs your network requires. To do so, you must account for every WAN connection and subnet on the network. Every node and router interface requires a host address, or ID. There's no hard and fast rule on how you should dole out your allotted IP addresses. Commonly, though, the lowest numbers (1 through 10) are assigned to routers and servers, but how you assign addresses is strictly up to you and your network policies and guidelines.

Configuring an IP address

The proper way to configure an IP address on the router is through the IP Address command, which assigns each router interface its unique IP address. A router with four interfaces needs four distinct IP addresses because, technically, each interface (and address) is on a different network. The IP Address command is entered from the config-if mode because the action affects only that interface. Both the IP address and the subnet mask are defined in the command. Here is a sample IP Address command session:

```
CCNA_For_Dummies#config t
Enter configuration commands, one per line. End with
        CNTL/Z.
CCNA_For_Dummies(config)#int e0
CCNA_For_Dummies(config-if)#ip address 192.168.1.6
        255.255.255.0
CCNA_For_Dummies#term ip netmask-format decimal
CCNA_For_Dummies#show int e0
Ethernet0 is up, line protocol is up
Some display deleted for clarity
Internet address is 192.168.1.6 255.255.255.0

CCNA_For_Dummies#term ip netmask-format bit--count
CCNA_For_Dummies#show int e0
Ethernet0 is up, line protocol is up
Some display deleted for clarity
Internet address is 192.168.1.6/24
```

The subnet mask is entered in dotted decimal notation as shown in the fourth line of this example. However, it may be displayed in the dotted decimal notation by using the decimal option on the Term IP Netmask-Format command. It can also be displayed in the Bit-count format by entering the bit-count option of that same command. Bit-count format refers to a standard, commonly used with the Classless Interdomain Routing (CIDR), that expresses the subnet network address in the form "/n," where "n" represents the number of bits in the network address. For example, an 8-bit network addresses (255.0.0.0) is expressed as /8, a 16-bit address (255.255.0.0) is expressed as /16, and a 24-bit address (255.255.255.0) is represented /24. Classless or bit-count format is not limited to class A, B, and C addresses. In fact, a network address can use any number up to 30 bits on a subnetted network, which would be expressed in bit-count format as /30.

Verifying an IP address

IP addresses are verified using PING, Trace, and Telnet. Learn these commands, their responses, and their meanings for the exam. It's important that you know that PING is used to verify IP address connections to the Network layer and that Telnet is used to verify network IP address connections to the Application layer.

Verifying with Telnet

The reason you need to verify IP addresses is to ensure that the various parts of a network can properly communicate with the other parts. For example, if you can Telnet (terminal emulation protocol) into a router from a remote location on the same network, you can verify that the interface and route are up and available. Because Telnet operates on the OSI Model's Application layer, when it's functioning, it's safe to assume that all lower layers are also functioning.

Here's a sample Telnet session used to verify the connection and route at IP address 205.7.5.1.

```
CCNA_4_DUMMIES#telnet 205.7.5.1
Trying 205.7.5.1 ... Open
Greetings from a Generic Cisco Lab
User Access Verification
```

Verifying with PING

The PING (Packet Internet Groper) command verifies OSI Layer 3 (Network layer) connectivity. PING sends out ICMP (Internet Control Message Protocol) messages to verify both the logical addresses and the physical connection. The PING command issued from a Cisco router responds with a number of single character responses. These responses, which you need to know for the CCNA exam, are listed in Table 12-7.

Table 12-7	Cisco PING Response Codes
Response	*Meaning*
! (exclamation mark)	Success
. (period)	Timed out waiting for reply
U	Destination unreachable
| (vertical bar)	Ping process interrupted
? (question mark)	Unknown packet type
C	Congestion-experienced
& (ampersand)	Time to live exceeded

Here are two sample PING sessions on a Cisco router, one successful, the other not so successful:

```
CCNA_4_DUMMIES#ping 205.7.5.1
Type escape sequence to abort.
Sending 5,100-byte ICMP Echoes to 205.7.5.1, timeout is 2
        seconds:
!!!!!
Success rate is 100 percent (5/5), round-trip min/avg/max
        = 104/110/128 ms

CCNA_4_DUMMIES#ping 205.7.5.5
Type escape sequence to abort.
Sending 5, 100-byte ICMP Echoes to 205.7.5.5, timeout is
        2 seconds:
.....
Success rate is 0 percent (0/5)
```

For some very good coverage on the PING command in general, visit www.freesoft.org/CIE/Topics/53.htm and for information specific to the Cisco PING, visit www.cisco.com.

Verifying with traceroute

The traceroute or trace command is used to show the complete route from a source to a destination. Trace sends out probe packets one at a time to each router or switch in the path between the source and the destination IP address entered. Traceroute displays the round-trip time for each packet sent to each upstream router. Traceroute has really only two results, time exceeded or destination unreachable. Trace is used to determine where a breakdown in a route may be occurring.

Here's an example of how trace is used: A network has four routers (A, B, C, and D). A trace command is issued on router A to trace the route from itself to router D. A timing response comes back from router B, but the next message indicates that router C is unreachable. You can be fairly certain that the problem lies somewhere on the route between router B and router C.

Like PING, trace has its own set of response codes, listed in Table 12-8, that you should know for the CCNA exam.

Table 12-8	Trace Command Response Codes
Response	*Meaning*
*	timed out
!H	router received packet but did not forward it (usually due to an access list)
N	network unreachable
P	protocol unreachable
U	port unreachable

Here are the results of a sample traceroute session in which all stations were reachable:

```
CCNA_4_DUMMIES#traceroute 192.5.5.1
Type escape sequence to abort.
Tracing the route to LAB-A (192.5.5.1)
1 LAB-D (210.93.105.1) 4 msec 4 msec 4 msec
2 LAB-C (204.204.7.1) 20 msec 32 msec 28 msec
3 LAB-B (199.6.13.1) 44 msec 48 msec 44 msec
4 LAB-A (201.100.11.1) 64 msec * 60 msec
```

Prep Test

1 Which of the following addresses is not a Data Link layer address?

- A ○ MAC
- B ○ Ethernet
- C ○ IP
- D ○ Physical
- E ○ Burned in

2 Who assigns each portion of the MAC address?

- A ○ First 24 bits IEEE, last 24 bits the manufacturer
- B ○ First 4 bytes IEEE, last 4 bytes the manufacturer
- C ○ First 12 bits the manufacturer, last 36 bits IEEE
- D ○ First 3 bytes Internic, last 3 bytes Cisco

3 Looking at an IPX address of 5ca9.0000.f0d3.76be, which portion is the network address and which is the node address?

- A ○ 5ca9.0000 network; f0d3.76be node
- B ○ 76be network; 5ca9.0000.f0d3 node
- C ○ 5ca9 network; 0000.f0d3.76be node
- D ○ 5ca9.0000.f0d3 network; 76be node

4 What is the binary equivalent of the dot decimal IP address 156.162.179.181?

- A ○ 10011100 10100010 10110011 10110101
- B ○ 10011101 10100010 10110011 10110101
- C ○ 10011100 10100011 10110011 10110101
- D ○ 10011100 10100010 10111011 10110010

5 An IP address starting with a bit sequence in the first octet of 110 would fall into what IP address Class?

- A ○ Class D or E
- B ○ Class C
- C ○ Class B
- D ○ Class A

6 Given a binary IP address of 11001110 10101111 10100010 00010010 and a dotted decimal subnet mask of 255.255.255.0 what is the network ID?

A ○ 205.175.162.0

B ○ 206.159.162.0

C ○ 206.175.162.18

D ○ 206.175.162.0

7 After entering the command show int e1 you read a line of output that reads "Internet address is 191.168.16.6/16". Which of the following is not true?

A ○ Your network number is 191.168.0.0

B ○ This is a Class B network

C ○ The netmask-format has been set to bit-count

D ○ You have configured 16 sub-interfaces on Ethernet port 1

8 When issuing a PING command from a Telnet session, what response would you expect to receive if the packet's TTL field was exceeded?

A ○ ! (exclamation point)

B ○ & (ampersand)

C ○ I (vertical bar)

D ○ . (period)

9 What does the response "C" mean to a ping command?

A ○ Can't reach destination

B ○ Congestion-experienced

C ○ Carrier loss

D ○ Consistent response

10 When issuing a traceroute command what does the response "!H" mean?

A ○ Network unreachable

B ○ Protocol unreachable

C ○ Access list prevents forwarding

D ○ Timed out

Answers

1 C. An IP is a Network layer address. The remaining answers are all variations of the same thing and as such are Data Link layer addresses. *See "MAC addresses."*

2 A. The first 24 bits (3 bytes) are assigned by the IEEE to identify the manufacturer, who in turn adds the last 24 bits (3 bytes) as a serial number for the network adapter. *Review "MAC addresses."*

3 C. 5ca9 represents the network and 0000.f0d3.76be represents the node. Remember that leading zeros on the beginning of the network portion are omitted. *Take a look at "A Novell idea."*

4 A. No cheating and using your calculator for this one. Be sure you know how to compute this without using a calculator. You will be called on to do this on the test. *Check out "Thinking in binary."*

5 B. Class C addresses use a three-bit identifier. Class B uses a two-bit (10), and Class A uses a single one-bit value (set to 1). *See "IP addresses."*

6 D. The network ID is 206.175.162.0, which is extracted because none of the last octet's bit are used. *Review "It's only a trial separation."*

7 D. You have not configured 16 sub-interfaces on Ethernet port 1. Review the configuration process used in this chapter and practice it if you have access to a router. *Look over "Configuring an IP address."*

8 B. The ampersand (&) character indicates the TTL value was exceeded. *Check out "Verifying with PING."*

9 B. The "C" character indicates that the PING packets experience congestion on the network. *See "Verifying with PING."*

10 C. This response indicates the access list entries have prevented the trace packets from being forwarded. *Review "Verifying with traceroute."*

Chapter 13

Subnetting

Exam Objectives

▶ Creating subnet masks
▶ Applying subnetting

*I*f you carefully consider the two exam objectives for this chapter, you discover that they're really just pieces of one larger exam objective. We decided to concentrate one whole chapter on just subnetting. If that sounds ominous, it should. It's our experience, supported by the input we received from many other examinees and with Cisco Networking Academy instructors, that the most difficult area of the CCNA exam to prepare for is subnet masks and subnetting.

You should expect several exam questions that test your knowledge of subnet masks and subnetting. Some are simple, covering only the basic concepts, but some are downright hard. There's simply no way to make this sound anything less than one of the most important areas on the test. If this area is one you find fairly easy, then you are ahead of the game, but you should still review it. However, if you're like most of us, this area is so full of numbers and lists to memorize that it can be overwhelming to try to learn it all sufficiently enough that you're ready for any question on the subject.

Yes, there are subnet calculators out in the real world, but as far as the CCNA exam is concerned, they don't exist. We recommend that you hit this chapter hard, put it aside, and then come back to it a couple of days later. It certainly can't hurt to review it the night before the test, if for no other reason than to build up your confidence.

You should really expect to see between three and six questions on the exam, depending on your draw from the question pool, that deal with subnetting. Needless to say, it's a good thing to have this topic down cold. Our advice is practice, practice, practice, and then practice some more.

There is stuff to be memorized in this chapter! Our best advice is just to memorize it and then cram right before the exam. Then, as soon as you get to the test station, do a brain dump and write down on the paper or plastic sheets you are provided as much of your memorized lists and names as you can. Even if you're given a dried-up marker and a worn-out tablet, as more than one of us experienced, you should still be able to scrawl some notes.

Quick Assessment

Creating
subnet
masks

1   The three classes of usable IP addresses are _____, _____ and _____.

2   In subnetting, _____ bits minimum must be left over for the host ID.

3   You may borrow up to _____ bits for subnetting a Class C address.

4   In a Class B address you may borrow up to _____ bits for subnetting.

5   The formula for calculating the number of hosts per subnet is _____.

6   You can use the formula _____ to calculate the number of subnets.

7   A Class C address with 5 bits borrowed for the subnet yields a subnet mask of _____ . _____ . _____ . _____

Applying
subnetting

8   If you have 255.255.254.0 subnet mask on a Class B address there can be _____ hosts on the subnet.

9   With a subnetted Class C address the maximum number of hosts possible is _____ and assuming a minimum of 2 bits used for the host, the lowest number of hosts possible is _____.

10 The two types of broadcasts supported by Cisco IOS are _____ and _____.

Answers

1 *Class A, Class B, and Class C.* See "Subnetting."

2 *2. Review "Borrowing bits to grow a subnet."*

3 *6. Take a look at "Borrowing bits to grow a subnet."*

4 *14. Check out "Borrowing bits to grow a subnet."*

5 $(2^{number\ of\ bits\ used\ for\ host}) - 2$. See "Calculating subnets."

6 $(2^{number\ of\ bits\ used\ for\ subnets}) - 2$. Review "Calculating subnets."

7 *255.255.255.248 (11111000).* Look over "Class C subnets."

8 *510 ($2^9 - 2$).* Check out "Class B subnets."

9 *62 ($2^6 - 2$), 2 ($2^2 - 2$).* See "Subnet planning problem."

10 *Flooded, directed.* Review "A short broadcast."

Subnetting

After hearing subnetting described for the first time, most people have the same reaction: Why? It can sound like so much smoke and mirrors, but subnetting is the foundation underlying the expansion of both local networks and the Internet in today's (and more importantly, in the CCNA exam's) world. Regardless of the results of your CCNA exam experience, subnetting has become essential knowledge for the administrator of any network.

There are two fundamental reasons why subnetting has so much importance in today's networking environment. First and foremost, the world is running out of available IP addresses. There just isn't an unlimited number of IP addresses available, and subnetting helps extend the existing addresses until either the next version of IP is rolled out or some other technology charges on the scene. The second reason for subnetting is that it reduces the size of the routing tables stored in routers. Subnetting extends the existing IP address base and restructures the IP address. As a result, routers must have a way to extract from an IP address both the network address and the host address.

There are three usable IP address classes: Class A, Class B, and Class C. Class A networks have the highest number of available hosts, and Class C networks have the fewest number of hosts. Of course, this means that Class B networks are somewhere in the middle.

Subnetting networks ID

In this section and the next couple of sections, we have included some basic examples of subnet masks in action. You should review these to be absolutely sure you understand the action and how the results were achieved.

Here is a three-step example of how the default Class A subnet mask is applied to a Class A address:

```
              Decimal            Binary
IP address  123.123.123.001    01111011 01111011 01111011
                                00000001
Subnet mask 255.0.0.0          11111111 00000000 00000000
                                00000000
Network ID  123.0.0.0          01111011 00000000 00000000
                                00000000
```

In this example, the default Class A subnet mask (255.0.0.0) is AND'd with the Class A address (123.123.123.001) using Boolean algebra (see Chapter 12 for more information), which results in the network ID (123.0.0.0) being revealed. The default Class B subnet mask (255.255.0.0) strips out the 16-bit network ID and the default Class C subnet mask (255.255.255.0) strips out the 24-bit network ID.

Review Chapter 12 for additional information of IP address classes, subnet masks, and the Boolean logic process used to apply the mask.

Subnetting, subnet, and subnet mask

Subnetting, a subnet, and a subnet mask are all different. In fact, the first creates the second and is identified by the third. *Subnetting* is the process of dividing a network and its IP addresses into segments, each of which is called a subnetwork, or *subnet*. The *subnet mask* is the 32-bit number that the router uses to cover up the network address to show which bits are being used to identify the subnet.

Subnetting for fun and profit

A network has its own unique address, such as a Class B network with the address 172.20.0.0, which has all zeroes in the host portion of the address. From the basic definitions of a Class B network and the default Class B subnet mask, you know that this network can be created as a single network that contains 65,534 individual hosts (see Chapter 12). However, through the use of subnetting, this network can be logically divided into subnets with fewer hosts on each subnetwork. Not only does this improve the available shared bandwidth, it cuts down on the amount of broadcast traffic generated over the entire network. The two primary benefits of subnetting are fewer IP addresses, often as few as one, are needed to provide addressing to a network, and subnetting usually results in smaller routing tables in routers beyond the local internetwork. Don't confuse the benefits of segmentation, which are improved bandwidth utilization and a reduction in broadcast traffic, with those of subnetting. An example of subnetting: When the network administrator divides the 172.20.0.0 network into five smaller networks — 172.20.1.0, 172.20.2.0, 172.20.3.0, 172.20.4.0, and 172.20.5.0 — the outside world stills sees the network as 172.20.0.0, but the internal routers now break the network addressing into the five smaller subnetworks. In this example, only a single IP address is used to reference the network, and instead of five network addresses, only one network reference is included in the routing tables of routers on other networks.

Borrowing bits to grow a subnet

The key concept in subnetting is borrowing bits from the host portion of the network to create a subnetwork. Rules govern this borrowing, ensuring that some bits are left for a host ID. The rules require that two bits remain available to use for the host ID and (read slowly) that all of the subnet bits cannot be all 1s or 0s at the same time. For each IP address class, only a certain number of bits can be borrowed from the host portion for use in the subnet mask.

Table 13-1 lists the number of bits that can be borrowed to create a subnet.

Table 13-1	Bits Available for Creating Subnets	
Address Class	Host Bits	Bits Available for Subnet
A	24	22
B	16	14
C	8	6

Subnetting a Class A network

The default subnet mask for a Class A network is 255.0.0.0, which allows for more than 16,000,000 hosts on a single network. The default subnet mask uses only 8 bits to identify the network, leaving 24 bits for host addressing. To subnet a Class A network, you need to borrow a sufficient number of bits from the 24-bit host portion of the mask to allow for the number of subnets you plan to create, now and in the future.

For example, to create two subnets with more than four millions hosts per subnet, you must borrow two bits from the second octet and use 10 masked (value equals one) bits for the subnet mask (11111111 11000000) or 255.192 in decimal.

Keep in mind that each of the 8-bit octets has binary place values, as shown in Table 13-2. When you borrow bits from the host ID portion of the standard mask, you don't change the value of the bits, only how they are grouped and used.

Table 13-2	IP Address Octet Binary Values	
Bit Number	Power of 2	Decimal Value
8	2^7	128
7	2^6	64
6	2^5	32
5	2^4	16
4	2^3	8
3	2^2	4
2	2^1	2
1	2^0	1

To structure a Class A network with a maximum of 254 subnets with 65,534 hosts on each subnet, you must borrow 8 bits from the host ID, creating a subnet mask with 16 masked bits, or 255.255.0.0.

Table 13-3 includes a sampling of subnet mask options available for Class A addresses.

Table 13-3	Class A Subnet Masks		
Subnet Mask	*Number of 1 Bits in Mask*	*Number of Subnets*	*Number of Hosts per Subnet*
255.0.0.0	8	0	16,777,214
255.192.0.0	10	2	4,194,302
255.240.0.0	12	14	1,048,574
255.255.0.0	16	254	65,534
255.255.128.0	17	510	32,766
255.255.240.0	20	4,094	4,094
255.255.255.128	25	131,070	126
255.255.255.240	28	1,048,574	14
255.255.255.252	30	4,192,302	2

All subnet masks contain 32 bits; no more, no less. However, a subnet mask cannot filter more than 30 bits. This means two things: one, that there cannot be more than 30 ones bits in the subnet mask, and two, that there must always be at least two bits available for the host ID. As listed in Table 13-3 above, the subnet mask with the highest value (255.255.255.252) has a binary representation of

```
11111111.11111111.11111111.11111100
```

The two zeroes in this subnet mask represent the two positions set aside for the host address portion of the address. Remember that the addresses with all ones (broadcast address) and all zeros (local network) cannot be used as they have special meanings. (See Chapter 12.) You should see a pattern (a bit pattern actually) in Table 13-3. As more bits are taken from the host ID and used in the subnet mask to identify subnets, more subnets are possible but at the cost of a fewer number of hosts per subnet. You should see a similar pattern in Tables 13-4 and 13-5, which show the subnet masks available for Class B and Class C IP addresses, respectively.

Subnetting Class B and Class C networks

The pattern shown in Table 13-3 is similar to that used for Class B and Class C IP addresses and subnet masks. The only differences are that you have fewer options (due to a fewer number of bits available) and that you're much more likely to work with Class B and C networks in real life. Table 13-4 lists a sampling of the subnet masks available for Class B networks, and Table 13-5 lists all of the subnet masks available for Class C networks.

Table 13-4		Class B Subnet Masks		
Subnet Mask	*Number of 1 Bits in Mask*	*Number of Subnets*	*Number of Hosts per Subnet*	*Binary Subnet Mask*
255.255.0.0	16	0	65,534	11111111.11111111.00000000.00000000
255.255.192.0	18	2	16,382	11111111.11111111.11000000.00000000
255.255.240.0	20	14	4,094	11111111.11111111.11110000.00000000
255.255.255.0	24	254	254	11111111.11111111.11111111.00000000
255.255.255.240	28	4,094	14	11111111.11111111.11111111.11110000
255.255.255.252	30	16,382	2	11111111.11111111.11111111.11111100

Table 13-5		Class C Subnet Masks		
Subnet Mask	*Number of 1 Bits in Mask*	*Number of Subnets*	*Number of Hosts per Subnet*	*Binary Subnet Mask*
255.255.255.0	24	0	254	11111111.11111111.11111111.00000000
255.255.255.192	26	2	62	111111111.11111111.1111111.11000000
255.255.255.224	27	6	30	111111111.11111111.1111111.11100000

Subnet Mask	Number of 1 Bits in Mask	Number of Subnets	Number of Hosts per Subnet	Binary Subnet Mask
255.255.255.240	28	14	14	111111111.11111111. 1111111.11110000
255.255.255.248	29	30	6	111111111.11111111. 1111111.11111000
255.255.255.252	30	62	2	111111111.11111111. 1111111.11111100

Any subnetting problems you see on the CCNA exam will most likely concentrate on Class B and C IP addresses. Be sure you know the binary place values for the 8-bit positons of each octet.

Knowing how to calculate subnets

Another calculation you need to know for the CCNA exam is how to determine the number of subnets and hosts per subnet available for any of the available subnet masks.

You can use two simple formulas to calculate these numbers:

```
Number of hosts per subnet = (2 number of bits used for
             host) - 2
and
Number of subnets = (2 number of bits used for subnets) - 2
```

Although they look identical, the key is to remember the number you're trying to calculate, hosts or subnets. Using these two formulas, you are ready should you run into a question that asks you to determine either how many subnets or how many hosts, or both, are possible on a network, given a particular subnet mask.

For example, suppose you are asked to determine the number of subnets available and the number of hosts available on each subnet on the network 192.168.1.0; with a subnet mask of 255.255.255.252. Using the subnet and hosts formulas, the answers are easily calculated. Of course, you must know your powers of 2 to calculate the answers.

Lab 13-1 details the steps you use to calculate both the number of subnets and hosts on a Class C network.

Lab 13-1 Calculating the Number of Subnets and Hosts Available from the Subnet Mask

1. **Calculate the number of subnets available on the Class C address 192.168.1.0 that has a subnet mask of 255.255.255.252.**

   The value 252 in the fourth octet of the subnet mask tells you that 6 bits have been borrowed to create subnets. In order to see this, you may need to "bit out" the last octet. The number 252 in binary is 11111100. Six bits have been used (borrowed) to create the subnet mask.

2. **Substituting 6 into the subnet formula as the power of 2 yields $(2^6) - 2$ or $(64) - 2$ or 62 subnetworks.**

3. **Another important step in this process, although not required by the question we are solving, but one you are sure to need on the test, is to calculate the valid subnet addresses of the subnets available. In Step 2, we determined that there are 62 subnets available. To determine the increment of the subnet values, subtract the subnet mask's last (right-most) octet value from 256. In this case, 256 minus 252 is 4. So, the valid subnets are 4, 8, 12, 16, ..., 244, 248, and 252.**

   If 6 bits have been borrowed for the subnet mask, then 2 bits remain to identify host addresses. This is evidenced by the two zeroes in the last two positions of the subnet mask.

4. **Substituting 2 in the host formula as the power of 2 yields: $(2^2) - 2$ or $(4) - 2$ or 2 hosts available in each subnet.**

5. **One more step that you may need to perform for test questions is to identify the valid host addresses within a subnet.**

   There are two basic rules to remember about subnets and hosts: The first address in a subnet is the local network address (the "all zeroes" address of the subnet) and the last address in a subnet is the broadcast address (the "all ones" address of the subnet). So, in the subnet 192.168.1.4, the valid host addresses are 192.168.1.5 and 192.168.1.6. This pattern is repeated within each subnet.

So the answer to the question of how many subnets are available is 62. The number of hosts available in each subnet is four, but only two hosts are available for use. Remember that you cannot use the zero address or the all ones addresses.

The general rule for calculating subnets and hosts is that the higher the mask is in decimal numbers, more subnets and fewer hosts per subnet are available. The reverse is true as well.

Class C subnets

Commit Table 13-6 to memory and then write it down on the paper provided at your testing station. Knowing the relationships in this table will significantly reduce the time you spend calculating subnetting problems on the exam. If you just can't remember everything in the table, commit the subnet and host formulas to memory instead. Remember that you don't get to use a calculator during the test.

Table 13-6	Class C Subnet Values		
Mask	**Subnet Bits Used**	**Number of Subnets**	**Number of Hosts/Subnet**
255.255.255.252	6	62	2
255.255.255.248	5	30	6
255.255.255.240	4	14	14
255.255.255.224	3	6	30
255.255.255.192	2	2	62
255.255.255.128	1	NOT A LEGAL SUBNET VALUE	
255.255.255.0	0 (Default)	1	254

To determine the total length of the subnet mask, add 24 to the number of borrowed (subnet) bits.

Class B subnets

To calculate the number of subnets and hosts available from a Class B subnet mask, you use the same host and subnet formulas described for calculating Class C values (see "Calculating subnets" earlier in this chapter). Using these formulas, we have constructed a table (see Table 13-7) that contains the Class B subnet and host values.

Table 13-7	Class B Subnet Values		
Mask	**Subnet Bits Used**	**Number of Subnets**	**Number of Hosts/Subnet**
255.255.255.252	14	16,382	2
255.255.255.248	13	8,190	6
255.255.255.240	12	4,094	14

(continued)

Table 13-7 *(continued)*

Mask	Subnet Bits Used	Number of Subnets	Number of Hosts/Subnet
255.255.255.224	11	2,046	30
255.255.255.192	10	1,022	62
255.255.255.128	9	510	126
255.255.255.0	8	254	254
255.255.254.0	7	126	510
255.255.252.0	6	62	1,022
255.255.248.0	5	30	2,046
255.255.240.0	4	14	4,094
255.255.224.0	3	6	8,190
255.255.192.0	2	2	16,382
255.255.128.0	1	NOT A LEGAL SUBNET VALUE	
255.255.0.0	0 (Default)	1	65,534

What good is memorizing these tables? There are two reasons to commit this information to memory. The first reason is that you now know the answers to at least two questions on the exam. The second reason is that you now have the information needed to determine valid IP addresses for subnets, hosts, and broadcasts.

A short broadcast

A broadcast is a message that every node on a network or subnetwork receives and examines. Cisco IOS supports two different types of broadcast messages: flooded and directed. Generally speaking, routers don't propagate broadcasts, which is one of the benefits of installing a router in the first place.

Flooded broadcasts (those with the nominal broadcast address of 255.255.255.255) are not forwarded by the router and are considered local traffic only. Directed broadcasts, which contain all 1s in the host portion of the IP address, are addressed to a specific subnetwork and are allowed to pass.

A Little Bit of Practice

In this section, we include some sample problems that are similar to what you'll encounter on the CCNA exam. You should practice these questions at least twice, once using the suggested steps, taking care to understand the answers and how we calculated each, and then again and again without the book until you are able to quickly and surely calculate the same result.

Calculating subnets, hosts, and broadcast addresses

Given the IP address of 192.168.1.65 that has a subnet mask of 255.255.255.192, determine its subnet. Lab 13-2 takes you through the steps used for this calculation.

Lab 13-2	Sample IP Address Problems

1. **Determine the subnet.**

   Looking at this problem in binary:

   Address 11000000 (192) 10101000 (168) 00000001 (1) 10000001 (65)

   Subnet 11111111 (255) 11111111 (255) 11111111 (255) 11000000 (192)

   Network 11000000 (192) 10101000 (168) 00000001 (1) 00000000 (0)

   2. **Calculate the valid number of subnets:**

   Using the formula $(2^2) - 2$ to calculate the subnets equals two subnets.

   Using the formula $(2^6) - 2$ to calculate the hosts per subnet equals 62 hosts.

   A Class C address with a subnet mask of 255.255.255.192 has 2 available subnets with 62 available hosts per subnet.

3. **Another way to calculate the valid subnets is to subtract the subnet mask value from 256 and count the number of times the difference can be added to itself before reaching the mask value. This count tells you the number of valid subnets available under this subnet mask.**

   For example, 256 – 192 = 64 and the valid subnets are 192.168.1.64 and 192.168.1.128, or two available subnets. Since these two addresses are the only valid subnets available under this subnet mask, they cannot be used as subnet masks themselves. Which is the reason why 192.168.1.128 was an invalid mask value in Table 13-7.

4. The broadcast address of a subnet is the highest number available in the subnet or one less than the next valid subnet's address. Remember that broadcast addresses are all 1s. Normally, the value 255 represents the broadcast address, but that's not always the case in subnet masking. For this particular situation, the broadcast addresses for the valid subnets are 192.168.1.127 and 192.168.1.191.

5. The available range of host addresses includes all of the addresses between the valid subnet addresses (excluding the subnet's network and broadcast addresses):

```
192.168.1.65 through 192.168.1.126
192.168.1.129 through 192.168.1.190
```

Another subnet problem, but just a little harder

You can expect to see subnet questions like this on the exam:

With an IP address of 192.168.10.115 and a subnet mask of 255.255.255.248 what is the class of address, the subnet address, and the broadcast address. Lab 13-3 details how you should go about solving this problem.

Lab 13-3   Solving IP Subnet Problems

1. First, check to see if any of the possible answers suggest that this is something other than a Class C address. If so, eliminate these answers immediately.

2. Now determine what numbers would be the subnet numbers:

```
256-248 = 8
```

3. The valid subnets would be 8, 16, 24, ... (leaving a bunch of numbers out here) ... 104, 112, 120... (more numbers left out) ... through 240.

4. The host ID in the IP address — 115 — falls between 112 and 120.

5. The subnetwork ID comes from the next lower valid subnet number. So its subnet ID is 192.168.10.112.

6. The broadcast number is 1 less then the next subnet address, so it would be 192.168.10.119.

So, the answers to the question are that 192.0.0.0 addresses are in Class C, the subnet address of 192.168.10.115 is 192.168.10.112, and the broadcast address of that subnet is 192.168.10.119.

A Class B subnet problem

Calculate the valid subnetwork and broadcast addresses for a Class B address of 172.16.1.128 with a subnet mask of 255.255.255.0. Lab 13-4 details the steps used to calculate the answers to this problem.

Lab 13-4	Calculating the subnet and broadcast addresses for a Class B address

1. **First of all, using the information you memorized from Chapter 12, you know that 172.0.0.0 networks are Class B networks.**

2. **From the subnet value in the third octet, 255, we know that 8 bits are in use for the mask (out of a possible 14 available).**

3. **Using the subnet formula, we get $2^8 - 2$ or 254 subnets, which in this case is also the number of hosts per subnet.**

4. **Adding the 254 hosts and the one broadcast address means that the entire fourth octet is used for each subnet.**

5. **To determine the valid subnetworks, subtract 256 – 255 = 1. The valid subnetwork numbers are 172.16.1.0, 172.16.2.0, ... through 172.16. 254.0.**

6. **The answers to this problem are that the subnetwork address is a Class B address of 172.16.1.0 and the broadcast address is 172.16.1.255.**

Subnet planning problem

On the exam, you may encounter a question similar to this scenario:

> Your company has been assigned a Class C address with a network number of 192.168.250.0. Your boss wants you to plan for network expansion but doesn't want to have more than 20 people on any LAN. Come up with a networking scheme.

The key to this question is the number of hosts per subnet. A Class C network can have a maximum of 62 hosts on each of two subnets or a minimum of two hosts on each of 62 subnets, depending on the subnet mask used.

To allow for 20 hosts per subnetwork (LAN) requires a subnet mask of 255.255.255.224. Remember that to discover the number of host addresses on a subnet, take 2 to the power represented by the number of bits in the host portion of the subnet mask, and then subtract 2 from this number:

```
2^5 - 2 = 30
```

Thirty hosts is about as close as you can get to 20 and still allow for 20 hosts. This uses 5 bits in the mask for hosts, which leaves 3 bits for the subnetwork, or 6 subnets (see "Class C subnets" earlier in this chapter). To figure out the subnet numbers, subtract 256 − 224 = 32. This would result in the network scheme shown in Table 13-8.

Table 13-8	Networking Scheme for Subnet Planning Problem	
Subnet Address	*Valid Hosts*	*Broadcast*
192.168.250.32	.33 - .62	.63
192.168.250.64	.65 - .94	.95
192.168.250.96	.97 - .126	.127
192.168.250.128	.129 - .158	.159
192.168.250.160	.161 - .190	.191
192.168.250.192	.193 - .222	.223

Prep Test

1 Given a Class A address of 120.40.168.13 and a subnet mask of 255.0.0.0, what is the network address?

A ○ 120.40.168.0
B ○ 120.40.0.0
C ○ 120.0.0.0
D ○ 0.40.168.13

2 What is the binary equivalent of the subnet mask 255.255.224.0?

A ○ 11100000
B ○ 11111111 11100000 00000000
C ○ 11111111 11111111 11110000 00000000
D ○ 11111111 11111111 11100000 00000000

3 Using a Class B address with a 255.255.255.248 how many bits are being borrowed from the host portion of the address?

A ○ 11
B ○ 10
C ○ 12
D ○ 5
E ○ None of the above

4 Given a Class C address of 194.16.121.1 and a subnet mask of 255.255.255.224 how many subnetworks can there be and how many hosts can be on each subnetwork?

A ○ 30 subnets and 6 hosts
B ○ 16 subnets and 16 hosts
C ○ 14 subnets and 14 hosts
D ○ 6 subnets and 30 hosts

5 Given an IP address of 204.200.106.1 and a subnet mask of 255.255.255.240 what is the broadcast address for subnet three?

A ○ 204.200.106.48
B ○ 204.200.106.63
C ○ 204.200.106.47
D ○ 204.200.106.79

6 Using a Class C address of 192.168.1.0 with a subnet mask of 255.255.255.248 how many subnetwork addresses are available?

A ○ 64

B ○ 32

C ○ 30

D ○ 16

7 If you have a need for no more than 12 subnetworks with at least 15 hosts per subnet which address scheme would be best?

A ○ Class C with 255.255.255.224 subnet mask

B ○ Class B with 255.255.224.0 subnet mask

C ○ Class B with 255.255.255.240 subnet mask

D ○ Class B with 255.255.240.0 subnet mask

8 Which series includes only valid subnets of a 192.168.1.0 IP address with a subnet mask of 255.255.255.224?

A ○ 192.168.32.0, 192.168.128.0, 192.168.228.0

B ○ 192.168.0.0, 192.168.64.0, 192.168.160

C ○ 192.168.1.64, 192.168.1.160, 192.168.1.192

D ○ 192.168.33.0, 192.168.99.0, 192.168.193.0

9 What is the dotted decimal equivalent of the binary IP address 10101100 00010000 1100100 111111010?

A ○ 172.32.100.250

B ○ 172.16.100.250

C ○ 172.16.104.249

D ○ 172.8.50.250

10 How many hosts are available on a Class B network that uses 27 bits for the network address in its subnet mask?

A ○ 30

B ○ 62

C ○ 16

D ○ 126

Answers

1 *C.* No guessing allowed. You must know how this is computed. If you're still having problems, go back over the Labs in this chapter, substituting different values until you get it. *See "Subnetting network IDs."*

2 *D.* This is computed as 255 = 128 + 64 + 32 + 16 + 8 + 4 + 2 + 1, 255 = 128 + 64 + 32 + 16 + 8 + 4 + 2 + 1, and 224 = 128 + 64 +32. *Review "Subnetting a Class A network."*

3 *E.* Thirteen bits were borrowed: 8 (255) from the third octet plus 5 (248) from the fourth octet. *Take a look at "Borrowing bits to grow a subnet."*

4 *D.* There can be 6 subnets and 30 hosts: 3 bits are used for 224 (128 + 64 + 32), $(2^3)-2 = 6$, leaving 5 bits for the hosts $(2^5)-2 = 30$. *Check out "Subnetting Class B and Class C networks."*

5 *B.* This is calculated as 256 – 240 = 16, 16 x 3 = 48, 48 + 15 = 63. Make sure you understand the logic of this calculation for the exam. *Really study Lab 13-2 in "Calculating subnets, hosts, and broadcast addresses."*

6 *C.* This was calculated as $(2^5) - 2 = 32 - 2 = 30$. *See "Calculating subnets."*

7 *D.* A Class B scheme with a 255.255.240.0 subnet mask yields 14 subnets with up to 4,094 hosts. Answers A and B only provide 6 subnets and answer C only allows 14 host addresses. *Review "Calculating subnets."*

8 *C.* Be absolutely sure you get this. *Pour over Lab 13-2 in "Calculating subnets, hosts, and broadcast addresses."*

9 *B.* Study the binary equivalents table in Table 13-2. Check out *"Subnetting a Class A network."*

10 *A.* This is calculated as $(2^{(16-11)}) - 2$. *See "Calculating subnets, hosts, and broadcast addresses."*

Chapter 14

TCP/IP

· ·

Exam Objectives

▶ Identifying TCP/IP Transport layer protocol functions

▶ Detailing TCP/IP Network layer protocol functions

▶ Explaining the functions of the ICMP

▶ Defining data encapsulation

· ·

*T*CP/IP (Transmission Control Protocol/Internet Protocol) is by far the most commonly used protocol in the world. It's considered one of the important catalysts for the rapid growth of the Internet as well as internal networks. However, the history of TCP/IP is intertwined with that of the Internet.

For the CCNA exam, you don't need to know the history of TCP/IP or the Internet, but you should know that TCP/IP is not just one or two protocols, but rather a suite of protocols that work together to enable Internet, intranet, and networking communications over local and wide area networks. Although the CCNA exam focuses more on the seven layers of the OSI model (see Chapter 2), you can expect to see several questions designed to test your knowledge of the TCP/IP protocol suite.

Specifically, make sure you know the difference between TCP and UDP. This is definitely on the test. You should know what and how ICMP packets are used and how data packets are encapsulated for each layer of the OSI model. You also need to know about the well-known port numbers, even if they aren't as well known to you.

This chapter could be subtitled TCFOA (The Chapter Full Of Acronyms). What with UDP, TCP, TCP/IP, FTP, HLEN, IP, SMTP, DNS, SNMP, ICMP, ARP, RARP, and PING, if this chapter has nothing else, it has TLAs (three-letter acronyms) and FLAs (four-letter acronyms) galore. We certainly understand why you may be PTO (Plain Tuckered Out) at the end of this chapter. Hang in there, you're well into your test preparations. If you've gotten this far, things are going great and it won't be long before you'll have the one grand-and-glorious FLA you're seeking — CCNA. From there, it's just a short trip to fame, fortune, clear skin, white teeth, lots of dates, and a better, more fulfilling job. Well, maybe we can't really promise you all that (forget the part about the dates), but getting a CCNA certification is certainly worth the effort to learn about TCP/IP.

Quick Assessment

Identifying
TCP/IP
Transport
layer proto-
col functions

1   TCP/IP is a _____ stack.

2   FTP is a _____-oriented protocol.

3   A Cisco router uses _____ to store and retrieve its configuration files from a server with the same name.

4   The main functions that the Transport layer of the TCP/IP protocol stack serves are _____ and _____.

5   UDP is a _____ protocol.

6   TCP is considered to be _____ while IP is considered to be _____.

7   TCP and UDP both use _____ to move information along to the application layer.

Detailing
TCP/IP
Network
layer proto-
col functions

8   IP provides for _____ addressing.

Explaining
the func-
tions of the
ICMP

9   ICMP is a _____ layer protocol that is used primarily for control and messaging services.

Defining
data encap-
sulation

10   A _____ is the term used for the combination of the header, trailer, and data that is encapsulated so that it can be moved onto the network.

Answers

1 *Protocol.* See "TCP/IP protocol stack."

2 *Connection.* Review "File Transfer Protocol (FTP)."

3 *TFTP.* Take a look at "File Transfer Protocol (FTP)."

4 *Reliability, flow control.* Check out "Transport Layer Protocols."

5 *Connectionless.* See "Connecting ways."

6 *Connection-oriented; connectionless.* Review "Connecting ways."

7 *Port numbers.* Look over "Well-known ports."

8 *Logical.* Check out "Internet Protocol (IP)."

9 *Network.* See "Internet Control Message Protocol (ICMP)."

10 *PDU.* Review " Data Encapsulation."

The TCP/IP Suite

The Transmission Control Protocol/Internet Protocol (TCP/IP) suite, also known as just the Internet Protocol suite, has quickly become the standard for network communications at both the global and local levels. TCP/IP was developed with portability and universal support in mind. Its adaptability and open structure have been important reasons for its rapid and wide-spread growth.

The TCP/IP protocols

TCP/IP is actually a suite, or stack, of protocols that interconnect and work together to provide for reliable and efficient data communications across an internetwork. The major protocols of the TCP/IP protocol suite are:

- Transmission Control Protocol (TCP)
- User Datagram Protocol (UDP)
- Domain Name System (DNS)
- Internet Protocol (IP)
- Address Resolution Protocol (ARP)
- File Transport Protocol (FTP)
- Simple Mail Transport Protocol (SMTP)
- Post Office Protocol (POP3)
- Interactive Mail Access Protocol (IMAP)
- Internet Control Message Protocol (ICMP)
- Routing Information Protocol (RIP)
- Open Shortest Path First (OSPF)
- Hypertext Transfer Protocol (HTTP)
- TCP/IP Utilities (PING, Telnet, IPCONFIG, ARP, and more)

Don't waste your time memorizing all of the protocols in the TCP/IP protocol suite. We haven't listed them all anyway. Look over the preceding list and mentally note the first six or seven. It's far more important to know the functions of certain protocols (TCP, UDP, and ICMP) than to memorize this list.

TCP/IP protocol stack

In addition to being a suite (or collection) of protocols, TCP/IP is also a protocol stack. This means that the TCP/IP protocol suite can be broken up into groups of smaller suites that can be stacked or layered on each other to cooperatively complete a task or activity.

The best way to see the makeup of the TCP/IP protocol stack is to view it in contrast to the OSI and DOD (Department of Defense) models. The TCP/IP stack contains one or more protocols to function at each layer of these models. The primary difference between the DOD and the OSI models is that the DOD is a more compact model and was the model to which TCP/IP was originally developed.

Table 14-1 shows how the TCP/IP protocol stack maps to the OSI model.

Table 14-1	The TCP/IP Protocol Stack
OSI Layers	*TCP/IP Protocols*
Application, Presentation, Session	Telnet, FTP, SMTP, SNMP, DNS, HTTP
Transport	TCP, UDP
Network	IP, ICMP, ARP, RARP
Data Link, Physical	Ethernet, Token Ring, FDDI*

* These are networking technologies that function at the Data Link and Physical layers. They aren't TCP/IP protocols or a part of the TCP/IP protocol stack. They're included only to show the technologies that function on that level of the models.

Application layer protocols

The TCP/IP Application layer protocols you can expect to see on the CCNA exam are listed in Table 14-1 on the OSI Application, Presentation, and Session layers. You should be familiar with the function and usage of each of these protocol, but don't waste the time to become expert on them.

File Transfer Protocol (FTP)

The File Transfer Protocol (FTP) is a reliable, connection-oriented (see "Connecting ways" later in this chapter) tool used to copy files from one computer to another over a TCP/IP network, such as the Internet or an intranet. FTP includes functions that allow it to log onto a remote network, navigate its directory structure, list the contents of its directories, and copy files by downloading them to the local computer.

Another flavor of FTP is the Trivial File Transfer Protocol (TFTP), which is an unreliable (meaning delivery is not guaranteed) file transfer protocol. Cisco routers use TFTP to store and retrieve configuration files from a TFTP server (a file source that supports TFTP).

Telnet

Telnet is a terminal emulation protocol used on TCP/IP-based networks to remotely log onto a remote device to run a program or manipulate data. Telnet was originally developed for ARPAnet and is an inherent part of the TCP/IP communications protocol. In the Cisco world, Telnet is used to access and configure routers from remote locations.

Other protocols you should know

You should be aware of other Presentation/Application layer protocols just in case they're mentioned in passing on the exam. They include Hypertext Transport Protocol (HTTP), Simple Network Management Protocol (SNMP), Domain Name System (DNS), and SMTP (Simple Mail Transfer Protocol).

Novell NetWare networks that use the IPX/SPX protocol stack have two protocols that perform the same functions as the TCP/IP application layer protocols — SAP (Service Advertising Protocol) and NCP (NetWare Core Protocol).

Don't get caught up in this last bunch of protocols when preparing for the exam. Most likely you'll see them in scenarios and questions on other topics, such as a question on well-known port numbers. (See Table 14-3 later in this chapter.)

Transport Layer Protocols

There are two TCP/IP protocols that function at the OSI model's Transport layer that you can expect to see on the exam: Transmission Control Protocol (TCP) and User Datagram Protocol (UDP).

Transmission Control Protocol (TCP)

TCP is a connection-oriented (see "Connecting ways" later in this chapter), reliable, delivery protocol that ensures that packets arrive at their destination error-free. Using TCP is similar to sending a registered letter. When you send the letter, you know for sure that it will get to its destination and that you'll be notified that it got there in good condition. Of course, like registered mail, you pay a higher price to use TCP. The higher price doesn't involve money, but rather the amount of bandwidth and time used to complete the transmission.

Creating TCP sockets

FTP, Telnet, SMTP, and HTTP are some of the Application layer protocols that use the transport services of TCP. These protocols use TCP to open a socket between two computers.

There are actually two types of sockets. The socket that works with TCP is called a _stream socket_ and the other, which works with IP, is called a _datagram socket._ A stream socket works with connection-oriented (see "Connecting ways" later in this chapter) protocols, like TCP, to transfer data between two computers.

TCP provides reliable, point-to-point communications that two devices on a TCP/IP network can use to communicate with each other. To communicate, each device must create a connection to the other by binding a socket to the end of the connection it controls. The devices read and write from and to the socket bound to the connection.

To get back to our original point, Application layer protocols use TCP to open a socket by recording the TCP protocol in use, the destination IP address, and the port number of the application (see "Well-known ports" later in the chapter) to be used on the destination device to process the information being transferred.

Connecting ways

Network protocols are either connection-oriented or connectionless.

- ✔ **Connection-oriented protocols** require that a direct connection be established between two devices before data can begin to transfer between the devices. Packets are transferred using a prescribed sequence of actions that include an acknowledgment to signal when a packet arrives, and possibly resending the packet if there are errors. This method is reliable and, as a result of its reliability and the overhead involved, much slower than connectionless protocols. TCP is a connection-oriented protocol.

- ✔ **Connectionless protocols** are largely based on your faith in the technology. Packets are sent over the network without regard to whether they actually arrive at their destinations. There are no acknowledgments or guarantees, but you can send a _datagram_, what connectionless protocol packets are called, to many different destinations at the same time. Connectionless protocols are fast because no time is used in establishing and tearing down connections. A fair analogy is mailing a first-class letter with the postal service. UDP is a connectionless protocol.

Connectionless protocols are also referred to as _best-effort_ protocols. This type of delivery system is common to protocols that do not include some form of acknowledgment system to guarantee the delivery of information.

You need to understand the primary difference between connection-oriented and connectionless protocols, but more importantly, you need to know that TCP is a connection-oriented protocol and that UDP is a connectionless protocol.

Table 14-2 lists some of the TCP/IP protocols and whether they are connection-oriented or connectionless. You may want to review this just for background information.

Table 14-2	Connection-Oriented and Connectionless Protocols
Protocol	*Type*
FTP	Connection-oriented
IP	Connectionless
IPX	Connectionless
TCP	Connection-oriented
UDP	Connectionless
SPX	Connection-oriented

Making a three-way handshake

Establishing a connection-oriented connection involves the process of setting up sequence and acknowledgment fields and agreeing upon the port numbers to be used. This is accomplished by a three-step handshake process that works like this:

- ✔ **Handshake one:** Host 1 sends a synchronization message to Host 2
- ✔ **Handshake two:** Host 2 acknowledges Host 1's synchronization message and sends back its own synchronization message
- ✔ **Handshake three:** Host 1 acknowledges Host 2's synchronization message

At this point, the connection is successfully established and the applications can begin transferring data. Throughout the communications session, TCP manages the transfer of data packets, ensuring that they reach their destination and if errors occur, TCP supervises the retransmission of the packet.

Ensuring reliability

If TCP ever has a retirement dinner, when they give it the gold socket, they'll say "You could always rely on good old TCP!" TCP data transfers are reliable. This isn't an opinion, it's a technical characteristic that was designed into TCP. TCP uses two mechanisms to provide its high level of reliability: error-checking and received segment acknowledgments.

Error-checking is accomplished through the use of two numbers stored in the packet header: a checksum and the number of bits in the packet payload. The checksum is calculated through an algorithm and the bit count is a straight tally. These two values are stored in the packet header and sent along as a part of the packet. The receiving end recalculates and recounts and checks its numbers against those in the packet header. If they are not equal, a request is sent to the sending station to resend the packet.

The acknowledgment of segment receipts is accomplished through a process called *windowing*, which is a form of flow control. In windowing, a window, which is represented as a number of packets, sets the interval before an acknowledgement must be sent back to the sending station by the receiving stations.

Windowing works like this:

1. Host 1 tells Host 2 that it has a window size of three (for example) and sends, in this case, three segments.

2. If Host 2 receives all three segments, it sends back an acknowledgment saying send segment 4 and the size of the window Host 2 can accept. As the transmission proceeds, the receiving station slowly increases the window size as long as segments are received without errors.

3. Had Host 2 failed to receive, for example, segment 3, it would resend an acknowledgment for segment 2, which means that Host 1 should send segment 3 again. At this time, the window would be reset to the minimum window size and the trust relationship would be rebuilt.

This example uses a *sliding window,* so called because the window can be adjusted on-the-fly to meet the needs of either the sending or receiving device.

After the connection is open, it remains open, providing a virtual circuit. TCP supports full-duplex transmission, which means that both the sender and receiver can transfer data simultaneously over the same connection. To accommodate this, the devices at each end of the connection must maintain two windows, one for sending and one for receiving.

TCP allows for multiplexing, which is the ability for more than one application to use an open transport connection. This is possible for two reasons: each TCP segment is self-contained, with its data and addresses encapsulated in the segment packet; and segments are sent on a first-come-first-served basis without regard to what came before or comes after each segment.

In summary, here's a list of what you should know and remember about TCP:

- ✔ Connection-oriented
- ✔ Reliable transfer
- ✔ Error-checking

✔ Full-duplex transmission

✔ Flow control

✔ Multiplexing

Getting to know the well-known ports

A *port* is a logical connection device that allows the system to assign the incoming data to a particular application for processing. Each port is assigned a *port number,* which is a way to identify the specific process to which the message is to be passed. For example, if you request a file from a remote FTP server, to communicate to the remote server the nature of the request, TCP sets the port number field in the header to 21 (the standard FTP port number). The remote server sees the request for port number 21 and forwards your request to its FTP program. Both TCP and UDP use port numbers to move information along to the application layer.

The registering body, IANA (Internet Assigned Numbers Authority), divides port numbers into three groups:

✔ **Well-known ports** are the most commonly used TCP/IP ports. These ports are in the range of 0 through 1023. These ports can be used only by system processes or privileged programs. Well-known ports are TCP ports but are usually registered to UDP services as well.

✔ **Registered ports** are in the range of 1024 through 49151. Registered ports are used on most systems by user programs to create and control logical connections between proprietary programs.

✔ **Dynamic (private) ports** are in the range of 49152 through 65535. These ports are unregistered and can be used dynamically for private connections.

Here's some additional information that you should know about port numbers:

✔ Port numbers below 256 are assigned to public applications (such as FTP, HTTP, etc.)

✔ Port numbers 256 – 1023 are assigned to companies for saleable applications

✔ Port numbers above 1023 are dynamically assigned in the host application

✔ Source and destination port numbers don't have to be the same

On the CCNA exam, you may be asked to identify the application associated with a well-known port number. Table 14-3 lists the port numbers and their corresponding applications that you should know for the test. This information may also be useful when doing access lists.

Table 14-3	Well-Known Ports
Port Number	**Application**
21	FTP
23	Telnet
25	SMTP
69	TFTP
80	HTTP

Formatting the TCP segment

You can expect one or two questions on the fields that make up the format of the TCP segment. On the Transport layer, packets are referred to as segments.

Figure 14-1 depicts the format of the TCP segment and Table 14-4 describes its contents. Compare this to the UDP segment presented in the next section.

```
TCP Segment

  16 bits   16 bits   32 bits   32 bits   4 bits   4 bits
 ┌────────┬────────┬────────┬────────┬───────┬──────────┐
 │ Source │ Dest.  │  Seq   │  ACK   │ HLEN  │ Reserved │
 │  Port  │  Port  │ Number │ Number │       │          │
 └────────┴────────┴────────┴────────┴───────┴──────────┘
                                                        0 or
                    6 bits   16 bits   16 bits  16 bits 32 bits    ?
                  ┌─────────┬────────┬────────┬────────┬────────┬──────┐
                  │Code Bits│ Window │ Check- │ Urgent │ Option │ Data │
                  │         │        │  sum   │Pointer │        │      │
                  └─────────┴────────┴────────┴────────┴────────┴──────┘
```

Figure 14-1:
The format
of the TCP
segment.

Table 14-4	TCP Segment	
Field	**Length in Bits**	**Purpose**
Source port	16	The number of the calling port
Destination port	16	The number of the called port
Sequence number	32	Used to ensure correct sequencing of data

(continued)

Table 14-4 *(continued)*

Field	Length in Bits	Purpose
Acknowledgment number	32	Sequence number of the next expected TCP octet
HLEN	4	Header length
Reserved	6	Set to zero
Code bits	6	Functions that set up and terminate the session
Window	16	Size of window sender can accept
Checksum	16	Error correction feature, sum of header and data fields
Urgent pointer	16	End of the urgent data
Option	0 or 32	Maximum TCP segment size
Data	—	Data from upper layers

User Datagram Protocol (UDP)

User Datagram Protocol (UDP) is the other major Transport layer protocol in the TCP/IP protocol suite. In contrast to TCP and its reliability, UDP is unreliable, which means it doesn't monitor the transmission of its segments (which, as you probably guessed, are called datagrams), and it doesn't require confirmation of datagram delivery. UDP is a best-effort, connectionless protocol best know for its speed. UDP also doesn't provide for windowing. As shown in Figure 14-2, a UDP header frame, which includes all of the fields before the data in the UDP segment, is only 8 bytes long compared to the TCP header frame that can be up to 24 bytes long. The primary protocols using UDP are SNMP, NFS, TFTP, and DNS.

For the exam, remember that UDP is connectionless and unreliable.

The UDP datagram

If you compare the UDP datagram's format and contents, shown in Figure 14-2 and detailed in Table 14-5, you should notice now how much less overhead, in the form of extra fields, there is in a UDP segment. Remember this comparison for the exam.

Figure 14-2:
The format
of the UDP
datagram.

UDP Datagram

16 bits	16 bits	16 bits	16 bits	?
Source Port	Dest. Port	Length	Check-sum	Data

Table 14-5		UDP Datagram
Field	*Size in Bits*	*Purpose*
Source port	16	The number of the calling port
Destination port	16	The number of the called port
Length	16	The length of the datagram
Checksum	16	Error correction feature, sum of header and data
Data	–	Data from upper layers

Network Layer Protocols

A number of TCP/IP protocols operate on the Network layer of the OSI Model, including Internet Protocol (IP), Address Resolution Protocol (ARP), Reverse ARP (RARP), BOOTP, and the Internet Control Message Protocol (ICMP). The OSI Network layer (see Chapter 5) is concerned with routing messages across the internetwork.

Internet Protocol (IP)

Where TCP is connection-oriented, IP is connectionless. This is something you should tuck away in your memory for test day. IP provides for the best-effort delivery of the packets (or datagrams) that it creates from the segments it receives from the Transport layer protocols. The IP protocol provides for logical addressing on the Network layer.

Converting Transport layer segments

The primary benefit of converting Transport layer segments into Network layer packets is that the conversion helps reduce the overall size of the packet, which results in better efficiency. The size of IP packets is based on the maximum transmission unit (MTU). IP selects an appropriate packet size and then proceeds to fragment larger packets. This process, known as fragmentation, usually occurs on a router between the source and destination, and results in a fragment that's sized just right to fit into a single frame for shipment over the network. The fragments are then reassembled at the final destination.

IP also provides for logical addressing, which is the hierarchical addressing scheme used on the Network layer. Layer 2 hardware addressing defines only a particular node on a network, whereas logical addressing also defines the node's network and other location information. IP uses routing tables to determine the action to take on a packet. For a router, this means that it decides which port to send the packet to move it along its way.

IP packets

The IP packet (or datagram) is variable length, and its format is shown in Figure 14-3 and described in Table 14-6. Review the format of the IP packet so that you're aware of its fields and the purpose of each.

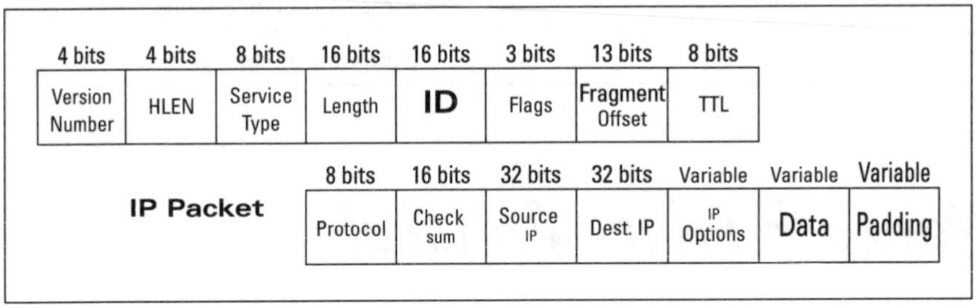

Figure 14-3: IP packet format.

Table 14-6		IP Packet
Field	*Size in Bits*	*Purpose*
IP Version number	4	Identifies the packet as IPv4 or IPv6
HLEN	4	Header length
Type of service	8	How packet should be processed
Length	16	The total length of the packet including the header and data
ID	16	Used for reassembly of fragmented packets
Flags	3	Used for reassembly of fragmented packets

Field	Size in Bits	Purpose
Flag offset		Used for reassembly of fragmented packets
TTL	8	Time-to-live value
Protocol	8	Identifies the Transport layer protocol that passed this packet to IP
Checksum	16	Error correction feature, sum of header and data
Source IP	32	IP address of sending node
Destination IP	32	IP address of destination node
IP Option	Variable	Optional use for testing and debugging
Padding	0 or 8	Used in the calculation of the checksum
Data	Variable	Data from application

The key points to remember about the IP and its packet format are:

✔ IP is primarily concerned with routing

✔ IP is a connectionless, unreliable, best-effort delivery service

✔ IP manages the fragmentation and reassembly of upper-layer segments

Internet Control Message Protocol (ICMP)

The Internet Control Message Protocol (ICMP) is another Network layer protocol. It's used primarily for control and messaging services and, as such, it carries messages between systems regarding status, passing control codes, and delivering error codes and messages. ICMP is also the underlying protocol to many TCP/IP utilities, such as PING, traceroute.

Some of the common messages that ICMP uses are:

✔ Echo request — tests connectivity

✔ Echo reply — replies to echo messages

✔ Buffer full — indicates a router's memory is full

✔ Destination unreachable — indicates a destination IP is unreachable

✔ Source quench — a flow control message

✔ Redirect — use a better route for a message

✔ Time Exceeded — TTL (time-to-live) field time exceeded

✔ Hops — message failed to reach destination in allotted hops

✔ Ping — Packet Internet Groper (See Chapter 12)

Address Resolution Protocol (ARP)

The ARP (Address Resolution Protocol) maps IP addresses to physical or hardware addresses. The Show arp command displays the contents of the ARP cache in a router's memory. Here's the result of a sample session:

```
Dummies#show arp
Protocol Address  Age (min)  Hardware Addr  Type  Interface
Internet 192.168.1.2  0      0800.09b3.4ab6 ARP   Ethernet0
```

If a router can't find a physical (MAC) address in its ARP table, it sends out an ARP request. The request broadcasts the IP address for which it is seeking a hardware address. Because it's a broadcast, all devices on the local network examine the packet. The node that has the broadcast IP address responds with its hardware address. The requesting machine then updates its ARP cache.

Reverse ARP (RARP)

Stations that do not store their IP configuration data, such as a diskless workstation, use RARP to discover their IP address when they power up. As you may have guessed, RARP uses a process that is the reverse of ARP. Instead of sending out its IP address to discover the matching MAC address (which is what ARP does), RARP broadcasts its MAC address hoping to get back its IP address. In order for this to work, there must be a RARP server, to supply the IP address, on the network.

Data Encapsulation

When the header, trailer, and message data are encapsulated into a single entity, it's called a *Protocol Data Unit (PDU)*. A PDU is the unit that can be sent out on the network. Unfortunately, each layer in the TCP/IP protocol stack gives its PDU a different name, and even worse is that you're expected to know the PDU names and the layer that assigns them.

Cisco calls the process that moves data up and down the OSI and TCP/IP layers the Five Steps of Data Encapsulation. Table 14-7 lists the OSI layer and the name given to the data at that layer. Figure 14-4 shows these five data encapsulation levels.

Table 14-7	Data Encapsulation Levels
OSI Layer	*Data Encapsulation Level*
Application	Data
Transport	Segments
Network	Packets (Datagrams)
Data link	Frames
Physical	Bits

Figure 14-4:
Five steps
of data
encapsula-
tion.

Data	Data	Application Layer
Segment	Transport Header / Data	Transport Layer
Packet	IP Header / Segment	Network Layer
Frame	Data Link Header / Packet / Trailer	Data Link Layer
Bits	1100110101001001111000110100101	Physical Layer

Prep Test

1 The application layer protocols of the TCP/IP protocol stack map to which layers of the OSI Model?

A ○ Application

B ○ Application and Presentation

C ○ Application, Presentation, and Session

D ○ Application, Presentation, Session, and Transport

2 What are the Netware protocols that perform the functions of TCP/IPs application layer?

A ○ IPX and SPX

B ○ SAP and NCP

C ○ ICMP and ARP

D ○ MAC and UDP

3 What mechanisms provide TCP its reliability?

A ○ Checksum and sequence number

B ○ Sequence number and length

C ○ Source and destination port

D ○ Checksum and acknowledgment

4 TCP allows for more than one application to use a transport connection. This is known as what?

A ○ Multiplexing

B ○ Sliding window

C ○ Full-duplex transmission

D ○ Flow control

5 Which application is paired with the wrong port number?

A ○ HTTP ○ 80

B ○ SMTP ○ 25

C ○ TFTP ○ 53

D ○ SNMP ○ 161

6 Which statement is not correct regarding the use of port numbers with TCP and UDP?

A ○ Ports below 256 are for public applications

B ○ Ports 256 – 1023 are assigned by IANA to companies for saleable applications

C ○ Ports above 1023 are dynamically assigned in the host application

D ○ The source and destination ports numbers must be the same

7 Which of these protocols is connection-oriented?

A ○ FTP

B ○ SNMP

C ○ NFS

D ○ TFTP

8 What command is used to display the ARP cache in a Cisco router's memory?

A ○ Show mem

B ○ Show cache

C ○ Show arp

D ○ Dis arp

9 Which sequence represents the five steps of data encapsulation?

A ○ Data, Segments, Packets, Frames, Bits

B ○ Data, Segments, Datagrams, Frames, Bits

C ○ Datagrams, Segments, Packets, Frames, Bits

D ○ Datagrams, Segments, Data, Frames, Bits

E ○ A & B

F ○ C & D

10 What protocol is used by a diskless workstation to determine the IP address assigned to them?

A ○ SAP

B ○ RARP

C ○ ICMP

D ○ DARP

Answers

1 *C.* The TCP/IP application protocols, including FTP, TFTP, Telnet, and SNMP, relate to the Application, Presentation, and Session layers of the OSI model. Be sure you know the OSI layer for each of the TCP/IP protocols. *See "Application layer protocols."*

2 *B.* The Novell NetWare protocols that operate on the Application layer are SAP and NCP. *Review "Other protocols you should know."*

3 *D.* TCP provides error-checking through the use of an error-checking control checksum and ensures reliability throughout the acknowledgment of segments received. *Take a look at "Ensuring reliability."*

4 *A.* Multiplexing is the capability of more than one application to use an open transport connection at a time. *Check out "Ensuring reliability."*

5 *C.* DNS uses well-known port 53, and TFTP uses port 69. *See "Well-known ports."*

6 *D.* The source and destination ports numbers do not need to be the same in a TCP packet. *Review "Well-known ports."*

7 *A.* FTP is a connection-oriented, reliable protocol in the TCP/IP protocol suite. *Look over "File Transfer Protocol."*

8 *C.* Show or sh is the general Cisco IOS command for displaying the contents or configuration of a device or feature. *Check out "Address resolution protocol (ARP)."*

9 *E.* Both A and B are valid sequences for data encapsulation using both TCP and UDP message formats. *See "Data Encapsulation."*

10 *B.* RARP (Reverse Address Resolution Protocol) looks up the IP address assigned to a node's MAC address. *Review "Reverse ARP (RARP).*

Chapter 15

Security

Exam Objectives

▶ Configuring access lists

▶ Verifying access list operations

▶ Using IPX access lists and SAP filters

*N*early every network administrator has a horror story to tell that involves breaches in security, a hacker that got in and then got away, corrupted files, and other bits of nastiness. That's why security is always an important topic of discussion among those who oversee networks of all sizes and levels.

Security controls on routers is also an issue on the CCNA exam, and in this world, security means access lists and SAP (Service Advertising Protocol) filters. This can be a tricky subject and one that's definitely on the test, so be sure to spend some time going over the material in this chapter. This chapter doesn't contain a lot (in terms of the number of pages) to learn or review, but what's here is important for the test. We also recommend that you take time to use a router to actually work with access lists and, if possible, SAP filters as well.

We structured this chapter like a Cisco training course, with some lecture and some lab. It is to your benefit to work through the examples on a router. There's nothing like doing it to learn it. In other words, if you really want to understand access lists, you really should get on the router and get some practice working with routers.

One comment, though. We don't recommend that you begin your studies in this chapter, just in case you were thinking of doing that. You should save this chapter for near the end of your studies. There's a lot to know before you're ready to take the exam, and you should review the fundamentals in the early chapters before tackling such things as access lists and SAP filters. On the other hand, if you've been working right along through this book and are now in the home stretch of your studies, then keep on going.

To provide you with a little incentive, Cisco now lets CCNAs use a special logo on their business cards. Just one of the perks that comes with joining the in-crowd. So, buck up, eye on the prize, and steady going, you're almost there.

Quick Assessment

Configuring access lists

1 The purpose of an access list is to _____ or _____ traffic through the router.

2 When multiple statements are included in an access list, they are executed in _____ order.

3 Access lists may be identified with _____ or _____ names.

4 A _____ may be used to permit or deny traffic based upon a specific IP address or group of IP addresses.

5 It takes _____ steps to activate an access list.

6 Port denial must be performed using either _____ or _____.

Verifying access list operations

7 The command _____ will display all the interfaces that have access-groups setup on them.

8 The `show access list` command will show all access lists currently active on the router and how many times it has been _____.

9 The two types of Novell access lists are _____ and _____.

Using IPX access lists and SAP filters

10 IPX uses _____ advertisements to inform clients of network resources and services available.

Answers

1 *Permit, deny.* See "Configuring Access Lists."

2 *Sequential.* Review "IP access lists."

3 *Numeric, alphanumeric.* Take a look at "Access list rules and conditions."

4 *Wildcard mask.* Check out "Wildcard masking."

5 *2.* See "IP access lists."

6 *TCP, UDP.* Review "Filtering port traffic."

7 *Show running-config or show ip interface.* Look over "Verifying the access list."

8 *Enforced.* Check out "Verifying the access list."

9 *Standard, extended.* See "Novell IPX Access Lists."

10 *SAP (Service Advertising Protocol).* Review "SAP Filters."

Configuring IP Access Lists

In the context of the CCNA exam, the purpose of an access list is to permit or deny traffic through a router. An access list consists of formally structured statements that outline what a router is to do with a packet when it enters the router.

There are several types of access lists on a Cisco router, but there are only two types you need to worry about for the CCNA exam: IP (Internet Protocol) access lists and IPX (Novell NetWare) access lists. Both access lists work like packet filters in that incoming packets are compared to the rules and conditions in the access list, and depending on the results of the comparison, acted upon. See "Novell IPX Access Lists" for details about IPX access lists.

IP access lists

IP access lists come in two types:

- ✔ **Standard IP access lists:** This type of access list analyzes the source IP address in a TCP/IP packet and then takes action to permit or deny the packet to pass through the router based on the outcome of its analysis.

- ✔ **Extended IP access lists:** This type of access list permits or denies a packet using a variety of factors, including:

    - Source address

    - Destination address

    - IP protocol (TCP, UDP, ICMP)

    - Specific Port (HTTP, FTP, Telnet)

Access lists can contain more than one filtering statement. If present, these statements are evaluated in sequence. Creating an access list requires that a certain amount of algorithmic logic be applied. If not carefully constructed, the actual results of an access list may be quite different from what was intended. An incoming packet is compared to the lines of an access list only until a match is found. After a match is made and acted upon, no further actions take place. Like a safety net, all access lists end with an implicit *deny any,* which means that if a packet hasn't matched any lines of the access list to that point, it is discarded. Only one access list per protocol per interface is allowed.

An access list can be many lines in length, which can present a maintenance problem. With numbered (not named) access lists, you cannot simply add a line in the middle of the list. If you want to change an existing access list, you first remove any preceding lines, line by line.

A two-step process exists to activate both standard and extended access lists. First, in global configuration mode, you define the access list by entering its lines. Second, in configuration-interface mode, you apply the access list to a specific interface (e0, s1, for example).

Standard access lists

The general syntax of a standard access list is:

```
Access--list number {permit | deny}[source address]
          [source mask]
```

After the access list is built, it's activated using the `protocol configuration` command. The option at the end of the command is used to indicate whether this access list entry is controlling incoming or outbound traffic (*out* is the default setting). The syntax of this command is:

```
ip access--group access--list number {in|out}
```

Here's the result of a sample session:

```
CCNA_For_Dummies(config)#access-list 1 deny 172.30.16.0
CCNA_For_Dummies(config)#int e0
CCNA_For_Dummies(config--if)#IP access--group 1
```

The first command creates access list 1 with an entry to deny access to 172.30.16.0. Next, interface configuration mode is entered and e0 (Ethernet0) is selected. Finally, the IP access-group command is used to assign access list 1 to e0 as an IP outbound access list. Remember that *out* is the default value.

Using these commands denies any traffic from IP address 172.30.16.0 from going out router's interface e0. Traffic addressed to that network will still be allowed in, but it won't be permitted to go out interface e0.

Access list rules and conditions

When an access list is created, a unique number is assigned so that the router knows which list to check for a particular protocol and interface. As with everything else in the router, rules govern how access list numbers are assigned.

Each type of access list has a block of numbers assigned to it. When any access list is created, the number it is assigned specifies its type to the operating system. Beginning with Cisco IOS release 11.2, standard and extended IP access lists can be given an alphanumeric name. Prior to that, access lists were designated only with a number, and the number had to come from the block of numbers for that type of access list. Table 15-1 lists the access list types with the block of numbers assigned to each block that you may see on the CCNA exam.

An implied *deny any* command should be placed at the end of any access list to deny all traffic not specifically meeting the conditions in the filter statements in the access list.

Table 15-1	Access List Types
Access List Type	*Number Block*
IP Standard	1–99
IP Extended	100–199
Protocol type-code	200–299
48-bit MAC address	700–799
IPX Standard	800–899
IPX Extended	900–999
IPX SAP	1000–1099

You can expect to see the access list type numbers in a straightforward question along the lines of "IP Standard Access list numbers are in the range of?" Another might be, "What is the correct form for an IP Extended Access list?" followed by a list of possible answers, some with the wrong number.

Remember that IP Extended access lists are in the range of 100 to 199. If you see a question that asks you to pick which of a selection of commands is used to create an IP Extended access list, be sure you pick the one with the correct access list number.

Wildcard masking

Wildcard masks are used to permit or deny traffic based upon a specific IP address or group of IP addresses. Think of a wildcard mask as the exact opposite of the subnet mask. Binary numbers are still used, but now the 0s mean check the number to see whether it's valid, and 1s mean ignore the number. Here are some examples to help you understand this new twist:

You want to deny all traffic from IP address 192.168.1.6, but from only this address. What wildcard mask would you use?

Decimal	*Binary*
IP Address	192.168.1.6 11000000 10101000 00000001 00000110
Wildcard Mask	0.0.0.0 00000000 00000000 00000000 00000000

A wildcard mask of all zeroes indicates that the router must check every bit to make sure that it matches exactly to the address in the access list.

What if you want to deny traffic from the specific network of 192.168.0?

Decimal	Binary
IP Address	192.168.1.0 11000000 10101000 00000001 00000000
Wildcard Mask	0.0.0.255 00000000 00000000 00000000 11111111

The effect of this wildcard mask is that the router checks each of the first three octets, and if they match the network address, it's denied regardless of what the last octet may be.

Here's a tip for figuring out what the wildcard mask should be: First, determine the subnet mask and then subtract it from 255.255.255.255, or the end of a range. This gives you the appropriate wildcard mask. For example, if you want to permit traffic between only 192.168.15.0 and 192.168.32.255, the wildcard mask you'd use is 0.0.17.255.

Words have meanings, too

Every time you type a number, chances are excellent that you'll make a mistake. To avoid making number entry mistakes and blocking all of your users from the Internet when you meant to block another network, you can use the wildcard words *any* and *host* when building an access list entry.

Entering the word *host* is the equivalent of the wildcard mask 0.0.0.0, which means that the check is for a specific address. The word *any* is the equivalent of the 255.255.255.255 wildcard mask, which says that you aren't concerned about the IP address. You can use this option when you want to limit access by port number instead.

Note that in the access-list command, while a numeric mask follows the address that it qualifies, the word masks *any* and *host* precede the address that they qualify.

Extended access lists

Extended access lists filter packets using other data than just the source address, including destination address, source port, destination port, and the specific protocol in use (UDP, ICMP, or TCP). As with a standard access list, applying an extended access list is a two-step process: create the list and then apply it to an interface(s).

The command syntax for the Extended IP access list statement is:

```
Access--list number {permit | deny} protocol source mask des-
           tination mask [operator operand] [established]
```

Here's the result from a sample session creating an Extended IP access list that permits IP traffic from the specific host 172.16.0.1 to any host on 192.168.1.0:

```
Dummies(config)#access-list 101 permit ip host 172.16.0.1
        192.168.1.0 0.0.0.255
Dummies(config)#int e0
Dummies(config-if)#access-group 101 in
```

Filtering port traffic

Extended access lists can also deny traffic by port number. A common error made when setting this up is forgetting that the port number can't be denied by IP; it has to be done with TCP or UDP.

The command structure used to permit or deny traffic using the port number adds the port, operator operand, and the established parameters to the extended access list command:

```
Access--list number {permit | deny} protocol source mask
        destination mask [operator operand] [established]
```

The port number (see Chapter 14 for more information) indicates the port number to be permitted or denied. The established option permits TCP traffic to pass only if the packet is using an established connection. The operator operand options are:

- ✔ lt = less than
- ✔ gt = greater than
- ✔ eq = equals
- ✔ neq = not equal

Here's a sample command that denies telnet (port number 23) access from IP address 10.1.1.1 into 10.1.1.2:

```
Dummies(config)#access--list 102 deny tcp 10.1.1.1 0.0.0.0
        10.1.1.2 0.0.0.0 eq 23
```

Named access lists

Beginning with Cisco IOS version 11.2, IP access lists can be assigned an alphanumeric name instead of a number, which is required on previous IOS releases. There are two primary advantages to using a named access list:

✔ The limitation of only 99 standard access lists and 100 extended access lists is removed.

✔ Access lists can be edited.

Two general rules exist concerning using named IP access lists in place of numbered access lists:

✔ A name can be used only once, which means the same name can't be used for multiple access lists or different types (an extended and a standard access list can't have the same name).

✔ Cisco IOS releases before 11.2 can't use named IP access lists.

Removing an access list

Removing an access list uses essentially the same procedures, only in reverse. First you remove the access list from the interface with the `no ip access-group` command, and then you remove the access list itself with the `no access list` command.

A word of caution: If you remove the access list from an interface, any packets attempting to cross that interface will be passed along unscathed. The effect of not having an access list that specifically denies access is to permit any access. So, before removing an access list, be very sure that's what you really want to do.

Here's the result from a router session that removes the standard access list entered earlier in the chapter (see "Standard access lists"):

```
Dummies#config t
Enter configuration commands, one per line. End with CNTL/Z.
Dummies(config)#int e0
Dummies(config-if)#no ip access-group 1
Dummies(config)#no access-list 1
```

In configuration mode, the `no ip access-group 1` command removes the assignment of access list 1 from the ethernet0 interface, and then the `no access-list` command removes the access list.

Verifying the access list

After an access list has been properly configured and attached to an interface, it's necessary to verify that it actually has been put into operation. The `show IP interface` command lists the access lists that are set. Here's a sample display generated by this command (some of the display has been deleted for space):

```
CCNA_For_Dummies#show ip interface
Ethernet0 is up, line protocol is up
...
Outgoing access list is 1
Inbound access list is not set
```

The command `show run`, which displays the running configuration, also shows which interfaces have access-groups set on them.

The `show-access list` command, which can be executed from user exec mode, displays all of the access lists currently active on a router and how many times (since the last clear counter command) the access list has been enforced. Of course, this information is only available if logging has been activated on the router. Logging captures the events necessary to provide you with this type of information. To enable logging on an access list, you merely add the command parameter `log` to the end of the last line of an access list.

Once logging is engaged, you can use the `access-list` command to view the results of the access list's instructions. To see the performance of a specific access list, modify this command by adding the specific access list you want to see; for example, `show access list 101`. Here's two samples of displays produced by this command:

```
Dummies>show access-list
Standard IP access list 1
  deny   172.30.16.0
  (10 matches)
Extended IP access list 101
  permit ip host 172.16.0.1 192.168.1.0 0.0.0.255
  (22 matches)
```

Novell IPX Access Lists

IPX access lists, like IP access lists, can be either standard or extended. However, standard IPX access lists, unlike standard IP access lists, can deny or permit based upon both source and destination addresses. (This may be a good time to review IPX addressing in Chapter 12.)

On the CCNA exam there's less emphasis on IPX access lists than on IP access lists. You also don't need to be concerned with IPX wildcard masks.

Table 15-2 lists the access list numbers used for IPX access lists.

Table 15-2	IPX Access List Numbers
Access List Type	*Number Range*
Standard IPX access lists	800–899
Extended IPX access lists	900–999
IPX SAP access lists	1000–1099

The named access list option is not available on IPX.

Standard IPX access lists

IPX access lists are basically the same as IP access lists. One major difference is that on an IPX access list, source and destination addresses are entered in hexadecimal.

The syntax and structure of the IPX standard access list command looks like:

```
Access list number{permit|deny} sourcenetwork [.network--
      node][source--node--mask] destination network
      [.network--node][destination--node--mask]
```

A couple of shortcuts are available in the IPX access list command. In place of the local network number you can substitute the number 0 and the number –1 (minus 1) matches all networks. Here are the results of some sample command entries:

```
Dummies(config)#access--list 801 deny FF 0
Dummies(config)#access--list 801 permit -1 -1
```

The first entry denies traffic from network FF to the local network, and the second entry permits all other traffic.

IPX extended access lists

In addition to filtering the source and destination IPX addresses that can be included on IPX standard access lists, IPX extended access lists can filter on the IPX protocol (SAP and SPX, for example) and the source and destination socket numbers.

The command structure and syntax for creating an IPX extended access list is:

```
Access--list number {permit/deny} protocol {source}
        {socket} {destination} {socket}
```

The codes that can be used for the common protocols and sockets are listed in Tables 15-3 and 15-4, respectively.

Table 15-3	IPX Protocol Type Numbers
Protocol	*Code*
Any	−1
Undefined	0
RIP	1
IPX	4
SPX	5
NCP	17

Table 15-4	IPX Socket Numbers
Socket	*Code*
All	0
NCP	451
SAP	452
RIP	453

The syntax and structure of the command used to activate an IPX access list is:

```
CCNA_4_Dummies(config--if)#ipx access--group access--list
        number [in|out]
```

SAP filters

No, this isn't a new device to keep your brother-in-law away! IPX informs clients of changes in network resources and services availability through SAP (Service Advertising Protocol) advertisements. Routers don't forward these SAP broadcasts (advertisements). They build SAP tables and then broadcast this information every 60 seconds. Setting up SAP filters, the amount of information that is sent out in the SAP updates can be limited. Limiting the services that are advertised, you can also limit who can access them.

SAP filters can be either input or output. An input filter reduces the number of services entered into the SAP Table, which results in a reduction in the size of the SAP Table itself. Output filters reduce the number of services propagated from the SAP Table.

To configure a SAP filter to an interface, you use the `ipx input-sap-filter` or the `ipx output-sap-filter` command, followed by the `access list number` command in interface configuration mode. Remember that SAP filters are numbered 1000–1099. Here's a sample of the commands used to configure a SAP filter:

```
Dummies(config)#access--list 1050 permit 15.0000.0100.0001 0
Dummies(config)#int e0
Dummies(config)#ipx input--sap--filter 1050
```

These commands create an access list with the number 1050, which is reserved for IPX SAP filters that let the outside world see only the network indicated in the command over the ethernet0 interface. Any packets entering this port are included in SAP updates.

Prep Test

1 An IP extended access list can permit or deny based on all but which item?

   A ○ Specific Port

   B ○ IP protocol

   C ○ Destination address

   D ○ Source address

   E ○ All of the above

   F ○ None of the above

2 The proper syntax to activate a standard access list is what?

   A ○ Access list [number][permit or deny][source address]
Protocol access-group access-list-number {inlout}

   B ○ Access list [number][permit or deny][destination address]
Protocol access-group access-list number {inlout}

   C ○ Access list [number][permit or deny][source address]
Protocol access-group access-list number {inlout}

   D ○ Access list [number][permit or deny][source address]
Protocol access-group access-list number {inlout}

3 Given a router named Fred and an access list numbered 17, which command line is correct for assigning the access group to an interface?

   A ○ Fred(config)>IP access group 17

   B ○ Fred(config)#IP access group 17

   C ○ Fred(config-if)#IP access group 17

   D ○ Fred(config-if)#IP access-group 17

4 What statement is implied at the end of any access list?

   A ○ permit host

   B ○ permit any

   C ○ deny any

   D ○ deny host

5 What is the impact of the implied statement at the end of any access list?

   A ○ All requests not meeting the preceding filter statements from any IP address are denied.

   B ○ All requests not meeting the preceding filter statements from internal hosts are denied.

C ○ All requests not meeting the preceding filter statements from internal hosts are permitted.

D ○ All requests not meeting the preceding filter statements from any IP address are permitted.

6 What command mode must you be in to define an access list?

A ○ User Exec

B ○ Setup

C ○ Privileged Exec

D ○ Global Configuration

7 Which block of numbers is not associated with IPX?

A ○ 700–799

B ○ 800–899

C ○ 900–999

D ○ 1000–1099

8 The number block 200–299 is associated with what type of access list?

A ○ IP Extended

B ○ Protocol type-code

C ○ 48-bit MAC address

D ○ IPX Standard

9 Given the access list below, which statement most accurately describes the effect of applying the access list?

```
access--list 20 deny 126.200.30.1
access--list 20 deny 168.35.4.0 0.0.0.255
```

A ○ It will deny outward traffic directed to network 126.200.30.1

B ○ It will deny all IP traffic

C ○ It will deny inward traffic directed to any host on the 168.35.4.0 network

D ○ It will deny all traffic directed to the host 126.200.30.1

10 When no access list has been activated on an interface what is the impact to data packets attempting to cross the interface?

A ○ They will be discarded

B ○ They will be returned to the source

C ○ They will be passed on

D ○ They will be denied

Answers

1 *F.* Answers A, B, C, and D are all factors on which an extended access list can permit or deny access. Pay close attention to what's being asked in the question. *See "IP access lists."*

2 *A.* There really is a difference among the choices given. The correct answer includes the source address. The other answers either use destination addresses or leave out or put in extra dashes. *Review "Standard access lists."*

3 *D.* You must be configuring an interface and there's a dash in access-group. *Take a look at "Standard access lists."*

4 *C.* The default Deny any is implied to stop all traffic not meeting the criteria contained within the access-list filter statements. *Check out "Access list rules and conditions."*

5 *A.* All requests not meeting the preceding filter statements from any IP address are denied. *See "Access list rules and conditions."*

6 *D.* You must be in global configuration mode and the prompt should look like routername(config)#. *Review "Standard access lists."*

7 *A.* The block 700–799 is associated with 48-bit MAC addresses. *Look over "Access list rules and conditions."*

8 *B.* This block is associated with protocol type-code access lists. Be sure you memorize the access list numbers for the CCNA exam. *Check out "Access list rules and conditions."*

9 *B.* It will deny all IP traffic. This is a standard IP access list (20 falls between 1 and 100) and does not filter based on destination address because of the implicit deny and no explicit permit all traffic is denied. *See "Filtering port traffic."*

10 *C.* Without an access list to filter them, they will be passed on. There's no requirement for access lists to be applied to an interface for the interface to pass data on. *Review "Removing an access list."*

Part V
LANs and WANs

The 5th Wave   By Rich Tennant

WE'RE HERE TO
SERVICE YOUR
LOCAL AREA NETWORK.

In this part . . .

The two halves of routing and switching are routing (see Part III) and switching (covered in this part of the book). We cover the ways a network switch is used to segment a network as well as the benefits of doing so. We also include a brief overview of the other ways you can segment a network: using a router and using a bridge.

You must also know the full range of WAN protocols supported on a Cisco router, as well as the makeup, performance, and benefits of using an ISDN line with a router. And if that doesn't seem like enough, you should be ready to answer questions on the exam about how different WAN protocols are configured on the CISCO router, including such fun facts as encapsulation, defaults routes, DLCIs, PVCs, and more.

And you thought we put the really easy stuff in the back of the book!

Chapter 16

LAN Switching

Exam Objectives

▶ Listing the advantages of LAN segmentation

▶ Segmenting a LAN with a switch

▶ Describing switching methods

▶ Defining a virtual LAN

1 f the CCNA exam had a subtitle, it would be "Routing and Switching," because that's what it's about. In fact, Cisco is in the process of developing two distinct tracks for its career certifications: routing and switching and WAN (Wide Area Networks) switching. As you can probably guess, routing and switching deals more with local area networks (LANs) and WAN switching with interconnections between LANs, MANs (Metropolitan Area Networks), and WANs. Although routing is the focus of the majority of the CCNA exam, switching isn't far behind. Routing is a very important element of Cisco's overall business, but anyone certified as a Cisco networking associate should also be well versed in the other major Cisco products, especially switches and their applications. We won't be surprised if in the not-too-distant future, there are separate CCNA exams for "Routing and Switching" and "WAN Switching."

For more information on Cisco Career Certifications and the various emphases available, visit:

```
www.cisco.com/warp/public/10/wwtraining/certprog/
```

This chapter focuses on Cisco switches and how you apply them. One area of special attention is LAN segmentation. In Chapters 4 and 8 we cover how a LAN is segmented using bridges and routers, respectively, as well as the benefits of LAN segmentation. In this chapter, we cover segmenting a LAN with a switch and why you would want to do it. But there's more to switching than just segmenting LANs, and we include information on the other switching areas you need for the exam.

Quick Assessment

Listing the advantages of LAN segmentation

1 Three primary benefits of LAN segmentation are _____, _____, and _____.

Segmenting a LAN with a switch

2 The three device choices that can be used to implement LAN segmentation are _____, _____, or _____.

3 Routers operate at the _____ of the OSI model.

4 The two major methods of bridging are _____ and _____.

5 Cisco switches store the _____ and the _____ in the CAM table.

6 By default, trunking protocols are _____ on Cisco switch ports.

Describing switching methods

7 The three most common switching methods are _____, _____, and _____.

8 _____ switching has the lowest latency.

Defining a virtual LAN

9 The primary benefits offered by VLANs are _____, _____, and _____.

10 Four methods that can be used to assign a VLAN are _____, _____, _____, and _____.

Answers

1 *Increased bandwidth per user, smaller collision domains, overcoming distance limitations.* See "Segmenting a LAN."

2 *Bridges, routers, switches.* Review "Segmenting a LAN."

3 *Network layer (Layer 3).* Take a look at "Segmenting a LAN with a router."

4 *Transparent, source-route.* Check out "Segmenting a LAN with a bridge."

5 *Source MAC address, port ID.* See "Segmenting a LAN with a switch."

6 *Disabled.* Review "Trunking together VLANs."

7 *Cut-through, store-and-forward, fragment-free.* Look over "Applying Three Methods to Gain Switching Success."

8 *Cut-through.* Check out "Applying Three Methods to Gain Switching Success."

9 *Broadcast control, functional workgroups, enhanced security.* See "Reaping the benefits of a VLAN."

10 *Port address, MAC address, user ID, network address.* Review "Configuring the VLAN one way or another."

Switching Around the Network

A switch is a Data Link layer (Layer 2) connectivity device used in networks to help move data to its destination. A switch's capability ranges from not much more than a smart hub to functions that are virtually the same as a router. But by and large, a switch is used to select the path that a data packet should use to reach its destination address. In comparison to a router, a switch is simpler in construction and logic and, as a result, is a much faster device than a router. A router must have knowledge of the network and the routes through the network to be effective. To do its job, a switch only needs to know whether a destination address can be found on a network segment attached to the switch.

Talking about switches

You may find that some of the same terms used to describe a router are used for switches as well. When data moves from one switch to another, it takes a *hop*. A switch also has *latency*, which is the time it takes the switch to determine where to send a packet.

This is as good a place as any to discuss the types of switching: among port switching, circuit switching, and packet switching. You need to know how these types of switching differ. You won't see specific exam questions about these terms, but you'll definitely find them used as references in questions.

Switching IP packets

First of all, when only the word switching is used, it refers to LAN switching. Packet switching is the *type* of switching used on LANs and most WANs. Packets are switched between parts of the network depending on their source and destination addresses. Cisco switches are packet switching switches, also referred to as IP switches. An IP switch uses the Internet Protocol (IP) addressing in each packet to determine the best route the packet should use, which is exactly what packet switching devices do.

Switching circuits

Circuit switching involves creating a circuit or connection for the exclusive use of two or more parties for a period of time, at which point the circuit is switched and assigned to another set of parties. If this sounds something like the telephone system, it is. Circuit switching is used for standard voice traffic, but it's also used for broadband technologies such as Frame Relay.

Switching from port to port

A port-switching device is an intelligent network device that can be attached to multiple LAN segments. Using software, a port-switching device connects one of its station ports to one particular LAN segment to create a form of virtual LAN (VLAN). (See "Virtually Segmenting the LAN" later in this chapter for more information on VLANs.) The most common port-switching devices are called hubs, but Cisco Catalyst switches also include port-switching capabilities.

On the CCNA exam, which focuses on LAN routing and switching, you shouldn't run into circuit switching. We just wanted you to be sure of the differences between packet and circuit switching.

Switches and LANs

Like a router (see Chapter 8) or a bridge (see Chapter 4), a LAN can be segmented for performance purposes using a switch (see the next section, "Segmenting a LAN"). For the CCNA exam, you need to concentrate on the use of a switch to segment a LAN. You should expect to find a few questions on the exam about the internal functions of a switch, primarily about switching types (see "Applying Three Methods to Switching Success" later in this chapter), so you should know some of the features of a switch.

Switches provide the following services to a LAN:

- ✔ Full-duplex networking
- ✔ Multiple simultaneous connections
- ✔ High-speed networking support featuring low latency and high data rates
- ✔ Dedicated and adaptable bandwidth per port

The switch's ability to connect to and support virtual LANs using different bandwidths on separate port connections is its most valuable feature, not to mention its value in LAN segmentation.

Segmenting a LAN

Depending on how LAN segmentation is implemented, several benefits can result. The primary benefits of segmentation are:

- ✔ Increased bandwidth per user
- ✔ Creating smaller collision domains
- ✔ Overcoming the maximum node and distance limitations associated with shared media networks, such as Ethernet

For the exam, your three choices for implementing LAN segmentation are the installation of a bridge, a router, or a switch.

Segmentation: A quick overview

Probably the first thing we should establish for you is why would you want to segment a LAN in the first place. Just because the CCNA exam wants to ask you lots of questions about this practice and process doesn't mean it's like a real thing, does it? Well, yes and no. Not every LAN needs to be segmented, but it's a technique that can be applied to ensure the network's performance as it grows.

Dealing with traffic jams

Just like the highways and freeways around cities, when too many cars try to occupy the roadway at one time, there is congestion. There are no gawker blocks in networks, thank goodness, but when too many users are demanding too much bandwidth from a network, it can become congested. On the roads, other factors can contribute to the problem besides too many cars. A slow traffic light or a car blocking the lane may be the problem, much like a slow server or too little RAM can slow the throughput on a network.

Whatever the cause of the congestion, one of the best and most efficient ways to solve the problem is to break up the network into smaller subnetworks, called segments, which maximizes network resources over smaller groups, usually of common or compatible resource needs.

The ways to segment a network

There are two ways to segment a network that you should know for the CCNA exam. They are:

- **Physical segmentation:** A router or bridge is used to create more, but smaller, collision domains, which minimizes the number of workstations on the same network segment. This reduces the demand for bandwidth by simply limiting the nodes on a segment.

- **Network switching:** A switch can be used to further divide a physical segment by providing packet switching, which relieves bandwidth congestion on the network segments attached to it.

Segmenting a LAN with a bridge

Using a bridge to segment a network is one of the physical segmentation techniques. A bridge, which operates on the Data Link layer (Layer 2) of the OSI model, can be used to create two or more physical or logical segments. The network nodes on a bridged network segment are on the same subnet (logical network), and any broadcast messages generated on a bridged network segment are sent only to the nodes on the same network segment. This serves to keep local traffic local, and relieves other segments of unnecessary traffic. However (and this is one of the bad things about using a bridge to segment a LAN), if a destination node is unknown to the bridge, the message is broadcast to all connected segments. Only a single path exists between bridged networks, and there is usually no provision for redundancy in the bridge. There are two major methods of bridging: transparent and source-route.

You and the port you came in on

Transparent bridging occurs primarily on Ethernet networks (the focus of the exam), where the bridge is responsible for determining the path from the source node to the destination node. A transparent bridge examines the incoming frame and reads the destination MAC address. It then looks in its bridging table and, if it finds the address, sends the packet to the appropriate port. Otherwise, the frame is sent to all ports except the one it came in on.

Bridging from the source

Token Ring networks use source-route bridging (SRB). In this bridging method, the responsibility of determining the path to the destination node is placed on the sending node, not on the bridge.

In a SRB environment, Token Ring devices send out a test frame to determine whether the destination node is on the local ring. If there is no answer, which means the destination node is not on the local ring, the sending node sends out a broadcast message, which is called an *explorer frame*. The bridge forwards the explorer frame across the network through the network's bridges. Each bridge adds its ring number and bridge number to the frame's routing information field (RIF), which is a sort of Hansel and Gretel breadcrumb trail, so it later retraces its route. Eventually, the destination device, if it exists, receives and responds to the explorer frame. When the sending node gets this response, it initiates communications between the two devices with each intermediate bridge using the RIF value to determine the path between the two nodes. Because SRB uses RIF information to determine its routes, no bridging table is created.

Segmenting the LAN with a router

Routers, which operate on the Network layer (Layer 3) of the OSI model, enable you to create and connect several logical networks, including those using different topologies or technologies, such as Token Ring and Ethernet, into a single internetwork. Inserting a router into a network, which is a physical segmentation, creates separate network segments, which the router manages independently. Routers provide multiple paths between segments and map the nodes on the segments and the connecting paths with a routing protocol and internal routing tables.

Routing over a segmented network is no different than routing over any inter-network. When the router receives a frame, it looks at the destination network address. If the destination is on a network segment directly connected to the router, the router forwards the frame over the appropriate port interfacing to that segment. Otherwise, the routing table is searched to determine whether the router has a forwarding address for the packet or if the default route should be used. If multiple segments are attached to the router, chances are the frame will remain in the physical and logical structure connected to the router and not be broadcast throughout the entire network.

Segmenting a LAN with a switch

A switch, which operates on the Data Link layer (Layer 2) of the OSI model, typically has a high-capacity backplane (commonly in the Gigabit range), which serves as a buffer to temporarily store message frames. A switch's backplane provides an additional pool of available bandwidth to each node on each segment attached to the switch.

When a data frame enters a port, the switch reads its source MAC address and stores this information along with the port ID in the CAM (content-addressable memory) table, if the information isn't already in the table. The CAM table is stored in volatile RAM, which means that if the power is interrupted, the CAM table must be rebuilt. Using the data in the CAM table, a switch can readily look up a node using its MAC address should anything come into the switch addressed to it. In this way, the switch keeps track of which nodes are on which segments.

Using a switch to segment a LAN increases the chances that a message will be forwarded to the right segment without the need for network-wide broadcasts. Fewer broadcast messages means more bandwidth for other traffic, which translates to more bandwidth for everyone.

The ports on a switch can be configured to support a virtual LAN (VLAN). A VLAN is a logical network segment with a unique configuration to that of the segments on the other ports of the switch. Simply put, a VLAN is a way to flock birds of a feather together. Each port on the switch can be uniquely configured to provide adjustments for data speed, transmission mode, and any other special LAN characteristics used by the logical network segment represented by the VLAN.

Applying Three Methods to Switching Success

The three most common methods used to forward data packets through a switch are cut-through (a.k.a. real-time), store-and-forward, and fragment-free.

✔ **Cut-through switching:** This type of switching method has lower latency because it begins to forward a frame as soon as the source and destination MAC addresses are read, which is typically within the first 12 bytes of an Ethernet frame.

✔ **Store-and-forward switching:** This type of switching has higher latency because it reads the entire frame into its buffer before beginning to forward the frame out another port. The benefits of the increased latency are filtering, management, and traffic control. In addition, a store-and-forward switch can recognize and discard runts (frames missing segments), giants (frames with extra segments), and damaged frames, which reduces traffic on the network.

✔ **Fragment-free switching:** This switching method is a hybrid of cut-through switching that receives just a little more of the frame before beginning to forward the frame. The amount of the frame received is called the collision window. The frame isn't sent out until 64 bytes have been received so that frames shorter than 64 bytes, which may be mistaken for collision fragments, aren't transmitted.

You really need to know store-and-forward and cut-through switching techniques for the CCNA exam. You aren't likely to run into fragment-free switching, which is a hybrid switching method anyway, on the exam.

Cisco Catalyst 5000 series switches use store-and-forward switching only.

Virtually Segmenting the LAN

A VLAN (virtual LAN) is a logical grouping of networked nodes that communicate directly with each other on Layers 2 and 3. VLANs are also called logical LANs because they aren't created physically using Layer 1 media and devices. Instead, they're created logically or virtually through the configuration on a router or switch. A VLAN is not geographically or functionally fixed in place (such as within a single department of a company or for all account representatives). It's created and managed on either a router or switch, which serves as the VLAN controller.

VLANs are created usually in the process of segmenting a network with the objective of load-balancing traffic over the network and managing bandwidth allocations more easily than with the physical management of a LAN. Each station port on a switch can host a separate VLAN with its own data speeds, modes, technologies, and other characteristics.

Reaping the benefits of a VLAN

The primary benefits offered by VLANs are:

- ✔ Functional workgroups
- ✔ Broadcast control
- ✔ Enhanced security

Building workgroups

Study Figure 16-1 and remember the following scenario for the test.

Figure 16-1 shows an example of a VLAN implementation. In this example, Switch A is located in the MDF (Main Distribution Frame) and Switches B and C are located in IDFs (Intermediate Distribution Frames) on two different floors, connected by fiber optic media through a trunking protocol. The alpha character on the workstation represents the switch to which each node is connected, and the numeral indicates a workgroup. Because members of workgroups tend to communicate more with other members of the workgroup than with outsiders, it makes sense to group them logically into VLAN1, VLAN2, and VLAN3 despite the fact that they're physically located on different floors.

Distribution frames are where the physical wiring from multiple network components is concentrated. A main distribution frame is the central wiring location for a network, such as the telephone closet in a building. An intermediate distribution frame is a connecting point located between the main distribution frame and network workstations.

Broadcasting to smaller domains

A VLAN can be looked upon as a broadcast domain with logically defined perimeters that are unconstrained by physical location, media, addressing, or transmission rates. The virtual broadcast domain created by the VLAN may contain workstations with different characteristics, including its location, network medium, its MAC addressing scheme (IP versus IPX), and bandwidth. By limiting broadcast messages to smaller and more manageable logical broadcast domains or virtual workgroups, or VLANs, the performance of the entire non-virtual network is improved.

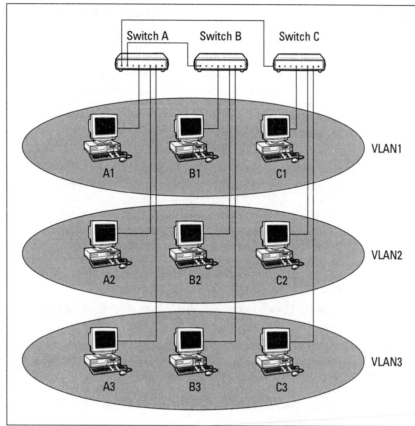

Figure 16-1:
A VLAN workgroup created across three physical LAN segments.

Improving security

Implementing a VLAN improves a network's security automatically. Members of one VLAN can't access data being transmitted on other VLANs or on any circuits outside the VLAN. This means that in Figure 16-1, the users of the workgroup on VLAN3 are in their own virtual network and are prevented from seeing any of the data being transmitted across either VLAN1 or VLAN2.

Configuring the VLAN one way or another

The assignment of a VLAN can be made in four different ways on the switch:

- ✔ **Port address:** Port-assigned VLANs are the most commonly implemented. The ports of a switch can be assigned individually, in groups, in rows, or even across two or more switches, provided the switches are properly connected through a trunking protocol. Port-based VLANs are the simplest to implement and are typically used in situations where DHCP (Dynamic Host Control Protocol) is used to assign IP addresses to network hosts.

- ✔ **MAC address:** MAC address-assigned VLANs are rare, primarily due to the increased popularity and use of DHCP on networks. MAC-based VLANs enable a user to belong to the same VLAN at all times, even when connecting to the network with a different MAC address or through a different port on the switch. The MAC addresses in a MAC-based VLAN must be entered into the switch and configured as a part of a specific VLAN. While great for users that may move about, this type of VLAN can be very complex and difficult for the administrator to manage and troubleshoot.

- ✔ **User ID:** User ID-assigned VLANs are also quite rare because they are complex to set up, administer, and troubleshoot. All VLAN users must be identified and entered into the switch and configured as a part of a specific VLAN. On a user-based VLAN, the user remains a part of the same VLAN regardless of where on the network or on which host they log onto the network.

- ✔ **Network address:** Network address-assigned VLANs are configured much like a MAC-based VLAN with the exception that nodes are registered using their logical or IP addresses. Network address-based VLANs are uncommon primarily because of the use of DHCP to assign workstation IP addresses. Like the MAC-based VLAN, this type of VLAN allows the user to remain part of the same VLAN even when they relocate to a different physical port connection to the network, provided of course that they keep the same IP address.

Trunking together VLANs

Normally, segmenting a LAN with switches involves the creation of at least two VLANs across two or more switches. After the VLANs are created, any information about them is shared between the switches using a trunking protocol. Sharing information allows all of the switches involved in a VLAN to be fully aware of the VLAN, its hosts, and their locations so that each switch is ready to support it. By default, trunking protocols, which are used to pass information between switches, are disabled on all ports. Before a VLAN can be configured between two switches, trunking be must enabled on the ports to be used to connect the switches together.

For the exam, you should be familiar with these trunking methods:

  ✔ **Inter-Switch Link (ISL):** ISL is a proprietary Cisco protocol that's supported only between Cisco Devices. ISL supports transportation across Ethernet, FDDI, or Token Ring environments. A physical router interface to each VLAN is unnecessary with a Cisco router running ISL.

  ✔ **IEEE 802.1Q:** The 802.1 subcommittee defines this as an industry standard protocol that allows VLAN information exchange between dissimilar manufacturers' equipment.

Two other trunking methods are used on Cisco equipment — IEEE 802.10 and an ATM-based protocol called LANE (LAN Emulation). These methods are advanced topics and aren't within the scope of the CCNA exam. If you run across them in your studies, don't waste time with them.

Prep Test

1 What bridging method is common to Ethernet topologies?

A ○ Transparent

B ○ Source-route

C ○ Cut-through

D ○ Store-and-forward

2 What bridging method is common to Token Ring topologies?

A ○ Transparent

B ○ Source-route

C ○ Cut-through

D ○ Store-and-forward

3 Which switching methodology has the lowest latency?

A ○ Transparent

B ○ Source-route

C ○ Cut-through

D ○ Store-and-forward

4 What are four ways that a VLAN be implemented? (Choose four.)

A ❑ Port address

B ❑ MAC address, and network address

C ❑ User ID

D ❑ Network address

E ❑ Physical connection

F ❑ Layer 2 bridge

5 Which of the following is not a common method used to forward data packets through a switch?

A ○ Trunking protocols

B ○ Cut-through

C ○ Store-and-forward

D ○ Fragment-free

6 Of the following which is the most common VLAN implementation?

A ○ Port address
B ○ User ID
C ○ MAC address
D ○ Network address
E ○ Segment address

7 Due to the increased usage of DHCP which of the following VLAN methodologies is not frequently used?

A ○ Network address
B ○ MAC address
C ○ User ID
D ○ Segment address

8 When a frame is received by a switch what is stored from it along with the port it came in on?

A ○ Source network address
B ○ Destination network address
C ○ Destination MAC address
D ○ Source MAC address

9 The type of switching used on most local area networks is

A ○ Packet-switching
B ○ Route-switching
C ○ Cell-switching
D ○ Circuit-switching

10 Which of the following is not a benefit of segmenting a LAN?

A ○ Increased bandwidth per user
B ○ Larger collision domains
C ○ Overcoming node limitations
D ○ Overcoming segment distance limitations
E ○ None of the above

Answers

1 *A.* Transparent bridging occurs primarily on Ethernet networks. *See "You and the port you came in on."*

2 *B.* Source-route bridging occurs on Token Ring networks. *Review "Bridging from the source."*

3 *C.* Cut-through switches have lower latency because they begin to forward a frame as soon as the source and destination MAC addresses are read. *Look over "Applying Three Methods to Gain Switching Success."*

4 *A,B,C,D.* The four ways that a VLAN can be assigned are port address, MAC address, user ID, and network address. *Check out "Configuring the VLAN one way or another."*

5 *A.* A trunking protocol is used to update switches attached to the same trunking line. The other answers listed are all methods used to switch messages on a network. *See "Applying Three Methods to Gain Switching Success."*

6 *A.* Because it is the simplest to implement and maintain, port address implementations are the most commonly used way to define a VLAN on a switch. *Review "Configuring the VLAN one way or another."*

7 *A. or B.* Network address and MAC addressed VLANs are both less common because of the use of DHCP for IP address assignment. *Take a look at "Configuring the VLAN one way or another."*

8 *D.* The source node MAC address is mapped to the port the message came in on and is entered in the CAM table when a switch receives a frame. *Check out "Segmenting a LAN with a switch."*

9 *A.* Packet-switching involves the movement of protocol data units (PDUs) across a network. Cell-switching and circuit-switching are other forms used in WAN implementations. *See "Talking about switches."*

10 *B.* Segmenting a LAN results in the creation of smaller collision domains. The other answers listed are also benefits of segmenting a LAN. *Review "Segmenting a LAN."*

Chapter 17

Connecting with WAN Protocols

• •

Exam Objectives

▶ Differentiating WAN services

▶ Recognizing Frame Relay terms and features

▶ Configuring Frame Relay LMIs, maps, subinterfaces

▶ Monitoring Frame Relay operation in a router

▶ Detailing PPP WAN encapsulation

▶ Identifying ISDN protocols, characteristics, and uses

▶ Describing Cisco's implementation of ISDN BRI

• •

*T*his chapter isn't at the end of the book because it doesn't matter. Instead, this chapter is one of those "... last and certainly not least" things. One of the compelling reasons to have a router on a network is to connect to a WAN. Most networks are small and simple enough that they do not require more than a single router to connect them to the outside world. So, how the router interacts with the various WAN services and protocols is a very important part of a CCNA's life and this is reflected on the CCNA exam.

The object of this chapter is to help you review the concepts, technologies, and router operations that are used together to connect a LAN to a WAN. There is less memorization in this chapter than in many of the other chapters of this book, but you really need to get a good understanding of each WAN service included and then lock in on their interactions and interfaces.

If you have access to a router that is supporting Frame Relay, ISDN, or PPP interfaces, we recommend, as we do with all router operations in this book, that you at least review its configuration. If you are so lucky to have access to a router on which you can actually change the configuration, do so!

Quick Assessment

Differentiating WAN Services

1 The five primary WAN services are _____, _____, _____, _____, and _____.

Recognizing Frame Relay terms and features

2 _____, _____, and _____ are the three steps associated with a Switched Virtual Circuit.

Detailing PPP WAN encapsulation

3 The default serial encapsulation method on Cisco routers is _____.

4 PPP can use either _____ or _____ for authentication.

Configuring Frame Relay LMIs, maps, subinterfaces

5 Frame Relay operates at the _____ and _____ layers of the OSI model.

6 Frame Relay uses _____ and _____ for congestion notification.

Monitoring Frame Relay operation in a router

7 Information about the network's current DLCI values, whether the DLCIs have local or global significance, and the status of virtual circuits are included _____ messages.

Identifying ISDN protocols, characteristics, and uses

8 _____ is available in either a BRI or a PRI format.

Describing Cisco's implementation of ISDN BRI

9 The three basic ISDN protocols are designated by the letters _____, _____, and _____.

10 ISDN transmits traffic on _____ channels and signaling on _____ channel.

Answers

1 X.25, Frame Relay, ISDN/LAPD, HDLC, PPP. *See "Differentiating WAN Services."*

2 Call Setup, Information Transfer, Call Clear. *Review "Working with virtual circuits."*

3 HDLC (High-Level Data Link Control). *Check out "High-level communications."*

4 PAP (Password Authentication Protocol) or CHAP (Challenge Handshake Authentication Protocol). *See "Getting point-to-point."*

5 Physical (Layer 1), Data Link (Layer 2). *Review "Recognizing Frame Relay."*

6 FECN (Forward Explicit Congestion Notification), BECN (Backward Explicit Congestion Notification). *Look over "Flagging congestion in Frame Relay."*

7 LMI (Local Management Interface). *Check out "So what the LMI?"*

8 ISDN (Integrated Services Digital Network). *Take a look at "Putting ISDN to use."*

9 E protocols, I protocols, Q protocols. *See "ISDN protocols."*

10 B (Bearer) and D (Data). *Review "Identifying the ISDN twins: PRI and BRI."*

Differentiating WAN Services

WAN services are used to access the Internet or to interconnect LAN networks within a single enterprise. You don't need to be an expert on WAN services to pass the exam, however you must know and be familiar with the basics of these protocols.

You can choose from among many different WAN services when connecting to the outside world. Don't waste your time memorizing them all. Focus your study time on the WAN services you need to know for the CCNA exam. They are:

- X.25
- Frame Relay
- ISDN/LAPD
- HDLC
- PPP

Connecting with the mysterious X.25

Way back in the 1970s, many so-called public data networks were actually owned by private companies and government agencies. In most cases, the wide area network of one company or agency was unique and often incompatible with the network of another company or agency. Naturally, when it became necessary for these networks to interconnect, some form of common network interface protocol became necessary.

In 1976, the International Consultative Committee for Telegraphy and Telephony (CCITT), which by the way is now called the ITU (International Telecommunication Union), thank goodness, recommended a protocol it called X.25. This protocol defined a packet-switched networking protocol for exchanging data over a connection-oriented service.

X.25 also defines the control information that is passed between a user device, called the Data Terminal Equipment (DTE), and another network node, called Data Communications Equipment (DCE). DTE equipment typically consists of terminals, PCs, routers and bridges that are owned by the customer. DCE equipment is typically carrier-owned internetworking devices.

You also find DCE referred to as Data Circuit Terminating Equipment in some Cisco materials. We use Data Communications Equipment in this book, but these two meanings are interchangeable.

Addressing the X.25 world

On both the X.25 and LAPB layers an emphasis is placed on flow control and error-checking, which reduces the need for these functions outside of X.25, very important on an unreliable analog dialup service. However, in a more reliable digital environment, because of the increased overhead associated with flow control and error-checking, these functions are a drawback.

Each X.25 link consists of a DTE (Data Terminal Equipment) at one end and a DCE (Data Communications Equipment) at the other. The DTE is typically a router or PAD (Packet Assembler/Disassembler), while the DCE is a switch or concentrator on the public data network.

The X.25 addressing scheme consists of a four decimal digit DNIC (Data Network Identification Code) and a NTN (Network Terminal Number) that's up to 11 decimal digits in length. The DNIC includes the country code and a provider number that's assigned by the ITU (International Telecommunication Union).

The combination of the last digit of the DNIC and the first eight digits of the NTN make up the unique address that's allocated to an X.25 network. Because there is no Address Resolution Protocol (ARP) incorporated in an X.25 network, X.25 addresses must be manually mapped to Layer 3 (IP) addresses in a router.

Working with virtual circuits

X.25 uses a virtual circuit (VC). Other terms you may encounter on the test that are interchangeable with virtual circuit are virtual circuit number (VCN), logical channel number (LCN), and virtual channel identifier (VCI). A VC may consist of a permanent virtual circuit (PVC) or commonly a switched virtual circuit (SVC). An SVC is a temporary virtual circuit that is created especially for and exists only for the duration of a particular data communications session. This contrasts to a PVC, which is called a "nailed up" circuit, a permanent, dedicated, and continuous VC.

Three steps are associated with creating, using, and clearing an SVC:

- ✔ **Call setup:** Before any of the data is sent, the sending DTE sends a circuit request packet to its local PSE (packet-switching equipment, usually at the phone company) that contains, in addition to the network address of the destination DTE, a VCI reference number. The PSE forwards the packet through the network. At the destination PSE, a second VCI is assigned to the request and it is forwarded to the destination DTE. When the destination DTE connects, in effect accepting the call, a virtual circuit exists between the two DTEs.

- ✔ **Information transfer:** After the SVC is created, the information transfer phase assigns each packet the same VCI numbers as were used to create the circuit. This enables the DTEs to differentiate packets from multiple sessions arriving on the same link. Because error and flow control are provided at the packet level, data reliability is very high.

> ✔ **Call Clear:** At the end of the session, the circuit is cleared by the source DTE sending a clearing request to the PSE which relays it to the destination PSE and DTE. If the circuit is a permanent virtual circuit (PVC), this step is not performed.

Routers and X.25

A single X.25 interface on a router can be configured to support up to 4,095 SVCs. By combining multiple SVCs for a single specific protocol, the throughput can be increased provided that the protocol provides its own packet resequencing. A maximum of eight SVCs may be combined into one path for a protocol.

When implementing X.25 on a Cisco router, you must configure three interface items.You do this by using the following commands:

```
encapsulation x25 dte or dce (dte is the default)
x25 address x.121-address
x25 map protocol address x.121-address [options]
```

The layers of the X.25 cake

X.25 has three layers that track to the lower three layers of the OSI model (Network, Data Link, and Physical). The three layers of X.25 services are:

> ✔ **X.25** (Layer 3), which is also called the packet level, describes the data transfer protocol in the packet switched network. It's similar to the OSI Network layer (Layer 3) model and similarly creates network data units called packets which contain both control information and user data. The packet level also includes procedures for establishing virtual circuits (temporary associations) and permanent virtual circuits (PVC) which is a permanent association between two DTEs, and defines datagrams, self-contained data units that include the information needed to route the unit to its destination.
>
> ✔ **LAPB** (Layer 2), which is also called the link level, ensures the reliable transfer of data between the DTE and the DCE using a sequence of frames that contain address, control, and data fields. The functions performed by the link level also include link synchronization and error detection and recovery. The protocols used on this level of X.25 protocols are:
>
>> • **LAPB (Link Access Procedure, Balanced)** is a derivative of HDLC (High-Level Data Link Control) that is the most commonly used X.25 Link level protocol.
>>
>> • **LAPD (Link Access Procedure, D Channel)** is an ISDN protocol (not to be confused with the Los Angeles Police Department).
>>
>> • **LLC (Logical Link Control)**, which is an IEEE 802 protocol used to transmit X.25 packets over a LAN.

• **LAP (Link Access Protocol)** is the precursor to LAPB and is no longer commonly used.

✓ **Physical level** (Layer 1) describes interfaces with the physical environment much like the OSI model's Physical layer.

X.25 protocols

By using a tunneling process, almost any Network layer protocol can be transmitted across X.25 virtual circuits. Tunneling is a process whereby the Layer 3 packets or datagrams are encapsulated within the X.25 Layer 3 packet for transmission across the virtual circuits.

The following protocols and services support X.25 WAN services:

✓ IP (Internet Protocol)

✓ AppleTalk

✓ Novell IPX

✓ Banyan Vines

✓ XNS (Xerox Network Systems)

✓ DECnet

✓ ISO-CLNS (Connection-less Mode Network Service)

✓ Apollo

✓ Compressed TCP (Transmission Control Protocol)

✓ Bridging

The framer in the DLCI

One of the CCNA objectives is to differentiate the various WAN services. Here's an overview of Frame Relay aimed at helping you achieve that objective for the exam. Frame Relay is discussed in more detail in the section, "Recognizing Frame Relay," later in this chapter.

Compared to X.25 (see "Connecting with the mysterious X.25" earlier in the chapter), Frame Relay is a next-generation protocol. Frame Relay is a Layer 2 (Data Link) technology that is optimized for high performance and efficient frame transmission. As opposed to being a specific interface type, Frame Relay is an encapsulation method that can operate across almost any serial interface. It utilizes upper-layer protocols for flow control and error correction and was designed specifically for use on fiber optic cables and digital networks. In Frame Relay, the DTE (also called customer premises equipment or CPE) is typically a router and the PSE (packet-switching equipment) at the network service provider takes the form of the DCE.

Frame Relay uses statistical multiplexing to combine multiple virtual circuits and transmits them over a single transmission circuit, assigning each set of DTEs (source and destination) a data-link connection identifier (DLCI, pronounced "delcie"). The DCE maps the DLCIs to outbound ports. When a frame enters the PSE, the DLCI is analyzed and the frame is directed toward the appropriate outbound port. This means that the entire path to the destination is known before the first frame is sent out. Because the VCs may not all belong to the same customer, such as on a shared media circuit, Frame Relay offers users a committed information rate (CIR). The CIR is the minimum bandwidth a customer receives, but additional bandwidth is available for customers who may need additional periodic bandwidth to handle bursts of data above their CIR on occasion.

ISDN and the LAPD

ISDN (Integrated Services Digital Network, not It Still Doesn't Network) consists of digital services that are capable of transmitting voice, data, and other source traffic over existing telephone lines. LAPD (Link Access Procedure on the D channel, not the Los Angeles Police Department) is the derivative of the LAPB (Link Access Procedure Balanced) protocol and primarily satisfies the signaling requirements of basic ISDN access.

High-level communications

HDLC (High-Level Data Link Control) is an ISO (International Standards Organization, you know — the OSI folks) standard that may not be totally compatible between devices from different manufacturers because of the way each vendor may have chosen to implement it. HDLC provides support for both point-to-point and multipoint services over synchronous serial data links and ISDN interfaces. HDLC is the default serial encapsulation method on Cisco routers. Figure 17-1 shows the contents of the HDLC frame format.

Figure 17-1:
The HDLC frame format.

Cisco HDLC					
Flag	Address	Control	Proprietary	FCS	Flag

HDLC supports four different transfer modes:

✔ **NRM (Normal Response Mode)** allows a secondary device to communicate with a primary device, but only when the primary device initiates the request.

> ✔ **ARM (Asynchronous Response Mode)** allows either the primary or the secondary device to initiate communications.
>
> ✔ **ABM (Asynchronous Balance Mode)** allows a device to work in what is called "combined" mode, which means it can work as either a primary or secondary device.
>
> ✔ **LAPB (Link Access Procedure, Balanced)** is an extension of the ABM transfer mode, but allows circuit establishment with both DTE (data terminal equipment) and DCE (data communications equipment).

Getting point-to-point

On a Cisco network, PPP (Point-to-Point Protocol) is used for router-to-router and host-to-network communications over synchronous and asynchronous circuits, including HSSI (High-Speed Serial Interface, pronounced "hissy") and ISDN interfaces. PPP works with several network protocols including IP, IPX and ARA (AppleTalk Remote Access). The two protocols used by PPP to perform its functions are LCP (Link Control Protocol) and NCP (Network Control Protocol). Figure 17-2 shows the PPP frame format.

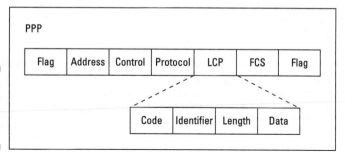

Figure 17-2:
The PPP frame format.

Authenticating passwords with PAP

The security features of PPP are CHAP (Challenge Handshake Authentication Protocol) and PAP (Password Authentication Protocol). The first step in establishing a PPP connection is authentication. If PAP is in use, the device requesting the connection sends an authentication request, which includes the username and password, to the processing router. If the router recognizes username and password as a valid combination, it returns an authentication acknowledgment. PAP offers very basic authentication security while CHAP offers a more robust authentication process.

Challenging passwords with CHAP

CHAP (Challenge Handshake Authentication Protocol) is an inbound authentication method that allows a receiving device to initiate a challenge sequence, which is then modified by the requesting device before the connection can be established.

Here's how CHAP works:

1. After a connection is made, the receiving device transmits a challenge message to the requesting device. The requesting device responds with an encrypted value calculated using a one-way math function.

2. The receiving device then checks the response by comparing it to its calculation of what should be the same calculated value.

3. If the two values match, authentication is acknowledged. If the values don't match, the connection is usually broken.

Recognizing Frame Relay

For the CCNA exam, you must be able to recognize both instances where a Frame Relay circuit is in use and those where it would be the best WAN service solution.

Frame Relay operates at the Physical and Data Link layers of the OSI reference model. It was originally designed to operate on ISDN networks, but is frequently implemented on numerous other network interfaces. The Cisco implementation of Frame Relay supports the following protocols:

- ✔ IP
- ✔ DECnet
- ✔ AppleTalk
- ✔ XNS (Xerox Network Services)
- ✔ Novell IPX
- ✔ CLNS (Connectionless Network Service)
- ✔ ISO (International Organization for Standards)
- ✔ Banyan Vines
- ✔ Transparent Bridging

Framing the Frame Relay frame

Like most WAN services, Frame Relay provides a communications interface between DTE and DCE devices. And like X.25, Frame Relay provides connection-oriented Data Link layer communications across a packet-switched network, although it is faster and more efficient than X.25. The Frame Relay frame format is shown in Figure 17-3.

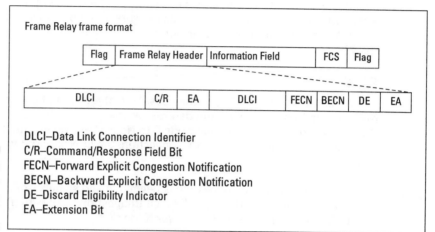

Frame Relay frame format

| Flag | Frame Relay Header | Information Field | FCS | Flag |

| DLCI | C/R | EA | DLCI | FECN | BECN | DE | EA |

DLCI–Data Link Connection Identifier
C/R–Command/Response Field Bit
FECN–Forward Explicit Congestion Notification
BECN–Backward Explicit Congestion Notification
DE–Discard Eligibility Indicator
EA–Extension Bit

Figure 17-3:
The Frame
Relay frame
format.

Flagging congestion in Frame Relay

Before we address ways to deal with network congestion on a Frame Relay network, we need to remind you about what causes network congestion in the first place. Put simply, network congestion is caused by too much data being sent over too little bandwidth. What this means in the Frame Relay world is that if the users on a Frame Relay circuit that has a CIR of 64K send a combined 96K of data, the network is congested with the extra 32K of data and must deal with it somehow.

Generally, on Frame Relay circuits, the data creating the congestion must either be delayed (retransmitted) or discarded (not forwarded). Retransmitted data may only serve to feed the congestion even more and discarding packets may cause data reliability issues between the sender and receiver. Frame Relay circuits depend on the constraint of its users to avoid problems. But, when that doesn't work, which it rarely does, Frame Relay has some built-in mechanisms to use.

As shown in Figure 17-3, the Frame Relay PDU (protocol data unit), which is called a frame, includes two mechanisms used by Frame Relay to reduce network congestion — the Explicit Congestion Notification (ECN) and Discard Eligibility (DE) fields. There are two types of ECN — Forward Explicit Congestion Notification (FECN) and Backward Explicit Congestion Notification (BECN).

Here's how Frame Relay attempts to reduce network congestion. For this next trick, we need you to give your full and undivided attention to the steps included in the next two sections. Let's suppose there is a Frame Relay network with 3 nodes: A, B, and C. On this network, node B is located between nodes A and C and network congestion is occurring in the direction of A to C. Okay?

FECN

When frames are sent by A to C, they pass over the PVC that connects A to B. Node B examines the frames and determines they need to be passed along to Node C over the PVC connecting Node B to Node C. However, should Node B detect a problem, such as network congestion, the ECNs are put into play, as follows:

1. Node B detects that congestion is beginning and signals Node C by changing the FECN (Forward Explicit Congestion Notification) bit from 0 to 1 on those frames addressed for Node C.

2. Node C, and any other nodes between B and C, learn from the FECN bit (set to 1) that there's congestion on the affected DLCIs.

In this way, Node B send notice to all upstream DLCIs that there is congestion on the network and an alternate route should be found until the congestion is eased.

BECN

What if network congestion is detected between Nodes B and A? What happens then? Node B can't use the FECN to notify A, because A is behind B, but through the use of the BECN, Node B can notify Node A and any nodes between B and A that there is a problem.

1. Node B also detects congestion on the circuit between C and A.

2. Node B then begins watching for frames coming from C toward Node A.

3. Node B signals Node A of the congestion by setting the BECN (Backward Explicit Congestion Notification) bit in those frames from 0 to 1.

4. Node A, and any other devices between A and Node B, knows from the BECN bit (set to 1) that congestion is building on the affected DLCIs.

FECN and BECN are used to alert Frame Relay nodes to problems with transmission over the network usually caused by network congestion.

In the ECN (Explicit Congestion Notification) method of congestion notification, the key point to remember for the exam is that if the FECN or BECN bit is set to 1, congestion exists on the network.

Throwing out everything over the limit

When a Frame Relay circuit becomes congested and frames must be discarded, it's better to have the sending device decide which frames can be discarded instead of the router just picking frames at random to throw out. The mechanism used to control which frames are discarded from a congested circuit is the Discard Eligibility (DE) bit. The DE bit is set to 1 (on) in those frames that are knowingly being sent in excess of the CIR (Committed Information Rate).

When the network becomes congested, those frames that have their DE bit set on are discarded until the congestion passes. However, if discarding these frames doesn't clear up the congestion, all bets are off and frames are discarded regardless of their DE bit setting. When there is no congestion, the DE bits of all frames are ignored.

For the exam, remember that when a Discard Eligibility bit in a frame's header is set to 1, the frame is knowingly being sent out above the CIR and can be discarded, if needed.

Configuring Frame Relay switching on a router

You may see an exam question on configuring a Cisco router for Frame Relay switching. Just remember that Cisco routers can be configured to perform Frame Relay switching and that doing so involves a series of things in pairs. There are two parts to Frame Relay switching — the Frame Relay DTE (router) and the Frame Relay DCE (switch) — and there are two types of switching that a Cisco router can be configured for — Local Frame Relay switching and Remote Frame Relay switching.

Configuring a router for Local Frame Relay switching enables it to forward frames based on the DLCI number found in the frames header. Configuring a router for Remote Frame Relay switching enables it to encapsulate frames into an IP packet and tunnel them across an IP backbone.

So what's the LMI?

LMI (Local Management Interface) is an interface type that was created by a consortium of four internetworking companies (Cisco, StrataCom, Northern Telecom, and Digital Equipment Corp.) in 1990. This group (called the "Gang of Four") enhanced the CCITT Frame Relay protocol by adding the capability for internetworking devices to communicate easily with a Frame Relay network. LMI messages include information about the network's current DLCI values, whether the DLCIs have local or global significance, and the status of virtual circuits.

To configure the LMI type, you need to set two values, the LMI type and the LMI keepalive interval. You also have an option to set the LMI polling and timer intervals. As indicated in Step 5 of Lab 17-1, in Cisco IOS versions 11.2 or later, the LMI type of interface is detected automatically. If you choose not to use the auto-sensing feature, you must configure the interface manually. The type you use depends on the type in use at the remote device. Your three choices are Cisco, ANSI, and Q933A. The default LMI type is Cisco, which is the Gang of Four LMI, and the default keepalive period is 10 seconds.

Mapping the IP to the DLCI

In order for IP devices to communicate with each other over a Frame Relay network, their IP addresses must be mapped to their DLCIs. Two methods ensure that this mapping occurs: manual and automatic.

Mapping the IP manually

The manual method, also known as static mapping, uses the frame-relay map command to enter the static IP mappings one by one. Static mapping is required when OSPF is used over Frame Relay, when inverse ARP is not supported on the remote router, or when you want to control broadcast traffic.

The command used to manually map the IP addresses to the DLCI is:

```
Router(config-if)#frame-relay map protocol protocol-address
          dlci broadcast][ietf|cisco|payload compress
          packet-by-packet]
```

Here is an example of what might be entered to map a DLCI manually:

```
CCNA_for_Dummies(config-if)#frame-relay map ip 192.168.1.1
          255.255.255.0 dlci cisco
```

Doing it automatically

The way to map IP addresses to their DLCIs automatically is by using the inverse ARP (IARP) function. IARP is enabled by default on an interface, but it's disabled automatically on a DLCI when the Frame-Relay map command is used. The IARP approach is much easier to configure than the static map approach. However, because configuration errors can occur when a virtual circuit is mapped to an unknown device, the static approach is more stable and less prone to configuration errors.

Lab 17-1 later in this chapter includes an example of the command used to automatically map an IP address to a DLCI.

Singing the subinterface homesick blues

When multiple virtual circuits are created on a single serial interface, each of the VCs is considered a subinterface. Using subinterfaces has several advantages, but the one you need to know for the test is that using subinterfaces provides the ability to implement different network layer characteristics on each virtual circuit. For example, one subinterface could be running IP routing while another (on the same serial interface) could be running IPX.

Subinterfaces are defined with the command

```
int s0.subinterface number
```

where the subinterface number can be any number in the range from 0 to 4,292,967,295. Typically, the DLCI number is assigned to an interface as the subinterface number.

There are two types of subinterfaces: point-to-point and multipoint. Point-to-point is used when connecting two routers over a single virtual circuit and multipoint is specified on the center router in a star topology of virtual circuits.

Configuring Frame Relay

Configuring a Frame Relay connection on a Cisco router is done by using a simple six-step process. Lab 17-1 describes the steps you use to configure a Frame Relay interface on a Cisco router.

Lab 17-1	Configuring a Frame Relay Interface on a Cisco Router

1. Select the interface to be configured.

```
CCNA_for_Dummies(config)#int s0
```

This command selects serial interface 0 and selects configuration interface mode.

2. **Configure a DLCI number to the interface.**

   ```
   CCNA_for_Dummies(config-if)#frame-relay interface-dlci 13
   ```

3. **Select the encapsulation type cisco or ietf (cisco is the default).**

   ```
   CCNA_for_Dummies(config-if)#encapsulation frame-relay
                ietf
   ```

Cisco encapsulation is the default type, and ietf encapsulation is used only when creating an interface that will be used to connection two routers of different manufacturers.

4. **Specify the LMI type (Cisco IOS 11.1 and earlier).**

   ```
   CCNA_for_Dummies(config-if)#frame-relay lmi-type cisco
   ```

In Cisco IOS versions 11.2 and later, the LMI type is auto detected by the router. Otherwise, LMI type "cisco" is the default value.

5. **Configure a subinterface.**

   ```
   CCNA_for_Dummies(config)#int s0.13 point-to-point
   ```

Create a subinterface number 13 that is a point-to-point link. Remember subinterfaces are specified as s0.n or e0.n, where n is the subinterface number.

6. **Map the Frame Relay interface using Inverse ARP.**

   ```
   CCNA_for_Dummies(config-if)#ip address 192.168.1.1
                255.255.255.0
   ```

Using inverse ARP, which is enabled by default, enables you to avoid entering mapping commands for each virtual circuit and use the dynamic mapping functions of the inverse-arp function.

Monitoring Frame Relay

You can use several commands to monitor the various aspects of a Frame Relay network. What do you know? These commands are the same ones you need to know for the exam. The commands used to monitor Frame Relay activities are:

- ✔ **frame-relay-inarp:** Dynamically clears any IP-to-DLCI mappings created through the inverse ARP function.

- ✔ **sh int type [number]:** Displays DLCI and LMI information.

- ✔ **sh frame-relay lmi [type number]:** Displays LMI statistics.

- ✔ **sh frame-relay map:** Displays the current map entries.

✓ **sh frame-relay pvc [type number [dlci]]:** Displays the current PVC statistics.

✓ **sh frame-relay traffic:** Display statistics about the Frame Relay traffic.

✓ **sh frame-relay route:** Displays the static routes configured in a Cisco router.

✓ **sh frame-relay svc maplist:** Displays all the SVCs under a specific map list.

PPP WAN Encapsulation

A serial port can also be configured to support a point-to-point protocol (PPP) interface. This configuration enables the port to emulate PPP data encapsulation, which allows Cisco devices to communicate with non-Cisco devices across a WAN link. To ensure that devices from different vendors are interoperable, PPP is considered a better tool, although more complex, than HDLC. PPP uses LCP (Link Control Protocol) to negotiate basic line interoperability as well as a whole family of network control protocols for negotiating individual Layer 3 protocols.

To enable PPP encapsulation on a serial connection, the serial line must be configured to use PPP. Then, the interface subcommand `encapsulation ppp` is used:

```
Router(config)# interface s0
Router(config-if)# encapsulation ppp
```

where s0 is the subinterface number being configured.

Here are a couple of URLs you may want to visit to learn more about Frame Relay and PPP protocols:

```
www.protocols.com/
www.rad.com/networks/tutorial.htm
```

Putting ISDN to Use

One of the best uses for ISDN PRI (Primary Rate Interface) services on a WAN (and one you should know for the exam) is providing RAS (Remote Access Service) to your network. An ISDN PRI service enables you to add 23 dialup access lines that can be used by remote workers to dial into the local network. ISDN PRI makes this possible in two ways.

First, an ISDN PRI line can have separate phone numbers assigned to each of the 23 B- (bearer) channels. Second, an ISDN PRI line can be terminated in an RJ-45 connector and directly connected to an ISDN PRI interface on a Cisco 7000 series router. Together, these two features simplify the deployment of dialup RAS connections by eliminating multiple phone lines, modems, and connecting cables.

Defining some ISDN basics

Several characteristics define and describe ISDN services, including the terminal type, reference points, protocols, channelization, and the type of service (BRI versus PRI).

ISDN terminal types

Two types of terminals connect to an ISDN network:

- ✔ **TE1:** Terminal equipment type 1 complies with the ISDN standards.

- ✔ **TE2:** Terminal equipment type 2 can be used only when a terminal adapter is applied because the type existed before the ISDN standards were developed.

ISDN reference points

Four reference points designate logical interfaces within an ISDN configuration. Logical interfaces are designated by the letters R, S, T, and U:

- ✔ **Reference point R:** Refers to the reference point between a non-ISDN device and a terminal adapter (TA).

- ✔ **Reference point S:** Refers to the reference point between a user terminal and an NT2 device.

- ✔ **Reference point T:** Refers to the reference point between an NT1 (network terminator 1) device, which terminates an ISDN line at the customers premise and an NT2 (network terminator 2) device, which provides multiple accesses to the ISDN line, such as a bridge or a PBX.

- ✔ **Reference point U:** Refers to the reference point between an NT device and the line-termination equipment on a provider's network.

ISDN protocols

There are three basic ISDN protocols, which are designated by the letters E, I, and Q in their first letter:

- ✔ **E Protocols** support ISDN on the PSTN (Public Switched Telephone Network).

- ✔ **I Protocols** define ISDN concepts, terminology, and services.

- ✔ **Q Protocols** define signaling and switching.

Save yourself some grief and just memorize these bullets and those in the preceeding sections ("ISDN terminal types" and "ISDN reference points"). Trust us, you need to know this for the exam.

Identifying the ISDN twins: PRI and BRI

ISDN service is defined to operate on a line that is comprised of multiple 64 Kbps B (bearer) channels which carry payload (voice and data) and either a 16 Kbps or 64 Kbps D (data) channel that really carries command signals. It may sound like the names assigned to the channels were switched somewhere along the way, but they weren't. The bearer channel bears the payload and the data channel carries the data about the payload. Remember this, because you're likely to be asked a question about this on the exam. There are two flavors of ISDN service: Primary Rate Interface (PRI) and Basic Rate Interface (BRI), which we cover in the next two sections.

Primary Rate Interface

PRI service consists of 23 B channels and one D channel, all of which are 64 Kbps. This adds up to 24 channels, the same number of channels available on a T1 circuit. What? You say that a T1 provides 1.544 Mbps of bandwidth and 24 times 64 Kbps only equals 1.536 Mbps? Where did the missing 8 Kbps go? When a T1 line is channelized, 8 Kbps are lost to the channelization and cannot be used for either data or control signaling.

Basic Rate Interface

BRI service consists of two B channels at 64 Kbps each and one D channel at 16 Kbps. This adds up to a combined bandwidth of 144 Kbps (128 Kbps for the actual data and 16 Kbps used for control signaling).

Working with ISDN BRI on a Cisco Router

ISDN BRI is usually configured as a dial-on-demand routing (DDR) link. To make calls on an ISDN network, you need specific network-wide configuration information, such as the following:

- **Directory numbers:** Regular telephone numbers (one for each B channel)
- **SPIDs:** Pronounced spidz, of course, and assigned by the ISDN service provider (one for each B channel)

> ✔ **Switch type:** Table 17-1 lists the common switch types used on Cisco routers to configure ISDN interfaces along with their configuration keywords. You will need to know the interface type of your service before configuring the router.

Remember that SPIDS are associated with ISDN Bearer (B) Channels.

In addition to directory numbers, SPIDs, and switch types, you need to configure the encapsulation type for the interface. If you're using PPP encapsulation, you will also need to designate an authentication type, which will normally be CHAP (Challenge Handshake Authentication Protocol), described earlier in this chapter in "Challenging passwords with CHAP."

Table 17-1	ISDN Switch Types
Switch Type	*Configuration Keyword*
AT&T 5ess	primary-5ess
AT&T 4ess	primary-4ess
AT&T basic rate	basic-5ess
ISDN PRI	primary-dms100
National ISDN-1	basic-ni1
Nortel DMS-100 basic rate	basic-dms100

Prep Test

1 Which of the following is not a layer of the X.25 WAN service?

A ○ X.25

B ○ LAPB

C ○ Transport

D ○ Physical

2 At what layer does the OSI model does Frame Relay operate?

A ○ Transport

B ○ Network

C ○ Data Link

D ○ Physical

3 Which protocol is used on what channel to satisfy signaling requirements for ISDN service?

A ○ LAPD: D

B ○ LAPD: B

C ○ LAPB: Bearer

D ○ LAPB: Signal

4 Which of the following is a transfer mode supported by HDLC?

A ○ ABM

B ○ ARM

C ○ LAPB

D ○ LAPD

E ○ NRM

5 Which is the correct sequence in a PPP frame?

A ○ Flag, Address, Control, Proprietary, Data, FCS, Flag

B ○ Flag, Address, Control, Protocol, LCP, FCS, Flag

C ○ Flag, Frame Relay Header, Information, FCS, Flag

D ○ Flag, Address, Identifier, Code, Length, Data, FCS, Flag

E ○ None of the above

6 Frame Relay is considered to be what type of connection?

A ○ Connectionless

B ○ Unreliable

C ○ Multicast

D ○ Connection-oriented

7 If the FECN or BECN bits are set to one in a Frame Relay frame what condition exists on the network?

A ○ The network is working properly.

B ○ The network is experiencing congestion.

C ○ The network carrier signal has degraded.

D ○ The frame is eligible for discard.

8 Which is not a valid LMI type?

A ○ 802.1Q

B ○ Cisco

C ○ ANSI

D ○ Q933A

9 ISDN BRI service consists of which components?

A ○ 23 D channels and 1 B channel

B ○ 2 D channels and 1 B channel

C ○ 2 B channels and 1 D channel

D ○ 23 B channels and 1 D channel

10 Which is the correct actual bandwidth of ISDN PRI?

A ○ 144 Kbps

B ○ 1.544 Mbps

C ○ 1.528 Mbps

D ○ 1.536 Mbps

Answers

1 C. Although Physical is an X.25 layer, transport is not. The three layers of X.25 are X.25 (layer 3), LAPB (Layer 2), and Physical (Layer 1). *See "The layers of the X.25 cake."*

2 C. Frame Relay is a Layer 2 technology optimized for high performance and efficient frame transmission. *Review "Recognizing Frame Relay."*

3 A. LAPD (Link Access Procedure on the D channel) is used by ISDN for signaling. The B (Bearer) channel is where the data traffic is carried. LAPD is a derivative of LAPB. *Take a look at "The layers of the X.25 cake."*

4 HDLC supports Normal Response Mode (NRM), Asynchronous Response Mode (ARM), Asynchronous Balance Mode (ABM), and Link Access Procedure Balanced (LAPB). LAPD is used on the D channel of ISDN for signaling. *Check out "High-level communications."*

5 B. Within the LCP (Link Control Protocol) are the Code, Identifier, Length, and Data fields. *See "Getting point-to-point."*

6 D. Frame Relay provides connection-oriented Data Link communications across a packet switched network just like X.25 does. *Review "Recognizing Frame Relay."*

7 B. In normal operation both of these bits are set to 0. Discard eligibility is set at the DE bit, 0 being not eligible and 1 being eligible. *Look over "Flagging congestion in Frame Relay."*

8 A. 802.1Q is a VLAN standard, Cisco is the default LMI type, the other two options are ANSI and 8933A. *Check out "So what the LMI?"*

9 C. BRI consists of two 64 Kbps Bearer channels and 1 16 Kbps D channel. PRI consists of 23 64 Kbps Bearer channels and 1 64 Kbps D channel. *See "Identifying the ISDN twins: PRI and BRI."*

10 D. 1.472 Mbps on the B channel (23 channels times 64 Kbps) plus 64 Kbps on the D channel (1 channel times 64 Kbps). 8 Kbps are used for channelizing the 1.544 Mbps T1 into the 24 channels. *Review "Primary rate interface."*

Part VI
The Part of Tens

The 5th Wave   By Rich Tennant

LOCO-AREA NETWORK

In this part . . .

After you have scheduled yourself to take the test, you can begin preparing for the test in earnest. This part includes some great places to get study guides, test demonstrations, and other information to help you prepare. We don't believe that you can see too many different styles of test preparatory materials, but we would use caution on which ones you buy. Some are definitely better than others. Visit the Web sites, try out the demonstrations, and use the tools that best work for you.

When your test day finally arrives, we have included a list of things you should think about or do before, during, and after the test. The CCNA test is administered online, and you cannot use study materials, notes, or anything besides good old brainpower to take the test. The test is not tricky. It is an honest measurement of your knowledge and understanding. So, remain calm. If you have carefully prepared yourself, you'll do just fine.

Chapter 18

Ten Really Great Sites
for Study Aids

*V*ariety is one of the keys to preparing for the CCNA exams. By using a number of different study tools and aids, you can see many ways of asking the same question. This helps prepare you for whatever wording and question formats you find on the CCNA exam.

A variety of sites on the Web simulate the test content and format fairly accurately. Some are free and some charge a nominal fee. The free ones are certainly worth the cost; the others — caveat emptor. You need to balance how much you want to spend on study aids to prepare yourself for a $100 test. Of course, if you don't pass, the cost of the test begins to multiply. Be cautious when buying study aids, and look for the bargains that are out there.

The web sites and other resources listed in this chapter are sites I believe you'll find helpful without having to spend a fortune. Please understand that all of these sites actually did exist at the time we wrote this book. If any of these sites have disappeared, you should search for others.

Cisco Systems, Inc.

```
www.cisco.com/warp/public/10/wwtraining/
```

This should be your first stop when preparing for the CCNA exams. This site is the proverbial "horse's mouth" for the CCNA tests. Cisco Systems keeps the information on this site up-to-date and it also has links to information about the exam, the career certification program, and for online test registration.

If you're looking for preparation courses, training courses, online materials, or practice tests, the Cisco site also lists the names and contact information for a number of training partners and commercial training companies.

BeachFront Quizzer

`http://ww.bfq.com/cisco.html`

One of the more popular practice test companies on the Web, BeachFront offers practice tests for nearly all certification exams. You can download a free sample to try out its test engine before you buy.

Boson Software, Inc.

`www.boson.com`

Boson Software, Inc. has practice tests for nearly all major vendor certifications. Its claim is that its test simulators have been written by networking professionals and that you're certain to be ready to pass the exam. Boson Software's CCNA practice test, which is just one of several Cisco exams available, is based on Cisco's published objectives and features more than 200 practice questions, all for a very reasonable price. The site also has a free demo test.

CramSession.com

`www.cramsession.com/cramsession/cisco/ccna/`

This site provides access to a summary of exam facts as well as a cram session study guide that's an excellent supplement to the cheat sheet included with this book for your last-minute studying.

As you get closer to the exam day, use this site to fine-tune your memory banks for the test. You also can use it to start outlining the areas you need to study.

MeasureUp, Inc.

www.measureup.com

This company boasts that more than 175,000 IT professionals have used its practice tests to become certified. Whether you believe that or not, the site does have a full list of practice exams, including the CCNA exam you need. It also has a free demo test that you can download.

MentorLabs

www.mentorlabs.com/vlab/access

MentorLabs' first offering is its vLab offering, which is a learning environment offering hands-on experience over the Web to state-of-the-art equipment. MentorLabs teams up with Cisco Systems to create the vLab's first application, a Cisco routing and switching laboratory. This method is especially useful if you don't have access to Cisco equipment.

SelfTest Software

www.selftestsoftware.com

This company offers what are arguably the best practice tests available on the Web. In fact, SelfTest Software practice tests are the ones most like the real thing. If you can afford to purchase a quality practice test, this is where you should start shopping.

Welcome.to/CCNA

http://welcome.to/ccna

This may be the most off-beat site we recommend, but you can find a lot of helpful hints and tips about taking the CCNA exam supplied by people who have taken the test. Its look and feel may be a little awkward, but it's full of good stuff.

The TechWeb Encyclopedia

www.techweb.com/encyclopedia

This site, operated by CMP Media, Inc., is another great site where you can enter a specific term or concept and get a well-worded definition as well as a few reference links that you can use to further your studies.

Whatis.com

www.whatis.com

Perhaps the best all-around reference on the Internet for computing, networking, and Internet terms and concepts, the Whatis.com site enables you to select the term you want to define by using a directory of terms at the top of the frameset. Use this site when all other sources for a definition fail you.

amazon.com, barnesandnoble.com, borders.com, and fatbrain.com

www.2prep.com/store
www.amazon.com
www.barnesandnoble.com
www.borders.com
www.fatbrain.com

What are booksellers doing in the list of CCNA sites, you ask? Well, whether you use the bookstore at Sylvan Prometrics, Amazon.com, Barnes and Noble, Borders, fatbrain, or another online bookstore, these sites can provide a list of the very latest CCNA exam guides, cram books, and question banks available in print. The test simulators are good, especially if you buy some of the complete test banks. But a study guide in print form is a good way to study when you're away from your PC, like on an airplane, in the bath, or out on a date (this is important stuff!).

Visit these sites and search for "CCNA."

And a Few More Good Sites to Visit

Here are a few more sites that have practice tests and study resources that you may find useful:

- Mason Technologies, Ltd., study guides and test tips:
  www.masontech.com

- Dave, and his friends give some tips on the CCNA exam: www.lilligren.com/cisco/leeccna.htm and www.henninger.net/ccna/

- CTIGuyz.com offers more tips on taking the test:
  http://207.212.98.71/html/CCNA.htm

- Learntosubnet.com offers a step-by-step tutorial on learning to subnet a network: www.learntosubnet.com/

- Cisco Systems Reseller resources include a CCNA notes page:
  www.cisco-resellers.com/ccnaprep.htm

- Another private party test preparation page:
  www.geocities.com/SiliconValley/Hub/5016/ccna.html

Chapter 19

Ten Things to Do on Your Test Day

*1*f you've never taken a Sylvan Prometric exam before, the whole process of scheduling the test, picking a test site, and showing up to take the test can make you feel like a complete outsider. Our advice is to remember that you are the customer. Ask your questions and get the information you need. The only dumb question is the one you didn't ask.

Sylvan Prometric and Cisco Systems do everything they can to make your testing experience successful. The computers on which you take the test are good, working, well-maintained, and situated in a comfortable setting. The setting at most test centers actually belies the security surrounding the testing center, and your comfort is utmost.

In this chapter, we list some tips on how to get the most of your test day experience, with the ultimate objective being for you to pass the test and receive your CCNA certification.

By far, how prepared you are has the most to do with your chances of passing. If you're ready, if you know your Cisco networking, your internetworking, and heed our test-day advice, passing may be a sure thing. We certainly hope so!

Get Me to the Test on Time

When you schedule your exam, you're asked first of all where you want to take the test. If you're uncertain, the friendly, helpful Sylvan Prometric counselor helps you choose the location closest to your home or find the most exotic location you want to visit. The only reason we mention location now is that your test location's operating days and hours are the only limits on when you can take the test. Taking the CCNA exam or any Sylvan Prometric exam isn't like taking the SAT, GMAT, or GRE, where you have to show up at a given time and date, or else. You're free to pick the time and date that works best for you.

All of us took the CCNA exam about four hours away at the same community college that offered extended evening hours Monday through Friday and morning hours on Saturdays. Our other choice was a location only one hour away, but with limited operating times. So, if your first choice (the nearest or most convenient) testing center doesn't meet your scheduling needs, look for another that does. If you're lucky enough to live in a larger city, you shouldn't have any trouble finding several testing centers from which to choose. However, if you live outside a metropolitan area, as we do, you may find your choices limited.

Remember that the time and place of the CCNA exam is strictly up to you. Set the time and place to provide you with ample time to get there and still have some last-minute cram time.

Arrive Early

Make sure that you get to the testing center at least a half hour before your test time, or perhaps earlier if you want to do some last-minute cramming. The last thing you want or need is to be rushing to make the test time (that you set yourself, remember) and be agitated and rushed when you begin the test. Get there early, find a quiet place, relax, have a cup of coffee, tea, Postum, or whatever helps you relax, go over the *CCNA For Dummies* Cheat Sheet included in the front of this book, and your notes.

Arrive early enough to allow time for such things as checking into the testing center or finding the right office for a parking permit. You may even want to get the test center's phone number from Sylvan Prometric and call before you leave home or the office to find out what you need to do about parking and checking in.

Review Your Notes One Last Time

In the time right before you check in, review the things guaranteed to be on the test: Layers 2 and 3 of the OSI model; TCP/IP protocols; network and physical addressing; subnetting; LAN, WAN, and networking concepts; and all the stuff marked with an Instant Answer icon throughout this book. In most cases, these items all have a list or sequence of things. Right before the test you should review any reminders you developed. You may not benefit by cramming conceptual topics, but a last-minute cram of lists and sequences can help you focus on the test.

Check In on Time

A few minutes before your scheduled test time, check in with the test administrator. Be sure that you have the two pieces of identification you must show. One form of identification needs to be a picture ID, so your driver's license, passport, or work badge (if it has both your picture and signature) should work. Your second identification just needs to contain your full name. A credit card, library card, or the like should be fine.

Because the test is closed-book, you can't carry your notes or books into the test area, so surrender them without whimpering. Don't play tug-of-war with the test administrator for your notes — you can't take them with you. Relax and focus on the test. Remember that taking the CCNA exam was your idea and is something you want to do. It's a good thing!

Keep one thing in mind: If you fail (it could happen), at least you've seen the test and you'll know what to study next time. In addition, the CCNA exam report shows how you performed in each area and what each area covers. So, regardless of the result, the test should be a positive experience. We know . . . this is easy for us to say; we aren't paying for your test.

Do a Brain Dump, But Do It on the Plastic

You're not allowed to bring in any paper at all. Most test centers give you sheets of plastic and a grease pen; a dry-erase board and a dry-erase pen; or one or two sheets of paper and a pencil. Use these items to make notes during the test. After the test, you must return any items you're given, whether it be the plastic sheets, paper, and any writing instruments. Ask for or take as much as you think you will need during the test. Once the test begins, you can't get more.

After you're situated at your assigned station and get your basic instructions, unload your lists by writing them down on the board, plastic, or paper. Write down as many of the lists and sequences and special relationships (such as the OSI Model's layers and the protocols that operate on each layer) as you can remember. You can then refer to your notes during the exam without getting flustered about whether you're remembering something correctly.

Do the Tutorial!

At the beginning of the test session, you're offered a tutorial on the different types of questions, illustrations, response types, and the Sylvan Prometrics testing system. Do yourself a favor and go through the tutorial. No matter how many times you've taken the driver's test on the testing machine, or even if you are a Sylvan Prometrics veteran with multiple certifications like our Mr. Gilster, the testing experience changes from time to time and may be very different from any you've experienced before. Don't think that if you've seen one online test, you've seen them all. Take the time to casually move through the tutorial. Your time doesn't begin until you finish the tutorial and actually start the test. So, use the tutorial as a way to relax, adjust your chair, keyboard, and mouse, and get ready for the exam.

Ready, Steady, Go

When you're ready to begin, take a deep breath, clear your head (or at least try), and start the exam. You have 90 minutes to answer the 79 to 81 questions on your exam. You can expect about 40 percent of the test to be on the OSI model, about 20 percent to cover Cisco router and IOS commands and syntax, 10 percent on WANs, and the remainder (around 30 percent) on LANs and miscellaneous routing and switching topics.

Take your time, but check the time remaining (it appears in the upper-right corner of the display) occasionally. Try not to spend too much time on any particular area. But, if you move along and stay on task, you should have enough time to finish the exam. Your time budget works out to well over one minute per question. It's not all day, but it is enough time — if you know your stuff.

A New Wrinkle: There's No Going Back!

Many Sylvan Prometric tests allow you to mark a question for later review. That option is no longer available on the CCNA exam. You must answer each question completely before advancing to the next.

You can expect to see some multimedia questions regarding the OSI model. These questions are in the form of drag and drop, in that you are asked to drag items into their proper sequence. Most of the questions on the test are multiple-choice questions. You can tell the questions that need more than one answer, because check boxes (little squares) are provided for you to select your answers. On questions that have only one right answer, option buttons (little circles) are provided for you to select. Don't worry about not getting all of the answers on the multiple answer questions; the test doesn't let you proceed to the next question until you provide the correct number of responses. How do you know how many answers to provide? After the question, you are told to choose a certain number of answers, and the number of correct answers required displays in the lower left-hand corner of the screen. On multiple-choice questions, be absolutely sure that you analyze each and every answer choice. More than one option can be, and often is, the correct response. You may see a few true/false questions as well.

Because you can't go back to review your work, analyze each question carefully before answering. Use the paper, plastic, or whatever note sheets you were provided to make notes as you analyze each option.

No Hootin' and Hollerin' Please

The good, and sometimes bad, part of taking a Sylvan Prometric interactive online test is that you get your results immediately. As soon as you finish the test, you not only know whether you passed but you also get a printed report that tells you how well you did on each area of the exam. Of course, if you pass, you won't care too much about the areas in which you can improve, at least not until later. However, if you fail, this information is the positive part of an otherwise disappointing time, and should provide you valuable and timesaving feedback for next time.

When you receive your passing test score, it's considered bad manners to celebrate boisterously at your terminal. When the time comes to celebrate, take along our congratulations and those of the entire *CCNA For Dummies* team for a job well done!

Part VII
Appendixes

The 5th Wave   By Rich Tennant

"AND JUST WHAT THE HECK PART OF THE NETWORK DID YOU SAY YOU'RE FROM?"

In this part . . .

This part contains sample questions for each topic of the CCNA exam to help you prepare for the test. We have tried to give you about the same number and type of questions as you will find on the actual exam. For many reasons (memory and the Cisco Systems Confidentiality Statement we accepted when we took the test being foremost), we are prevented from just giving you the exact questions for the test. The questions you see on your test are very likely different from those that we saw when we took the test, although the test covers the same material. Use these sample questions to measure the areas in which you need to study more. If you do fairly well on these questions, then you are probably reaching your peak.

Please remember that our questions are intended to help you find your weaknesses. They are not a list of the questions you'll find on the actual exam. If you can answer these questions fairly easily, then check to make sure that you can also explain why each wrong answer is wrong. Then, we think you'll be just about ready.

Included in this book is a CD-ROM that contains many tools to help you prepare for the test, including a test engine that will generate practice tests for you in a variety of combinations.

We've also included a handy glossary that contains the terms you should be familiar with for the CCNA exam. Use these terms to refresh your memory as you study and as a part of your last-minute studies.

Appendix A

Sample Test

· ·

*H*ere are sample questions representing all of the topic areas of the CCNA examination. The CCNA exam has 79–81 questions spread over eight testing topics (see Chapter 1). You must get 75 percent correct to receive your CCNA certification. We have provided you with about the same number and percentage of questions you should find on the actual test. Remember that the test you take is most likely not the same as the ones we took or the one your friends or co-workers were given. The test has many versions that are given at random.

These sample questions are not the exact questions you'll find on the exam. They are examples of the topics and questions you should see on the actual test. Practice with these questions and those on the CD-ROM. If you do well, you are probably just about ready to take the CCNA exam.

On at least one question, you may be given an illustration from which you're asked to identify certain characteristics or equipment. For example, you may be asked to identify a particular network device from a group of devices. So, study all of the network layout diagrams you can find, especially those using Cisco's symbols, and be sure you can identify all of the features and devices included.

As you go through these questions, it's also a very good idea to be sure that you know why an answer is correct, and perhaps more importantly, why an answer is wrong. Best of luck!

The OSI Reference Model

1 On the OSI model's Network layer, what data transport functions are performed for the sending node?

A ○ Data are formatted into datagrams and Network layer headers are added

B ○ Data are formatted into packets and Layer 2 headers are added

C ○ Data are formatted into frames and Layer 3 headers are added

D ○ Data are broken into packets and Network layer headers are added

2 Data encapsulation occurs on which layer(s)? (Choose all that apply.)

A ❑ Application layer

B ❑ Network layer

C ❑ Data Link layer

D ❑ Physical layer

E ❑ All of the above

3 Routing protocols allow routers to learn the state of networks not directly connected to them. Which of the following does not characterize a routing protocol?

A ○ The routed protocol for which it maintains information

B ○ The media used to interconnect internetworked routers

C ○ The algorithm and metrics used to determine best routes

D ○ The method used to communicate with other routers

E ○ The length of time it takes news of a change to be communicated throughout the network

4 On which OSI layer do e-mail, browser, and FTP clients operate?

A ○ Layer 4

B ○ Layer 6

C ○ Layer 7

D ○ Layer 5

5 Data conversion formats, such as ASCII, EBCDIC, JPEG, and data encryption, are found on which OSI layer?

A ○ Layer 4

B ○ Layer 6

C ○ Layer 7

D ○ Layer 5

6 Which of the following actions is defined on the Transport layer of the OSI model? (Choose one.)

A ○ Flow control and error recovery
B ○ Placing MAC addresses in the header
C ○ Encapsulating data into frames
D ○ Adding network addresses

7 Which of the following occurs when a connection is established?

A ○ Service request coordination
B ○ Response coordination
C ○ Synchronization and acknowledgment
D ○ Flow control and error recovery

8 Which of the following is a service provided by each OSI layer to the other layers?

A ○ Encapsulation for the layer below
B ○ Flow control to the layer above
C ○ Services to the layer above
D ○ Transmission of cells to the layer below

9 Which layer of the OSI model provides error-free and reliable packet delivery?

A ○ Session
B ○ Transport
C ○ Data Link
D ○ Physical

10 A MAC address is made up of six fields of _____ bits each

A ○ 2
B ○ 4
C ○ 8
D ○ 12

11 On which OSI Reference model layer are electrical and mechanical characteristics of networking media defined?

A ○ Layer 1
B ○ Layer 2
C ○ Layer 5
D ○ Layer 7

12 A receiving device prevents buffer overflow through what technique?

A ○ Sliding windows
B ○ Source-quench messages
C ○ Buffer queing
D ○ Shared memory

13 UDP is what type of network service?

A ○ Connectionless
B ○ Flow control
C ○ Error correction
D ○ Connection-oriented

14 The conversion of data from the sending node's format into that of the receiving node is performed on what layer of the OSI model?

A ○ Layer 1
B ○ Layer 2
C ○ Layer 6
D ○ Layer 7

15 Which layer of the OSI model fragments and reassembles packets while managing network layer connections?

A ○ Layer 5, Session
B ○ Layer 4, Transport
C ○ Layer 1, Physical
D ○ Layer 2, Data Link

16 TCP and UDP are defined on which layer of the OSI model?

A ○ Layer 2
B ○ Layer 3
C ○ Layer 4
D ○ Layer 5

WAN Protocols

17 An ISDN BRI line consists of

A ○ One 128K B channel and one 16K D channel
B ○ One 128K B channel and two 8K D channels
C ○ Two 64K B channels and two 8K D channels
D ○ Two 64K B channels and one 16K D channel

18 FECN and BECN provide for flow control in what internetworking protocol?

A ○ ATM
B ○ X.25
C ○ Frame Relay
D ○ PPP
E ○ SLIP

19 Which of the following commands is used to configure LMI for ANSI on a Cisco IOS router?

A ○ frame relay lmi-type ansi
B ○ set frame-relay lmi-type ansi
C ○ lmi-type ansi frame-relay
D ○ set frame-relay type ansi

20 The available bandwidth on an ISDN PRI connection is

A ○ 1.544 Mbps
B ○ 1.528 Mbps
C ○ 1.536 Mbps
D ○ 1.472 Mbps
E ○ None of the above

21 The X.25 standard encompasses which layers of the OSI model?

A ○ Physical and Data Link
B ○ Data Link and Networking
C ○ Networking and Transport
D ○ Physical, Data Link, Network, and Transport

22 X.25 connections are established between what two devices?

A ○ An SVC and a PVC
B ○ A master router and a slave router
C ○ A DTE and a DCE
D ○ An HDLC and an LAPB

23 _____ is a packet switching technology that identifies each logical data stream with a _____.

A ○ ATM, VPI
B ○ Frame Relay, DLCI
C ○ ATM, VCC
D ○ ATM, VCI

24 When would the command `encapsulation frame-relay ietf` be used on a Cisco router?

   A ○ To configure it on a Frame Relay network as both an interior and exterior transfer frame

   B ○ To configure it on a Frame Relay network to use interior encapsulation transfer frame

   C ○ To configure it on a Frame Relay network with a non-Cisco router on the other end

   D ○ None of the above

25 Which of the following are valid Frame Relay LMI types? (Choose all that apply.)

   A ❑ Cisco default

   B ❑ ANSI

   C ❑ q933a

   D ❑ All of the above

   E ❑ None of the above

26 The default serial encapsulation method on Cisco routers is

   A ○ SDLC

   B ○ HDLC

   C ○ PPP

   D ○ IETF

   E ○ None of the above

27 Which of the following are characteristics of X.25? (Choose all that apply.)

   A ❑ Is packet-switched and typically operates as a PVC

   B ❑ Uses built-in error correction and flow control

   C ❑ Offers high reliability and high performance

   D ❑ Packet destination is determined by either an LCI or an LCN

28 On which of the following physical interfaces can PPP be configured?

   A ○ ISDN

   B ○ Asynchronous serial

   C ○ Synchronous serial

   D ○ HSSI

   E ○ All of the above

29 Which of the following is not associated with Frame Relay?

   A ○ DLCI

   B ○ LMI

   C ○ TDM

   D ○ PVC

30 How is subinterface 3 on serial interface 1 referenced on a Cisco IOS router?

A ○ Serial1/3
B ○ Serial1 sub-int 3
C ○ Serial1 s3
D ○ Serial1.3

31 Multilink PPP works over all but which type of interface?

A ○ Synchronous serial interfaces
B ○ BRI
C ○ PRI
D ○ Asynchronous serial interfaces

32 A packet destined for every node on a network is a

A ○ broadcast
B ○ multicast
C ○ flexicast
D ○ unicast

Cisco IOS Commands

33 The command `show interface tokenRing 1` is entered from which mode?

A ○ Exec
B ○ Privileged Exec
C ○ Global configuration
D ○ Any of the above

34 What command is used to add static IP routes?

A ○ Router IP
B ○ Route IP
C ○ IP Router
D ○ IP Route

35 If your default route to the network is 190.170.20.0, what command would you enter?

A ○ Router IP default-network 190.170.20.0
B ○ Route default 190.170.20.0
C ○ IP default-network 190.170.20.0
D ○ IP default 190.170.20.0

36 Based on the following Cisco router entries, which of the statements below is incorrect?

```
dummies(config)#ipx routing
dummies(config)#interface ethernet 0.1
dummies(config-subif)#ipx network 201 encapsulation
        SAP
dummies(config)#interface ethernet 0.2
dummies(config-subif)#ipx network 202 encapsulation
        novell-ether
```

A ○ The script defines two subinterfaces: Ethernet 0.1 and 0.2.
B ○ Subinterface E0.1 is using IPX network 201 with Ethernet 802.2 encapsulation.
C ○ Subinterface E0.2 is using IPX network 202 with Ethernet II encapsulation.
D ○ None of the above.

37 Which of the following commands cannot be used to confirm the operations of an IPX enabled router?

A ○ dummies#show ipx interface [interface type][interface number]
B ○ dummies#show ipx interface brief
C ○ dummies#show ipx traffic
D ○ dummies#show ipx port

38 Which of the following modes provides a prompted dialog that can be used to establish an initial configuration?

A ○ User Exec Mode
B ○ Global Configuration Mode
C ○ SETUP Mode
D ○ Privileged Exec Mode

39 Which of the following modes enables a detailed examination of the router, as well as file manipulation, testing and debugging, and remote access?

A ○ User EXEC Mode
B ○ Global Configuration Mode
C ○ SETUP Mode
D ○ Privileged Exec Mode

40 Which of the following prompts is the prompt for interface configuration mode?

A ○ Router(config-if)#
B ○ Router(config-if)>
C ○ Router(config)>
D ○ Router(interface)#

Network Protocols

41 TCP and Port 25 are used by what TCP/IP service?

   A ○ NFS
   B ○ SMTP
   C ○ SNMP
   D ○ DNS

42 On the Transport layer, a socket consists of

   A ○ A MAC address plus a port
   B ○ A MAC address plus an IP address
   C ○ An IP Address plus a port
   D ○ An API plus a port

43 What is the NETSTAT command used for?

   A ○ To display the names and IP addresses of directly connected internet-working devices
   B ○ To display the current state of TCP/IP connections and protocol statistics
   C ○ To display protocol statistics and the link status of each router interface
   D ○ To display the IEEE 802.1d spanning-tree algorithm data

44 Match the reserved TCP port number (1) 15, (2) 21, (3) 69, (4) 79 with the appropriate application (A) FINGER, (B) NETSTAT, (C) TFTP, and (D) FTP.

   A ○ 1 with A, 2 with B, 3 with C, 4 with D
   B ○ 1 with B, 2 with D, 3 with C, 4 with A
   C ○ 1 with C, 2 with B, 3 with D, 4 with A
   D ○ 1 with D, 2 with C, 3 with A, 4 with B

Routing

45 What are the two basic categories of routing protocols?

   A ○ Path determination and static
   B ○ Distance vector and metric
   C ○ Distance vector and link-state
   D ○ Path determination and link-state
   E ○ Proximity vector and tie-state

46 What metric is used by a router to determine the best route to a network when it learns of routes from multiple routing protocols?

A ○ Administrative Distance
B ○ Managerial Expanse
C ○ Executive Distance
D ○ Administrative Expense

47 What is a static route's default administrative distance?

A ○ 1
B ○ 70
C ○ 90
D ○ 110

48 What is the default administrative distance for a RIP route?

A ○ 130
B ○ 120
C ○ 110
D ○ 100

49 What command is used to enter a default route of 192.179.2.0?

A ○ Router IP default-network 192.179.2.0
B ○ Route default 192.179.2.0
C ○ IP default-network 192.179.2.0
D ○ IP default 192.179.2.0 255.255.255.0

50 What command is used to display the current default route?

A ○ show route
B ○ show default route
C ○ show ip default
D ○ show ip route

51 How many bits are in the network number on an IPX network?

A ○ 32
B ○ 24
C ○ 48
D ○ 60

52 The Cisco IOS encapsulation frame type novell-ether represents which Novell frame type?

A ○ Ethernet II
B ○ Ethernet 802.2
C ○ Ethernet 802.3
D ○ Ethernet SNAP

53 Which of the following commands enable IPX routing on the router dummies?

A ○ dummies>ipx routing
B ○ dummies(config)>routing ipx
C ○ dummies(config)# ipx routing
D ○ dummies(config)# routing ipx

54 Which of the following shows the proper designation for an interface and subinterface

A ○ Ethernet 0, subinterface 1
B ○ E0.1
C ○ E0-2
D ○ All of the above

55 What is the node address in the IPX address 1022.00c0.4774.250a.453?

A ○ 1022
B ○ 00c0.4774.250a
C ○ 1022.00c0.4774
D ○ 4774.250a.453

56 Regarding DNS, which of the following statements is true concerning Cisco IOS?

A ○ DNS is enabled by default.
B ○ DNS is disabled by default.
C ○ The router must have a DNS name-server specified.
D ○ The router is able to access a maximum of four DNS name-servers.

57 Which of the following modes provides a limited examination of the router and remote access?

A ○ User EXEC Mode
B ○ Global Configuration Mode
C ○ SETUP Mode
D ○ Privileged Exec Mode

58 What command is used to determine the paths available for packets to use?

A ○ Trace

B ○ Ping

C ○ Show IP ro

D ○ IP route

59 What is the Cisco router command used to enable fast-switching, if it has been disabled?

A ○ enable fast-switching

B ○ ip fast-switching

C ○ enable ip fast-switchingx

D ○ ip route-cache

60 While in Global Configuration Mode, which command is used to enable password security for remote login sessions?

A ○ line console 0

B ○ enable-password

C ○ line vty 0 4

D ○ enable-secret

61 Which of the following are advantages of static routing? (Choose all that apply.)

A ❑ The router doesn't have to perform calculations on the route.

B ❑ The router doesn't have to send out updates about the path.

C ❑ Static routes are scalable.

D ❑ Paths between the two routes are always known.

Network Security

62 What sets the number of IP address bits used to make a match in an access list?

A ○ Range

B ○ Subnet mask

C ○ IP Class

D ○ Wildcard mask

63 Access lists are defined in which router mode?

A ○ Exec

B ○ Privileged Exec

C ○ Interface Configuration

D ○ Global Configuration

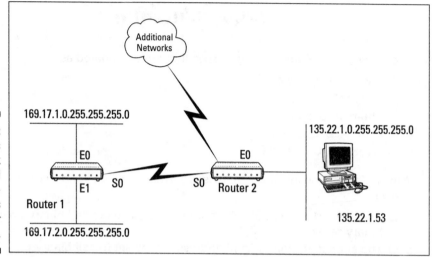

Figure A-1:
Use this network diagram and the following access list for Question 64.

169.17.1.0.255.255.255.0

135.22.1.0.255.255.255.0

EO

EO

E1   S0   S0   Router 2

Router 1

135.22.1.53

169.17.2.0.255.255.255.0

```
access-list 123 permit tcp 169.17.1.0 0.0.0.255 host
             135.22.1.53 eq telnet
access-list 123 permit tcp 169.17.2.0 0.0.0.255 host
             135.22.1.53 eq ftp
access-list 123 permit icmp 169.17.0.0 0.0.255.255 any
```

64 Which of the following statements is false, based on the access list and Figure A-1, regarding router 2's Ethernet 0 as an outbound packet filter?

A ○ Telnet traffic from network 169.17.1.0 destined for host 135.22.1.53 is permitted

B ○ FTP traffic from network 169.17.2.0 destined for host 135.22.1.53 is permitted

C ○ ICMP traffic to any destination on the 135.22.1.0 network is permitted

D ○ All other traffic is denied

E ○ None of the above

65 Access lists are most likely to be used for which of the following?

A ○ To deny all traffic

B ○ To identify priority packets for faster handling

C ○ To decrease the content in routing updates

D ○ To filter who is able to logon remotely to a router

LAN Switching

66 There are _____ IP addressing classes that are designated as _____.

A ○ Four: 1, 2, 3, and 4
B ○ Five: 1, 2, 3, 4, and 5
C ○ Three: A, B, and C
D ○ Four: A, B, C, and D
E ○ Five: A, B, C, D, and E

67 Which of the following statements is/are true regarding IP addresses? (Choose all that apply.)

A ❑ The network portion of an IP address can be set to "all binary ones" or "all binary zeros."
B ❑ The subnet portion of an IP address can be set to "all binary ones" or "all binary zeros."
C ❑ The host address portion of an IP address cannot be set to "all binary ones" or "all binary zeros."
D ❑ The network 127.x.x.x can be used as a network address.
E ❑ None of the above.

68 How many valid subnet numbers are available for the network at 186.116.0.0 that has a subnet mask of 255.255.252.0?

A ○ 60
B ○ 62
C ○ 64
D ○ 66

69 What is the first host address on the second valid subnet on the Class B network 191.16.0.0 with a subnet mask of 255.255.248.0?

A ○ 191.16.8.1
B ○ 191.16.16.1
C ○ 191.16.12.1
D ○ 191.24.16.1

70 The decimal equivalent of the binary number 11011011 is

A ○ 217
B ○ 219
C ○ 223
D ○ 215

71 The binary equivalent of the decimal number 139 is

A ○ 10001001
B ○ 10001010
C ○ 10001011
D ○ 10001111

72 What would the subnet mask be if we added 10 subnet bits to the default subnet mask for a Class A IP address?

A ○ 255.192.0.0
B ○ 255.255.224.0
C ○ 255.255.192.0
D ○ 255.240.0.0

73 _____ support multiple paths between network segments and _____ usually provide a single path between network segments.

A ○ Switches, routers
B ○ Hubs, bridges
C ○ Routers, bridges
D ○ Routers, hubs

74 In link-state routing, flooding refers to what?

A ○ Sending UDP packets to neighboring routers that are copied to their routing tables and forwarded to neighboring routers
B ○ Sending LSAs to their neighbors and all other routers in the autononomous system that are copied to their routing tables and forwarded to neighboring routers
C ○ Sending LSPs to master routers that update their routing table and then forward the routing table on to slave routers
D ○ Sending LSA to border gateway routers that update their routing tables and forward the LSA on to other autonomous systems

75 The maximum number of hops when using the Routing Information Protocol is

A ○ 12 hops
B ○ 15 hops
C ○ 32 hops
D ○ There is no limit

76 Of those listed, which VLAN assignment method is typically used?

A ○ Port
B ○ IPX address
C ○ IP address
D ○ MAC address

77 The distance limitation associated with any type of cable is due primarily to which of the following?

A ○ Propagation delay
B ○ Collisions
C ○ Attenuation
D ○ IEEE 802.3 standards

78 A bridge is what type of forwarding device?

A ○ Cut through
B ○ Link State
C ○ Store and forward
D ○ Distance Vector

79 Which of the following statements is not a characteristic of LAN segmentation with a switch?

A ○ Switches eliminate the impact of collisions through microsegmentation
B ○ Creates a large collision-free domain from smaller collision domains
C ○ Low latency and high frame-forwarding rates at each interface port
D ○ Works with existing 802.3-compliant NICs and cabling

80 Which of the following statements is not a characteristic of Full-Duplex Ethernet?

A ○ Allows the simultaneous transmission and reception of different data packets
B ○ Requires two pairs of cables and a switched connection between the nodes
C ○ Is considered a point-to-point connection and is nearly collision free
D ○ None of the above.

81 How many subnets and hosts are available on a network with the IP address of 172.17.2.0 and a subnet mask of 255.255.255.0?

A ○ 126 hosts and 510 subnets
B ○ 254 hosts and 254 subnets
C ○ 510 hosts and 126 subnets
D ○ 1022 hosts and 62 subnets

Answers

1 *D.* The Network layer receives datagrams from the Transport layer, breaks them into packets, adds Network headers, and sends these on to the Data Link layer. *See Chapter 5.*

2 *E.* Encapsulation, which involves the conversion of data into layer-specific PDUs and the adding of layer-specific headers and trailers, occurs on each of the lower layers of the OSI Reference Model. *See Chapter 3.*

3 *B.* Routing protocols are by necessity media independent, so the internetworking media used to connect them is not something that characterizes them. *See Chapter 11.*

4 *C.* E-mail, Web browser, and FTP clients operate on the Application layer (Layer 7) of the OSI model. *See Chapter 7.*

5 *B.* Data conversions, like ASCII, EBCDIC, and JPEG, and data encryption are found on the Presentation layer (Layer 6) of the OSI model. *See Chapter 7.*

6 *A.* Flow control and error recovery are performed on the Transport layer. Formatting data into frames and adding the network address are performed on the Network layer (Layer 3). The MAC address is added on Layer 2 (Data Link layer). *See Chapters 4, 5, and 6.*

7 *C.* The process of synchronization and acknowledgment between hosts takes place while a connection is being established. *See Chapter 6.*

8 *C.* Each OSI layer provides services to the layer immediately above it. Not all layers perform encapsulation or flow control functions, and only the Data Link layer encapsulates cells. *See Chapter 4.*

9 *B.* Layer 4 of the OSI reference model provides for the formation, preservation, and termination of virtual circuits, transport fault detection and correction, and flow control. *See Chapter 6.*

10 *C.* A MAC address is made up of six 8-bit fields, which are divided into two three-field combinations that respectively are used to store the manufacturer's ID number and a unique serialized device ID number. *See Chapter 4.*

11 *A.* The Physical layer (Layer 1) is responsible for the transmission of the raw bit stream and the definition of electrical signaling and hardware interfaces. *See Chapter 4.*

12 *B.* The receiving device sends source-quench messages to the sending device to notify it that the receiving device cannot receive data as fast as the source device is sending it. The sending device halts transmission until it is notified that it may proceed. *See Chapter 6.*

13 *A.* UDP (User Datagram Protocol) is a connectionless Transport layer protocol that exchanges datagrams without waiting for an acknowledgment. It does not guarantee delivery and assumes that error processing and retransmission will be handled by other protocols. *See Chapter 6.*

14 *C.* The Presentation layer (Layer 6) is responsible for formatting both inbound and outbound data into the appropriate format. This provides a common interface between the sending and receiving nodes. What the Presentation layer does, in effect, is make the data ready for presentation to the host to which it is addressed. *See Chapter 7.*

15 *B.* The Transport layer (Layer 4) is responsible for general data delivery in either connection-oriented or connectionless transmission mode, as well as flow control and error recovery services. *See Chapter 6.*

16 *C.* TCP (Transmission Control Protocol) and UDP (User Datagram Protocol) are Transport layer (Layer 4) protocols. TCP is connection-oriented and UDP is connectionless. *See Chapter 6.*

17 *D.* An ISDN Basic Rate Interface (BRI) is composed of 128 Kbps of traffic split on two 64 Kbps Bearer channels and uses one 16K Data channel for out of band control of the connection, for a total bandwidth of 144 Kbps. *See Chapter 17.*

18 *C.* FECN (forward-explicit congestion notification) and BECN (backward-explicit congestion notification) are the methods used for flow control in Frame Relay to maximize throughput. They are both 1-bit fields set to zero (off) when there is no congestion, and to one (on) when congestion is detected. *See Chapter 17.*

19 *A.* The command `frame-relay lmi-type ansi` configures Local Management Interface (LMI) for ANSI on a Frame Relay interface. *See Chapter 17.*

20 *C.* ISDN PRI is delivered over a channelized T1 line (1.544 Mbps over 24 channels). All channelized services use 8 Kbps for the channelization process (1.544 − .008 = 1.536 Kbps). *See Chapter 17.*

21 *D.* X.25 encompasses the first three layers of the OSI reference model. *See Chapter 17.*

22 *C.* At each end of an X.25 connection is a data terminal equipment (DTE) device and a data circuit-terminating equipment (DCE) device. *See Chapter 17.*

23 *B.* Frame Relay is an encapsulation method that operates on Layer 2 using packet switching technology across nearly any serial interface. To identify each virtual circuit created from the multiplexing of logical data streams, Frame Relay uses a Data-Link Connection Identifier (DLCI). *See Chapter 17.*

24 *C.* The command `encapsulation frame-relay ietf` configures the router interface for Frame Relay traffic and changes the encapsulation method from Cisco's methodology to the IETF standard. *See Chapter 17.*

25 *D.* Cisco default, ANSI, and q933a are all valid LMI standards implemented on a Cisco router. Be on the lookout for questions like this one on the exam. *See Chapter 17.*

26 *B.* HDLC (High-Level Data Link Control) is the default encapsulation mode on a Cisco router. *See Chapter 17.*

27 *A, B, D.* X.25 is highly reliable, but in order to realize its reliability, it must process the acknowledgments, buffering, and retransmission processes required to ensure packet delivery. *See Chapter 17.*

28 *E.* Point-to-Point Protocol (PPP) can be configured on all interface types, including ISDN, Asynchronous serial, Synchronous serial, and HSSI physical interfaces. *See Chapter 17.*

29 C. TDM (time division multiplexing) is not a characteristic of Frame Relay. In fact, it's the opposite of the form of multiplexing used by Frame Relay — statistical multiplexing. *See Chapter 17.*

30 D. The naming convention for subinterfaces is the same as for the interface with the addition of the subinterface number appended with a period. *See Chapter 17.*

31 A. Multilink PPP can work over single or multiple interfaces such as BRI, PRI, and Asynchronous serial interfaces. *See Chapter 17.*

32 A. Messages sent to every network node are broadcast messages. Messages sent only to many, but not all, nodes on a network are multicast. *See Chapter 16.*

33 B. The command `show interface TokenRing 1` must be entered in Privileged EXEC mode. *See Chapter 9.*

34 D. The command IP Route is entered from the global configuration to add static routes to a router. *See Chapter 11.*

35 C. The command `IP default-network 190.170.20.0` is entered from the global configuration mode, designated by the prompt "Router(config)# " to add the default route to a router. *See Chapter 11.*

36 C. Subinterface E0.2 is using IPX network 202 with Ethernet 802.3 (novell-ether) encapsulation. *See Chapter 11.*

37 D. There is no port command associated with the `show ipx` command. Each of the other commands listed can be used to display the configuration and activities of an IPX enabled router. *See Chapter 11.*

38 C. The SETUP Mode provides a simple-to-follow prompted dialog used to establish an initial configuration. *See Chapter 9.*

39 D. The Privileged EXEC Mode allows for detailed examination of the router, file manipulation, debugging and testing, and remote access. The User EXEC Mode provides for the limited examination of the router and remote access. *See Chapter 9.*

40 A. The interface configuration mode is represented by the prompt Router(config-if)#. *See Chapter 9.*

41 B. Simple Mail Transport Protocol uses transmission control protocol through port 25. *See Chapter 14.*

42 C. On the Transport layer, a socket is made up of an IP address and a port number in the form of NNN.NNN.NNN.NNN:XX, where the Ns represent the IP address and the Xs represent the port number. *See Chapters 6 and 12.*

43 B. The NETSTAT command displays protocol statistics and the state of current TCP/IP connections. This command is especially useful for determining the name of each physical interface on a system. *See Chapter 14.*

44 *B.* You need to remember which ports are used by which TCP/IP services. In this case, NETSTAT uses port 15, FTP uses port 21, TFTP uses port 69, and FINGER uses port 79. *See Chapter 14.*

45 *C.* Distance vector protocols require frequent broadcasts of their entire routing table over all interfaces. Link-state protocols discover their neighboring devices by using the Hello protocol and keep track of the updates and Hellos received from neighboring systems. *See Chapter 11.*

46 *A.* All routes, whether static or dynamic, are assigned an administrative distance. The route with the lowest administrative distance metric is used when multiple route sources exist. *See Chapter 11.*

47 *A.* The default administrative distance assigned to a static route is a value of one. *See Chapter 11.*

48 *B.* The default administrative distance for a RIP route is the value 120. *See Chapter 11.*

49 *C.* The command IP default-network 190.170.20.0 is entered from the global configuration mode, which is designated by the prompt "Router(config)#," to add the default route to a router. *See Chapter 10.*

50 *D.* To see the default route in a Cisco IOS router, you would enter **show ip route**. *See Chapter 10.*

51 *A.* The network number on an IPX network number is 32 bits long and is usually shown in hexadecimal format. *See Chapter 10.*

52 *C.* Ethernet 802.3, sometimes referred to as 802.3 raw, is called *novell-ether* by Cisco and is the default encapsulation for NetWare version 3.11 and earlier. *See Chapter 11.*

53 *C.* You must be in the global configuration mode to enable the routing of IPX frames using the command ipx routing. *See Chapter 11.*

54 *B.* A subinterface is designated in the format E0.2. *See Chapter 17.*

55 *B.* The node address is 00c0.4774.250a and the network ID number, which is always the first number, is 1022. If a socket number is included, it is last. *See Chapter 12.*

56 *A.* By default, DNS capability is enabled in the Cisco IOS. It's a good idea to specify the name-server(s) up to six to avoid the overhead of broadcast DNS requests. *See Chapter 12.*

57 *A.* The User EXEC Mode provides for the limited examination of the router and remote access. *See Chapter 9.*

58 *C.* The command Show IP route (ro is shorthand for route) displays the paths available for packets to use. *See Chapter 10.*

59 *D.* The command ip route-cache enables fast-switching on a Cisco router. To disable fast-switching, you would enter the command no ip route-cache. *See Chapter 10.*

60 *C.* The command line vty 0 4 creates password protection for incoming Telnet sessions. *See Chapter 10.*

61 *A, B, D.* One of the drawbacks to static routing is its lack of scalability. The administration overhead on large networks can be a burden. *See Chapter 10.*

62 *D.* The wildcard mask (a.k.a. inverse mask) and the source or destination IP addresses are used to identify a range of addresses to match. The wildcard mask tells the router how many bits of the IP address to examine when determining a match. *See Chapter 15.*

63 *D.* All access lists are defined in the global configuration mode identified by the prompt routername(config)#. *See Chapter 15.*

64 *E.* Statements A, B, and C are explicitly permitted, and statement D is implied because of the implicit denial associated with access lists. In addition to the question regarding access lists, this question makes two points: the level of detail you must analyze when looking for correct answers, and the use of diagrams and command lists as background information to a question or series of questions. Read questions carefully and be sure why or why not an answer is a good choice. *See Chapter 15 (for information on access lists).*

65 *C.* An access list is typically used to reduce traffic such as the content in routing updates. *See Chapter 15.*

66 *E.* Yes, there are five IP address classes; don't forget about classes D and E. Class A is limited to 126 of very large networks; Class B is limited to 16,383 of medium-sized networks; Class C is limited to 2,097,151 networks; Class D is a special class used for multicasting; and Class E is also a special class used for experimental or research. *See Chapter 13.*

67 *E.* Okay, maybe it is a trick question, but you need to be ready for this type of question. None of the statements are true about an IP address. Certain addresses in the IP address space have been reserved for special purposes and are not typically allowed as host addresses. For each of "A" through "D," the opposite is true. The network portion of an IP address *cannot* be set to "all binary ones" or "all binary zeros" and the subnet portion of an IP address *cannot* be set to "all binary ones" or "all binary zeros." However, the host address portion of an IP address *can* be set to "all binary ones" or "all binary zeros," the network 127.x.x.x *cannot* be used as a network address. *See Chapter 13.*

68 *B.* The binary equivalent of 252 is 11111100, resulting in a least significant bit value in decimal form of 4. The first valid subnet number then is 186.116.4.0. Counting by fours to the highest valid subnet number of 186.116.252.0 totals 62 valid subnet numbers. *See Chapter 13.*

69 *B.* The binary equivalent of 248 is 11111000, resulting in a least significant bit value in decimal form of 8. The first valid subnet number then is 191.16.8.0. Counting by eights to the next valid subnet number results in 191.16.16.0. Zero in the fourth octet is reserved for the subnet address, leaving 191.16.16.1 as the first available host in the second valid subnet. *See Chapter 13.*

70 *B.* Adding up the decimal equivalents of the binary values indicated, that is 128+64+16+8+2+1=219. *See Chapter 13.*

71 *C.* Starting from the leftmost binary value and setting each binary value position to one when there is enough remaining value for that position, you get 128 (1) + 64 (0) + 32 (0) + 16 (0) + 8 (1) + 4 (0) + 2 (1) + 1 (1) = 139 or 10001011. *See Chapter 13.*

72 *C.* The default subnet mask for a Class A is 255.0.0.0, and each octet consists of 8 bits. Adding 10 bits to the default would use the entire second octet (255.255.0.0) and leaves 2 bits to be used in the third octet. The first 2 bits (from the left) are 128 and 64; added together the sum is 192, resulting in a subnet mask of 255.255.192.0. *See Chapter 13.*

73 *C.* Routers offer multiple paths between network segments and may be implemented with redundancy while bridges offer a single path from one network segment to another. *See Chapter 16.*

74 *B.* Link-state routers send a hello message, called a link-state packet (LSP) or link-state advertisement (LSA), to neighboring routers that update their routing tables and forward the information to the rest of the network. This is also known as flooding. *See Chapter 16.*

75 *B.* RIP has a maximum number of hops of 16, which contrasts to EIGRP, which has a maximum hop count of 224. *See Chapter 11.*

76 *A.* The simplest, easiest to administer and most common VLAN assignments are made by switch port numbers. *See Chapter 16.*

77 *C.* Attenuation is the natural weakening of the signal due to the resistance found in the media being traversed. *See Chapter 4.*

78 *C.* Bridges must examine the destination address field of a frame to determine which interface it should forward the frame through, thus requiring the entire packet to be placed in memory. *See Chapters 4 and 16.*

79 *B.* Switches segment a LAN into smaller collision-free domains from a single large-collision domain. *See Chapter 16.*

80 *D.* All of the statements listed are characteristics of a properly implemented full-duplex Ethernet network. *See Chapter 17.*

81 *B.* In this class B address, 8 bits are being used to identify subnets, leaving 8 for the hosts: $(2^8) - 2 = 254$. *See Chapter 13.*

Appendix B

About the CD

● ●

*O*n the CD-ROM:

- ✔ Sample questions and test engine demos from some of the top names in test preparation materials
- ✔ Some great links I recommend for CCNA test information, study aids, and sample questions
- ✔ The great QuickLearn game — Outpost — to make test preparation fun
- ✔ The Dummies Certification test engine with lots of sample CCNA questions

System Requirements

Make sure that your computer meets the minimum system requirements shown in the following list. If your computer doesn't meet most of these requirements, you may have problems using the contents of the CD.

- ✔ A PC with a 486 or faster processor.
- ✔ Microsoft Windows 95 or later.
- ✔ At least 16MB of total RAM installed on your computer.
- ✔ At least 150MB of available hard drive space to install all the software on this CD. (You need less space if you don't install every program.)
- ✔ A CD-ROM drive — double-speed (2x) or faster.
- ✔ A sound card for PCs.
- ✔ A monitor capable of displaying at least 256 colors or grayscale.
- ✔ A modem with a speed of at least 14,400 bps.

If you need more information on the basics, check out *A+ Certification For Dummies* by Ron Gilster; *Networking For Dummies,* 4th Edition, by Doug Lowe; *Upgrading & Fixing Networks For Dummies,* 2nd Edition, by Bill Camarda; *Windows NT Networking For Dummies,* by Ed Tittel, Mary Madden, and Earl Follis; *Networking with NetWare For Dummies,* 4th Edition, by Ed Tittel, James E. Gaskin, and Earl Follis; *Windows NT Server 4 For Dummies,* by Ed Tittel; or *Novell's Encyclopedia of Networking,* by Kevin Shafer (all published by IDG Books Worldwide, Inc.).

Using the CD with Microsoft Windows

Note: To play the QuickLearn game, you must have a Windows 95 or Windows 98 computer — the game won't run on Windows NT. You must also have Microsoft DirectX 5.0 or a later version installed. If you do not have DirectX, you can download it at `www.microsoft.com/directx/homeuser/downloads/`.

To install the items from the CD to your hard drive, follow these steps:

1. **Insert the CD into your computer's CD-ROM drive.**
2. **Click Start⇨Run.**
3. **In the dialog box that appears, type** D:/setup.exe **and then click OK.**

   If your CD-ROM drive uses a different letter, type the appropriate letter in the Run dialog box.

4. **Read through the license agreement that appears, and then click the Accept button if you want to use the CD. After you click Accept, you'll never be bothered by the License Agreement window again.**

   The CD interface Welcome screen appears. The interface is a little program that shows you what's on the CD and coordinates installing the programs and running the demos. The interface basically enables you to click a button or two to make things happen.

5. **Click anywhere on the Welcome screen to enter the interface.**

   The next screen lists categories for the software on the CD.

6. **To view the items within a category, just click the category's name.**

   A list of programs in the category appears.

7. **For more information about a program, click the program's name.**

   Be sure to read the information that appears. Sometimes a program has its own system requirements or requires you to do a few tricks on your computer before you can install or run the program, and this screen tells you what you may need to do, if necessary.

8. **If you don't want to install the program, click the Go Back button to return to the previous screen.**

   You can always return to the previous screen by clicking the Go Back button. This feature enables you to browse the different categories and products and decide what you want to install.

9. **To install a program, click the appropriate Install button.**

   The CD interface drops to the background while the CD installs the program you chose.

10. **To install other items, repeat Steps 7 through 10.**

11. **When you finish installing programs, click the Quit button to close the interface.**

    You can eject the CD now. Carefully place it back in the plastic jacket of the book for safekeeping.

To run some of the programs on the *CCNA For Dummies* CD, you need to leave the CD in the CD-ROM drive.

What You'll Find on the CD

The following is a summary of the software included on this CD.

Dummies test prep tools

This CD contains questions related to CCNA Certification. The questions are similar to those you can expect to find on the exams. We've also included some questions on CCNA topics that may or not be on the current tests or even covered in the book, but you should know these things to perform your job.

QuickLearn Game

The QuickLearn Game is the *For Dummies* way of making studying for the Certification exam fun. Well, okay, less painful. OutPost is a DirectX, high-resolution, fast-paced arcade game.

Double-click Dxinstal.exe in the Directx folder on the CD, and it walks you through the installation. As part of the install, you must restart your computer.

Answer questions to defuse dimensional disrupters and save the universe from a rift in space-time. (The questions come from the same set of questions that the Self-Assessment and Practice Test use, but isn't this way more fun?) Missing a few questions on the real exam almost never results in a rip in the fabric of the universe, so just think how easy it will be when you get there!

Practice Test

The Practice Test is designed to help you get comfortable with the CCNA testing situation and pinpoint your strengths and weaknesses on the topic. You can accept the default setting of 60 questions in 60 minutes, or you can customize the settings. You can pick the number of questions, the amount of time, and even decide which objectives you want to focus on.

After you answer the questions, the Practice test gives you plenty of feedback. You can find out which questions you got right or wrong and get statistics on how you did, broken down by objective. Then you can review the questions — all of them, all the ones you missed, all the ones you marked, or a combination of the ones you marked and the ones you missed.

Self-Assessment Test

The Self-Assessment test is designed to simulate the actual CCNA testing situation. You must answer 60 questions in 60 minutes. After you answer all the questions, you find out your score and whether you pass or fail — but that's all the feedback you get. If you can pass the Self-Assessment test fairly easily, you're probably ready to tackle the real thing.

Links Page

I've also created a Links Page, a handy starting place for accessing the huge amounts of information about the CCNA tests on the Internet. You can find the page, `Links.htm`, in the root folder of the CD.

Commercial demos

IP Subnet Calculator

Windows 95, 98, NT, and 2000. Evaluation version.

The IP Subnet Calculator Release 3, from Net3 Group, Inc., is a handy utility that enables you to calculate information about IP addresses, including subnet and CIDR information. For more information, visit the web site at `www.net3group.com`.

AGNetTools for Windows

Windows 95, 98, and NT 4. Demo.

AGNetTools, from AG Group, Inc., is a menu-driven IP test utility. Using AGNetTools, you can calculate ping responses, find routes to specified servers, look up IP names and addresses, calculate throughput for Web pages and ftp servers, and scan for IP address names, ports, and services. For more information, visit the web site at `www.aggroup.com/`.

EtherPeek

Windows 95, 98, and NT 4. Demo.

EtherPeek, from AG Group, Inc., is a powerful network traffic and protocol analyzer for Ethernet networks. For more information, visit the Web site at `www.aggroup.com/`.

Note: To obtain a serial number that enables you to use EtherPeek, go to `www.aggroup.com`.

TokenPeek

Windows 95, 98, and NT 4. Demo.

Note: To obtain a serial number that enables you to use TokenPeek, go to `www.aggroup.com`.

TokenPeek, from AG Group, Inc., is a powerful network traffic and protocol analyzer for Token Ring networks. For more information, visit the web site at `www.aggroup.com/`.

If You've Got Problems (Of the CD Kind)

I tried my best to compile programs that work on most computers with the minimum system requirements. Alas, your computer may be somewhat different, and some programs may not work properly for some reason.

The two most likely culprits are that you don't have enough memory (RAM) for the programs you want to use, or that you have other programs running that are affecting installation or running of a program. If you get error messages such as `Not enough memory` or `Setup cannot continue`, try one or more of the following procedures and then try using the software again:

✔ **Turn off any antivirus software monitor that you may have running on your computer.** Installers sometimes mimic virus activity and may make your computer incorrectly believe that it is being infected by a virus.

✔ **Close all running programs.** The more programs you're running, the less memory is available to other programs. Installers also typically update files and programs; if you keep other programs running, installation may not work properly.

✔ **In Windows, close the CD interface and run demos or installations directly from Windows Explorer.** The interface itself can tie up system memory or even conflict with certain kinds of interactive demos. Use the Windows Explorer to browse the files on the CD and launch installers or demos.

✔ **Add more RAM to your computer.** This is, admittedly, a drastic and somewhat expensive step. However, if you have a Windows 95 or Windows 98 PC, adding more memory can really help the speed of your computer and enable more programs to run at the same time.

If you still have trouble installing the items from the CD, please call the nice people at Hungry Minds Customer Care, phone number 800-762-2974 (outside the U.S.: 317-572-3993), and they will help you solve your problems and continue your studies.

Appendix C

Glossary

• •

Access layer router: Routers on the Access layer direct network traffic to its destination and are used to segment LANs.

Access list: A table of entries used to permit or deny traffic through a router that consists of structured statements outlining what a router is to do with an incoming packet.

Active hub: Active hubs re-energize the signal before sending it on to its ports. Smart active hubs intelligently direct a signal to the port on which its destination exists.

Algorithm: The process used to determine the solution to a problem. In routing, algorithms are used to determine the best route for traffic to take to get to its intended destination.

Application layer: Layer 7 of the OSI Model. This layer defines services to application software.

ARP (Address Resolution Protocol): The protocol used to resolve physical addresses into network addresses.

ATP/NBP (AppleTalk Transaction Protocol/Name Binding Protocol): AppleTalk's data transport protocols.

Attenuation: The distance limit at which the electrical signal transmitted on a wire begins to weaken and is no longer recognizable.

Autonomous system: A network that operates under a single set of rules that may include one or more routing protocols.

Auxiliary password: This password is set to control access to the router on an auxiliary port.

Bandwidth: Maximum amount of data that can be transmitted over a network medium, expressed in bits-per-second.

Binary: A number system that uses two values (0 and 1) to represent numbers in positions representing increasing powers of 2.

Bootstrap: The bootstrap program finds a valid Cisco IOS image in the location specified by the router's configuration register and loads it to RAM.

BRI ISDN: This type of ISDN service consists of two 64 Kbps bearer (B) channels and one 15 Kbps data (D) channel for a combined bandwidth of 144 Kbps.

Bridge: A bridge, which is a Data Link layer (Layer 2) device, works with Layer 2 protocols and Layer 2 MAC sublayer addresses to forward messages within and outside of a network segment.

Bus topology: A fundamental network topology. Using this topology, network nodes are connected to a central cable, called a backbone, which runs the length of the network.

Cat 3: A 4-pair cable supporting bandwidth up to 10 Mbps. This cable is the minimum standard for 10BaseT networks. Wire category (cat) standards are developed by IEEE.

Cat 5: A 4-wire cable with bandwidth up to 100 Mbps, used for 100BaseTX and ATM (asynchronous transfer mode) networking.

CDP (Cisco Discovery Protocol): A proprietary Cisco protocol that is used to update information on a router about directly connected Cisco routers, bridges, and switches.

CHAP (Challenge Handshake Authentication Protocol): An inbound authentication method that allows a receiving device to initiate a challenge sequence, which is then modified by the requesting device before the connection can be established

Checksum: A form of error-checking where the one's complement is summed for all of the 16-bit words that make up a TCP segment or UDP datagram.

CIR (Committed Information Rate): The minimum bandwidth committed to a customer on a circuit.

Classless Interdomain Routing (CIDR): An addressing scheme that expresses the subnet network address in the form "/n," where "n" represents the number of bits in the network address.

Collision domain: A network segment on which networked devices share the same bandwidth and on which message collisions may occur.

Command Line Interface (CLI): The DOS-like user interface and prompt of Cisco routers.

Configuration mode: The command line mode that is used to manually configure a router or make changes to a router's status.

Configuration-register: The location from which the IOS software is to be loaded during the boot process is a hexadecimal value in the configuration-register.

Connectionless protocol: A connectionless protocol does not use a virtual circuit, or connection-oriented conduit, and no error-recovery functions are included.

Connection-oriented protocol: A protocol is considered connection-oriented if it meets one of two criteria: data is transmitted over a negotiated, established path, a virtual circuit, between two nodes, and the protocol includes a process for error-recovery.

Console password: This password is set to control access to the router through the console port.

Convergence: When all routers on a network have the same knowledge of the network, the network is said to have convergence.

Core layer router: Core layer routers are used to merge geographically separated networks. The focus of the core layer is on moving information as fast as possible, most often over dedicated or leased lines.

Cost: An arbitrary routing metric value assigned by the administrator for the crossing and intersection of networks.

CPE (Customer Premise Equipment): The equipment installed and operated from the customer end of a frame-relay circuit.

CRC (Cyclic Redundancy Check): A calculated amount that's used for error detection. It is placed into the Data Link trailer added to the message frame before it's sent to the Physical layer.

Cross-connect: The connection that interconnects the workstation cabling and the network cabling. A common method of creating network cross-connects is through a patch panel.

CSMA/CD (Carrier Sense Multiple Access/Collision Detection): The access method used on an Ethernet network.

Cut-through switching: This switching method begins to forward a frame as soon as the source and destination MAC addresses are read, typically within the first 12 bytes of an Ethernet frame.

Data Link layer: Layer 2 of the OSI Model. This layer defines the mechanisms used to move data about the network, including topology, such as Ethernet or Token Ring, and the ways in which data is reliably transmitted.

DCE (Data Communications Equipment): In a communications connection, DCE equipment is typically carrier-owned internetworking devices.

Default subnet mask: The default subnet mask for Class A IP addresses is 255.0.0.0. The default subnet mask for Class B IP addresses is 255.255.0.0. The default subnet mask for Class C IP addresses is 255.255.255.0.

Distance Vector: A distance vector routing protocol uses hop counts to determine the best route, views the network from its neighbors' perspective, and copies its routing table to neighboring routers. Examples of distance vector protocols are RIP, IPX RIP, and IGRP.

Distribution routers: Routers on the intermediate level (Distribution level). Distribution routers make the bulk of routing policy decisions and filter and forward packets to the other router layers.

DLCI (Data-Link Connection Identifier): A single circuit mapped to an outbound port that combines multiple virtual circuits.

DTE (Data Terminal Equipment): In a communications connection, DTE equipment typically consists of terminals, PCs, routers, and bridges that are owned by the customer.

Dynamic route: Dynamic routing enables a router to make route determinations using routing metrics and efficiencies. Any changes to the network are updated to the routing table automatically.

EIA/TIA wiring standards: The EIA/TIA 568 and 568B standards are the wiring standards used for network media. These two standards apply to the elements of LAN cabling, including telecommunications closets, equipment rooms, entrance facilities, work areas, backbone cabling, horizontal cabling.

EMI (Electromagnetic Interference): Interference generated by virtually all electrical devices that can cause interference and impair the signals of other devices. Also called electrical noise.

Enable Exec mode: Also called Privileged Exec mode, it is used to perform high-level testing and debugging, and updating or changing configuration files.

Enable password: This password is used when an Enable Secret password has not been set. It's also used for older router software versions.

Enable Secret password: This password adds a level of security over and above the Enable password.

Encapsulation: Also referred to as data encapsulation. The transformation process of data as it passes through the layers of the OSI Model.

Error detection: The process of detecting errors that occur during the transmission of the bits across a wire.

Ethernet: A network technology, defined in IEEE 802.3, that is the most popular networking technology for LANs. Ethernet networks are by definition built on a bus topology that operates on baseband rates of 10 Mbps, 100 Mbps, or 1,000 Mbps (1 Gbps).

FDDI (Fiber Distributed Data Interchange): an ANSI (American National Standards Institute) standard that defines a dual ring technology that operates at 100 Mbps over fiber optic cabling.

Flash: Router memory that holds the image and microcode of the router's operating system, which can be upgraded under software control, a process called *flashing.*

Flow control: Flow control meters the flow of data between network devices that may not be running at the same speeds.

Frame Relay: A Layer 2 technology optimized for high performance and efficient frame transmission. Frame Relay operates across serial interfaces and was designed specifically for use on fiber optic cables and digital networks.

FTP (File Transfer Protocol): A reliable, connection-oriented protocol used to copy files from one computer to another over a TCP/IP network.

Full-duplex: A transmission mode that allows communications to flow in two directions (from sender to receiver and from receiver to sender) of a session simultaneously. The PSTN (Public Switched Telephone Network) is an example of a full-duplex system.

Half-duplex: A transmission mode that transmits two directions (from sender to receiver and from receiver to sender), but only one way at a time. A citizens band (CB) radio is an example of a half-duplex system.

HDLC (High-Level Data Link Control): A standard that provides support for both point-to-point and multipoint services over synchronous serial data links and ISDN interfaces. HDLC is the default serial encapsulation method on Cisco routers

Hop Count: The number of routers a packet passes through to reach its destination.

Hostname: Every router on a network should have a unique identifying name. Cisco calls this name the hostname.

HSSI (High-Speed Serial Interface): A serial interface capable of transmitting data at more than 20 Kbps.

Hub: A hub is used to cluster workstations into a group. Hubs are either active or passive. When a hub receives a signal on one of its ports, it passes the signal on to all of its other ports.

ICMP (Internet Control Message Protocol): A Network layer protocol that's used for control and messaging services and carrying messages between systems regarding status, passing control codes, and delivering error codes.

IEEE 802.1Q: The 802.1 standard that defines VLAN information exchange between dissimilar manufacturers' equipment.

IEEE 802.2: This subcommittee of the IEEE 802 Project defines Logical Link Control (LLC) of the Data Link layer.

IEEE 802.3: This subcommittee of the IEEE 802 Project defines Ethernet and CSMA/CD.

IEEE 802.5: This subcommittee of the IEEE 802 Project defines logical ring topology, media, and interfaces (Token Ring).

IGRP (Interior Gateway Routing Protocol): A classful, distance-vector routing protocol very similar to RIP that must be identified to an autonomous system.

Infrastructure: all of a network's components, including its hardware, software, cabling, conceptual layout, and physical layout. The infrastructure of a network is its operating elements.

IP access list: There are two types of IP access lists: standard IP access lists that analyze the source IP address in a TCP/IP packet and then takes action to permit or deny the packet to pass through the router based on the outcome of its analysis, and extended IP access lists that permit or deny a packet using a variety of factors, including Source address, destination address, protocol, and port.

IP address classes: There are three usable IP address classes: Class A, Class B, and Class C. Two other IP address classes do exist, but they're set aside for special purposes. Each IP address class (A, B, and C) has a finite number of bits assigned to hold each of the network and host IDs.

IPX: A Novell proprietary protocol used by NetWare 4.x and earlier network operating systems.

IPX access list: Used to deny or permit a packet to the router using both the source and destination addresses.

IPX address: An address consisting of a 10-byte hexadecimal number that is made up of a 4-byte network number and a 6-byte node number.

IPX socket: A 16-bit number that's added to the end of the network and node addresses in the IPX header in the format of *network.node.socket*.

ISDN (Integrated Services Digital Network): A digital service capable of transmitting voice, data, and other source traffic over existing telephone lines. ISDN is available in two formats: PRI and BRI.

LAN (Local Area Network): A LAN supports data transfer on a physical infrastructure in a small, limited geographic area, such as within a single building or on a single floor of a building.

Latency: the delay introduced by network devices, such as a bridge, switch, or router, as they process packets.

Link State: Link State protocols use the shortest path algorithm to determine the best route and update the routing table using event-triggered updates and LSPs (Link State packets, a.k.a. "Hello" packets) sent to all neighboring network routers. Examples of link state protocols are NLSP, OSPF, and IS-IS.

LLC (Logical Link Control) sublayer: This sublayer of the Data Link layer creates connections between networked devices.

LMI (Local Management Interface): An interface type that enhances the Frame Relay protocol by adding the capability for internetworking devices to communicate with a Frame Relay network.

Logical address: An address that has a logical connection to all other addresses on its network, such as an IP address.

MAC (media access control) address: A MAC address is a 48-bit address made up of two parts: the manufacturer's ID number and a unique serialized number assigned to the device by its manufacturer.

MAC sublayer: The MAC sublayer of the Data Link layer provides a range of network services, including controlling access to the network and physical addressing.

MOTD (Message of the Day) banner: The banner message displayed when someone logs into the router.

NetBIOS/NetBEUI (Network Basic Input/Output System/NetBIOS extended User Interface): Microsoft's network protocols that work together to manage communications and provide data transport services.

NetWare Core Protocol (NCP): The Novell NetWare protocol that provides client-to-server connections and applications.

NetWare Link Services Protocol (NLSP): A link state routing protocol that is the default routing protocol on NetWare 4.11 and higher.

Network layer: The Network layer (Layer 3 of the OSI Model) is the layer on which routing takes place. This layer defines the processes used to route data across the network and the structure and use of logical addressing.

Novell Directory Service (NDS): Novell NetWare's directory services protocol.

NVRAM: A router memory type where the startup configuration file is stored.

Octet: An eight-bit binary number. IP addresses consist of four octets.

OSI Model (Open Systems Interconnection Reference Model): The OSI seven-layer model developed by the ISO (International Standards Organization) and released in 1984. The OSI model describes how information moves from one network to another.

PAP (Password Authentication Protocol): A challenge protocol used to verify username and password on a processing router.

Parity: An error-detection method. There are two types of parity used, odd-parity and even-parity. In either case, an extra bit is used to set the number of bits in a data block to either an even or add number.

Patch panel: A termination point for network cables. A patch cord is used to interconnect each port on the patch panel.

PDU (Protocol Data Unit): The package of data that moves through the OSI layers. A PDU has several forms as it moves (see encapsulation).

Physical address: A network address that has no relationship to any other address on a network, such as a Layer 2 MAC address.

Physical layer: Layer 1 of the OSI Model. This layer defines the electrical and physical specifications for the networking media that carry the data bits across a network.

PING (Packet Internet Groper): This command is used to verify Layer 3 connectivity. PING sends out ICMP messages to verify both the logical addresses and the physical connection.

Port: A logical connection that allows the incoming data to be assigned to a particular application or service for processing. Each port is assigned a *port number,* which is a way to identify the specific process to which the message is to be passed. See also Well-known port.

POTS (Plain Old Telephone System): The common public telephone system, also see PSTN.

POST: The router POST process checks the CPU, memory, and the interface ports to ensure they are present and operational.

PPP (Point-to-Point Protocol): A protocol used for router-to-router and host-to-network communications over synchronous and asynchronous circuits, including HSSI and ISDN interfaces

Presentation layer: Layer 6 of the OSI Model. This layer is concerned with data representation and code formatting. Data formatting, such as ASCII, EBCDIC, and encryption are supported on this layer.

PRI ISDN: An ISDN PRI line consists of 23 64 Kbps bearer (B) channels and one 16 Kbps data (D) channel.

Privileged Exec mode: see Enable Exec mode.

Protocol: A set of rules that defines how two devices communicate with one another and the format of the packets used to transmit data over communications lines.

PSTN (Public Switched Telephone Network): The common telephone system.

PVC (Permanent Virtual Circuit): A type of X.25 virtual circuit that is permanent, dedicated, and continuous.

RAM: Router memory where active program and operating system instructions, the running configuration file, and routing tables are stored.

RARP (Reverse ARP): The protocol used to resolve network addresses into physical addresses.

Repeater: A repeater is a device used on a network to solve attenuation problems in cable wire. A repeater cleans up the signal, gives it a boost, and sends it on its way.

RFI (Radio Frequency Interference): Devices that broadcast wireless or radio signals can produce interference through radio wave transmissions picked up by other electrical devices, which is the cause of EMI.

Ring topology: a fundamental topology. Using this topology, the primary network cable is installed as a loop, or ring, and the workstations are attached to the primary cable at points on the ring.

RIP (Routing Information Protocol): A classful, distance-vector routing protocol that uses information provided by neighboring routers to maintain the cost, in terms of hops and other metrics, of a particular route.

ROM: The router's read-only memory where the POST, bootstrap, and startup/power-up utilities, as well as a limited version of the Cisco IOS, is stored.

Route poisoning: a.k.a. poison reverse routing. This technique, which is used to avoid routing loops, assigns the maximum hop count plus one to the hop count metric of any route not available.

Routed protocol: Routed protocols are used to carry end-user traffic across the internetwork. Examples of routed protocols are IP and IPX.

Routing: The process of moving data along a path from a source to a destination.

Routing loop: A condition caused when routing tables are not updated accurately at the same time and erroneous route information is used. Also called Count to Infinity routing loops. A maximum hop count variable on the router is used to avoid routing loops.

Routing protocol: A routing protocol is used to pass messages between routers for maintaining and updating routing tables. Examples of routing protocols are RIP, IGRP, OSPF, and EIGRP.

Routing table: A routing table is stored in the RAM of a bridge or router and stores message addresses for later use in forwarding messages to those addresses.

RTS/CTS (Ready To Send/Clear to Send): This is also called hardware flow control. RTS/CTS uses two wires in a cable, one for RTS and one for CTS. The sending device uses the RTS signal to indicate when it's ready to send. The receiving device uses the CTS to indicate it's ready to receive. When either is turned off, the flow is interrupted.

Running configuration: The configuration in the router's RAM when it is operating.

SAP (Service Advertisement Protocol): A Novell NetWare protocol that is used to advertise (update) the services available over the network.

Segment: A subnetwork on a network created by the insertion of a router, switch, or bridge. Segments are created to increase bandwidth efficiency, reduce congestion, and create smaller collision domains.

Segmentation: Dividing a network into segments decreases congestion and reduces the chance of message collisions by creating smaller collision domains.

Session: A series of related connection-oriented transmissions between network nodes.

Session layer: The Session layer (Layer 5 of the OSI Model) establishes, maintains, and manages the communication session between computers.

Setup mode: The command line mode used to set the configuration of a router.

Spanning Tree Protocol: A bridging protocol that designates interfaces to be in Forwarding or Blocking State. In Blocking State, only special packets reporting the status of other bridges on the network are allowed through. In Forwarding State all packets are allowed to pass.

SPID (Service Profile Identifier): The number assigned by an ISDN service provider to each B channel of a BRI ISDN line.

Split horizon: A technique used to prevent bad routing information from being sent back to its source.

SPX (Sequence Package Exchange): A Novell NetWare protocol that provides connection-oriented packet delivery.

Star topology: Each workstation connects directly to a central device with its own cable, creating a starburst-like pattern.

Star-bus topology: A hub or switch is used as a clustering device that is then attached to the network backbone. This is a common topology of Ethernet networks.

Star-ring topology: A multistation access unit (MAU) clusters workstations and is connected to the next MAU on the network to create a ring structure.

Startup configuration: The configuration file loaded from NVRAM during startup. Contrasts to running configuration.

Static route: A router entry that is configured manually and by the network administrator for a network address for which only a single route is desired.

Store-and-forward switching: This switching method reads the entire frame into its buffer before forwarding it. This type of switching results in variable-length latency.

STP (Shielded twisted-pair): STP has its wires wrapped in a copper or foil shield to help reduce EMI and RFI interference, which makes it more expensive than UTP wire. STP is common in Token Ring networks.

Subinterface: Each of the virtual circuits on a single serial interface is a subinterface. There are two types of subinterfaces: point-to-point and multipoint.

Subnet mask: A binary bit pattern of ones and zeroes that is applied to an IP address to extract the network ID and Host ID portions of the address.

Subnetting: The standard address class structure is expanded by borrowing bits from the host portion to provide more bits for the network portion of the address.

SVC (Switched Virtual Circuit): A temporary virtual circuit that is created especially for, and exists only for, the duration of a X.25 data communications session.

Switch: A Layer 2 device used to move data to its destination with capabilities ranging from a smart hub to those virtually the same as a router.

TCP (Transmission Control Protocol): The TCP/IP protocol that provides connection-oriented, reliable delivery of packets.

TCP/IP (Transmission Control Protocol/Internet Protocol): A protocol suite of interconnected and interworking protocols that provide for reliable and efficient data communications across an internetwork.

Telnet: A terminal emulation protocol used on TCP/IP-based networks to remotely log onto a remote device to run a program or manipulate data.

TFTP (Trivial File Transfer Protocol): A best-effort file transfer protocol used by Cisco routers to store and retrieve configuration files from a TFTP server.

Token Ring: Token Ring networks, defined in IEEE 802.5, are laid out in a loop that starts and ends at the same node, forming a ring network that operates at either 4 Mbps or 16 Mbps.

Topology: The physical layout of the network.

Trace: a.k.a. traceroute. This command tests the route from a source to a destination by sending out probe packets one at a time to each router or switch in the path and then displays the round-trip time for each packet.

Transport layer: Layer 4 of the OSI Model. This layer defines the functions that provide for the reliable transmission of data segments, as well as the disassembly and assembly of the data before and after transmission.

TTL (Time to Live): A routing variable that indicates the remaining number of hops a packet can take before being expired.

Twisted-pair (TP) wire: Twisted-pair wire comes in two types: unshielded (UTP) and shielded (STP).

UDP (User Datagram Protocol): The TCP/IP best-effort protocol that isn't concerned with the reliable delivery of packets and doesn't bother with overhead such as acknowledgments.

User Exec mode: The command line mode available immediately after logging into a router. It is used to connect to other devices, perform simple tests, and display system information.

UTP (Unshielded twisted-pair): The most common type of cabling used in networks. UTP is commonly referred to as 10BaseT Ethernet cable.

Virtual circuit (VC): a.k.a. virtual circuit number (VCN), logical channel number (LCN), and virtual channel identifier (VCI). A VC can be a permanent virtual circuit (PVC) or a switched virtual circuit (SVC).

Virtual Terminal (vty) password: This password is set to restrict access to the router using a Telnet session. Unless this password, also known as the vty password, is set, you cannot Telnet into the router.

VLAN (Virtual LAN): A logical grouping of networked nodes that communicate directly with each other on Layers 2 and 3.

WAN (Wide Area Network): A WAN is a network that interconnects LANs and across a broad geographic area. A WAN uses a data transmission technology provided by a common carrier.

Well-known ports: Ports in the range of 0 through 1023 that are used only by system processes or privileged programs. Well-known ports are generally TCP ports but can be registered to UDP services as well.

Wildcard mask: This mask is used with access lists to filter specific IP addresses or groups of IP addresses by including a zero in a position to be checked and a one in positions to be ignored.

Windowing: A flow control method that establishes a window that allows a certain number of packets to be transmitted before an acknowledgment must be sent.

X.25: A packet-switched networking protocol for exchanging data over a connection-oriented service.

XON/XOFF: This roughly stands for transmission on/transmission off, and is also called software flow control. The sending device sends data until the receiving device signals with a control character to stop so that the receiving device can catch up. When the receiving device is ready to go, it signals the sending device to restart the transmission.

Index

• *Q* •

• *R* •

• *S* •

• *X* •

• *Z* •

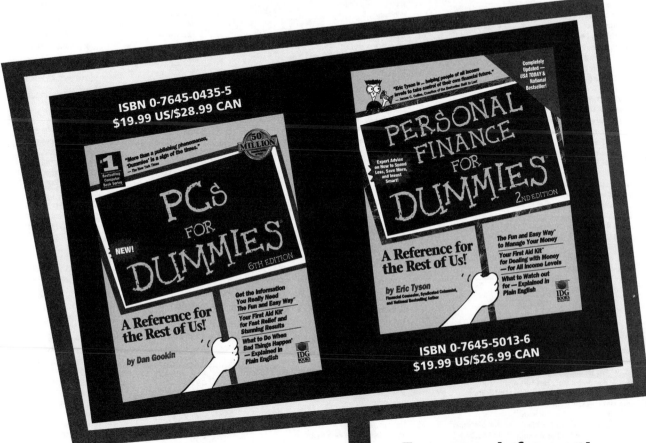

From PCs to Personal Finance, We Make it Fun and Easy!

ISBN 0-7645-0435-5
$19.99 US/$28.99 CAN

ISBN 0-7645-5013-6
$19.99 US/$26.99 CAN

For more information, or to order, please call 800.762.2974.

www.hungryminds.com
www.dummies.com

Dummies Books™
Bestsellers on Every Topic!

GENERAL INTEREST TITLES

BUSINESS & PERSONAL FINANCE

Title	Author	ISBN	Price
Accounting For Dummies®	John A. Tracy, CPA	0-7645-5014-4	$19.99 US/$27.99 CAN
Business Plans For Dummies®	Paul Tiffany, Ph.D. & Steven D. Peterson, Ph.D.	1-56884-868-4	$19.99 US/$27.99 CAN
Business Writing For Dummies®	Sheryl Lindsell-Roberts	0-7645-5134-5	$16.99 US/$27.99 CAN
Consulting For Dummies®	Bob Nelson & Peter Economy	0-7645-5034-9	$19.99 US/$27.99 CAN
Customer Service For Dummies®, 2nd Edition	Karen Leland & Keith Bailey	0-7645-5209-0	$19.99 US/$27.99 CAN
Franchising For Dummies®	Dave Thomas & Michael Seid	0-7645-5160-4	$19.99 US/$27.99 CAN
Getting Results For Dummies®	Mark H. McCormack	0-7645-5205-8	$19.99 US/$27.99 CAN
Home Buying For Dummies®	Eric Tyson, MBA & Ray Brown	1-56884-385-2	$16.99 US/$24.99 CAN
House Selling For Dummies®	Eric Tyson, MBA & Ray Brown	0-7645-5038-1	$16.99 US/$24.99 CAN
Human Resources Kit For Dummies®	Max Messmer	0-7645-5131-0	$19.99 US/$27.99 CAN
Investing For Dummies®, 2nd Edition	Eric Tyson, MBA	0-7645-5162-0	$19.99 US/$27.99 CAN
Law For Dummies®	John Ventura	1-56884-860-9	$19.99 US/$27.99 CAN
Leadership For Dummies®	Marshall Loeb & Steven Kindel	0-7645-5176-0	$19.99 US/$27.99 CAN
Managing For Dummies®	Bob Nelson & Peter Economy	1-56884-858-7	$19.99 US/$27.99 CAN
Marketing For Dummies®	Alexander Hiam	1-56884-699-1	$19.99 US/$27.99 CAN
Mutual Funds For Dummies®, 2nd Edition	Eric Tyson, MBA	0-7645-5112-4	$19.99 US/$27.99 CAN
Negotiating For Dummies®	Michael C. Donaldson & Mimi Donaldson	1-56884-867-6	$19.99 US/$27.99 CAN
Personal Finance For Dummies®, 3rd Edition	Eric Tyson, MBA	0-7645-5231-7	$19.99 US/$27.99 CAN
Personal Finance For Dummies® For Canadians, 2nd Edition	Eric Tyson, MBA & Tony Martin	0-7645-5123-X	$19.99 US/$27.99 CAN
Public Speaking For Dummies®	Malcolm Kushner	0-7645-5159-0	$16.99 US/$24.99 CAN
Sales Closing For Dummies®	Tom Hopkins	0-7645-5063-2	$14.99 US/$21.99 CAN
Sales Prospecting For Dummies®	Tom Hopkins	0-7645-5066-7	$14.99 US/$21.99 CAN
Selling For Dummies®	Tom Hopkins	1-56884-389-5	$16.99 US/$24.99 CAN
Small Business For Dummies®	Eric Tyson, MBA & Jim Schell	0-7645-5094-2	$19.99 US/$27.99 CAN
Small Business Kit For Dummies®	Richard D. Harroch	0-7645-5093-4	$24.99 US/$34.99 CAN
Taxes 2001 For Dummies®	Eric Tyson & David J. Silverman	0-7645-5306-2	$15.99 US/$23.99 CAN
Time Management For Dummies®, 2nd Edition	Jeffrey J. Mayer	0-7645-5145-0	$19.99 US/$27.99 CAN
Writing Business Letters For Dummies®	Sheryl Lindsell-Roberts	0-7645-5207-4	$16.99 US/$24.99 CAN

TECHNOLOGY TITLES

INTERNET/ONLINE

Title	Author	ISBN	Price
America Online® For Dummies®, 6th Edition	John Kaufeld	0-7645-0670-6	$19.99 US/$27.99 CAN
Banking Online Dummies®	Paul Murphy	0-7645-0458-4	$24.99 US/$34.99 CAN
eBay™ For Dummies®, 2nd Edition	Marcia Collier, Roland Woerner, & Stephanie Becker	0-7645-0761-3	$19.99 US/$27.99 CAN
E-Mail For Dummies®, 2nd Edition	John R. Levine, Carol Baroudi, & Arnold Reinhold	0-7645-0131-3	$24.99 US/$34.99 CAN
Genealogy Online For Dummies®, 2nd Edition	Matthew L. Helm & April Leah Helm	0-7645-0543-2	$24.99 US/$34.99 CAN
Internet Directory For Dummies®, 3rd Edition	Brad Hill	0-7645-0558-2	$24.99 US/$34.99 CAN
Internet Auctions For Dummies®	Greg Holden	0-7645-0578-9	$24.99 US/$34.99 CAN
Internet Explorer 5.5 For Windows® For Dummies®	Doug Lowe	0-7645-0738-9	$19.99 US/$28.99 CAN
Researching Online For Dummies®, 2nd Edition	Mary Ellen Bates & Reva Basch	0-7645-0546-7	$24.99 US/$34.99 CAN
Job Searching Online For Dummies®	Pam Dixon	0-7645-0673-0	$24.99 US/$34.99 CAN
Investing Online For Dummies®, 3rd Edition	Kathleen Sindell, Ph.D.	0-7645-0725-7	$24.99 US/$34.99 CAN
Travel Planning Online For Dummies®, 2nd Edition	Noah Vadnai	0-7645-0438-X	$24.99 US/$34.99 CAN
Internet Searching For Dummies®	Brad Hill	0-7645-0478-9	$24.99 US/$34.99 CAN
Yahoo!® For Dummies®, 2nd Edition	Brad Hill	0-7645-0762-1	$19.99 US/$27.99 CAN
The Internet For Dummies®, 7th Edition	John R. Levine, Carol Baroudi, & Arnold Reinhold	0-7645-0674-9	$19.99 US/$27.99 CAN

OPERATING SYSTEMS

Title	Author	ISBN	Price
DOS For Dummies®, 3rd Edition	Dan Gookin	0-7645-0361-8	$19.99 US/$27.99 CAN
GNOME For Linux® For Dummies®	David B. Busch	0-7645-0650-1	$24.99 US/$37.99 CAN
LINUX® For Dummies®, 2nd Edition	John Hall, Craig Witherspoon, & Coletta Witherspoon	0-7645-0421-5	$24.99 US/$34.99 CAN
Mac® OS 9 For Dummies®	Bob LeVitus	0-7645-0652-8	$19.99 US/$28.99 CAN
Red Hat® Linux® For Dummies®	Jon "maddog" Hall, Paul Sery	0-7645-0663-3	$24.99 US/$37.99 CAN
Small Business Windows® 98 For Dummies®	Stephen Nelson	0-7645-0425-8	$24.99 US/$34.99 CAN
UNIX® For Dummies®, 4th Edition	John R. Levine & Margaret Levine Young	0-7645-0419-3	$19.99 US/$27.99 CAN
Windows® 95 For Dummies®, 2nd Edition	Andy Rathbone	0-7645-0180-1	$19.99 US/$27.99 CAN
Windows® 98 For Dummies®	Andy Rathbone	0-7645-0261-1	$19.99 US/$27.99 CAN
Windows® 2000 For Dummies®	Andy Rathbone	0-7645-0641-2	$19.99 US/$27.99 CAN
Windows® 2000 Server For Dummies®	Ed Tittel	0-7645-0341-3	$24.99 US/$37.99 CAN
Windows® ME Millennium Edition For Dummies®	Andy Rathbone	0-7645-0735-4	$19.99 US/$27.99 CAN

Dummies Books™
Bestsellers on Every Topic!

GENERAL INTEREST TITLES

FOOD & BEVERAGE/ENTERTAINING

Title	Author	ISBN	Price
Bartending For Dummies®	Ray Foley	0-7645-5051-9	$14.99 US/$21.99 CAN
Cooking For Dummies®, 2nd Edition	Bryan Miller & Marie Rama	0-7645-5250-3	$19.99 US/$27.99 CAN
Entertaining For Dummies®	Suzanne Williamson with Linda Smith	0-7645-5027-6	$19.99 US/$27.99 CAN
Gourmet Cooking For Dummies®	Charlie Trotter	0-7645-5029-2	$19.99 US/$27.99 CAN
Grilling For Dummies®	Marie Rama & John Mariani	0-7645-5076-4	$19.99 US/$27.99 CAN
Italian Cooking For Dummies®	Cesare Casella & Jack Bishop	0-7645-5098-5	$19.99 US/$27.99 CAN
Mexican Cooking For Dummies®	Mary Sue Miliken & Susan Feniger	0-7645-5169-8	$19.99 US/$27.99 CAN
Quick & Healthy Cooking For Dummies®	Lynn Fischer	0-7645-5214-7	$19.99 US/$27.99 CAN
Wine For Dummies®, 2nd Edition	Ed McCarthy & Mary Ewing-Mulligan	0-7645-5114-0	$19.99 US/$27.99 CAN
Chinese Cooking For Dummies®	Martin Yan	0-7645-5247-3	$19.99 US/$27.99 CAN
Etiquette For Dummies®	Sue Fox	0-7645-5170-1	$19.99 US/$27.99 CAN

SPORTS

Title	Author	ISBN	Price
Baseball For Dummies®, 2nd Edition	Joe Morgan with Richard Lally	0-7645-5234-1	$19.99 US/$27.99 CAN
Golf For Dummies®, 2nd Edition	Gary McCord	0-7645-5146-9	$19.99 US/$27.99 CAN
Fly Fishing For Dummies®	Peter Kaminsky	0-7645-5073-X	$19.99 US/$27.99 CAN
Football For Dummies®	Howie Long with John Czarnecki	0-7645-5054-3	$19.99 US/$27.99 CAN
Hockey For Dummies®	John Davidson with John Steinbreder	0-7645-5045-4	$19.99 US/$27.99 CAN
NASCAR For Dummies®	Mark Martin	0-7645-5219-8	$19.99 US/$27.99 CAN
Tennis For Dummies®	Patrick McEnroe with Peter Bodo	0-7645-5087-X	$19.99 US/$27.99 CAN
Soccer For Dummies®	U.S. Soccer Federation & Michael Lewiss	0-7645-5229-5	$19.99 US/$27.99 CAN

HOME & GARDEN

Title	Author	ISBN	Price
Annuals For Dummies®	Bill Marken & NGA	0-7645-5056-X	$16.99 US/$24.99 CAN
Container Gardening For Dummies®	Bill Marken & NGA	0-7645-5057-8	$16.99 US/$24.99 CAN
Decks & Patios For Dummies®	Robert J. Beckstrom & NGA	0-7645-5075-6	$16.99 US/$24.99 CAN
Flowering Bulbs For Dummies®	Judy Glattstein & NGA	0-7645-5103-5	$16.99 US/$24.99 CAN
Gardening For Dummies®, 2nd Edition	Michael MacCaskey & NGA	0-7645-5130-2	$16.99 US/$24.99 CAN
Herb Gardening For Dummies®	NGA	0-7645-5200-7	$16.99 US/$24.99 CAN
Home Improvement For Dummies®	Gene & Katie Hamilton & the Editors of HouseNet, Inc.	0-7645-5005-5	$19.99 US/$26.99 CAN
Houseplants For Dummies®	Larry Hodgson & NGA	0-7645-5102-7	$16.99 US/$24.99 CAN
Painting and Wallpapering For Dummies®	Gene Hamilton	0-7645-5150-7	$16.99 US/$24.99 CAN
Perennials For Dummies®	Marcia Tatroe & NGA	0-7645-5030-6	$16.99 US/$24.99 CAN
Roses For Dummies®, 2nd Edition	Lance Walheim	0-7645-5202-3	$16.99 US/$24.99 CAN
Trees and Shrubs For Dummies®	Ann Whitman & NGA	0-7645-5203-1	$16.99 US/$24.99 CAN
Vegetable Gardening For Dummies®	Charlie Nardozzi & NGA	0-7645-5129-9	$16.99 US/$24.99 CAN
Home Cooking For Dummies®	Patricia Hart McMillan & Katharine Kaye McMillan	0-7645-5107-8	$19.99 US/$27.99 CAN

TECHNOLOGY TITLES

WEB DESIGN & PUBLISHING

Title	Author	ISBN	Price
Active Server Pages For Dummies®, 2nd Edition	Bill Hatfield	0-7645-0603-X	$24.99 US/$37.99 CAN
Cold Fusion 4 For Dummies®	Alexis Gutzman	0-7645-0604-8	$24.99 US/$37.99 CAN
Creating Web Pages For Dummies®, 5th Edition	Bud Smith & Arthur Bebak	0-7645-0733-8	$24.99 US/$34.99 CAN
Dreamweaver™ 3 For Dummies®	Janine Warner & Paul Vachier	0-7645-0669-2	$24.99 US/$34.99 CAN
FrontPage® 2000 For Dummies®	Asha Dornfest	0-7645-0423-1	$24.99 US/$34.99 CAN
HTML 4 For Dummies®, 3rd Edition	Ed Tittel & Natanya Dits	0-7645-0572-6	$24.99 US/$34.99 CAN
Java™ For Dummies®, 3rd Edition	Aaron E. Walsh	0-7645-0417-7	$24.99 US/$34.99 CAN
PageMill™ 2 For Dummies®	Deke McClelland & John San Filippo	0-7645-0028-7	$24.99 US/$34.99 CAN
XML™ For Dummies®	Ed Tittel	0-7645-0692-7	$24.99 US/$37.99 CAN
Javascript For Dummies®, 3rd Edition	Emily Vander Veer	0-7645-0633-1	$24.99 US/$37.99 CAN

DESKTOP PUBLISHING GRAPHICS/MULTIMEDIA

Title	Author	ISBN	Price
Adobe® In Design™ For Dummies®	Deke McClelland	0-7645-0599-8	$19.99 US/$27.99 CAN
CorelDRAW™ 9 For Dummies®	Deke McClelland	0-7645-0523-8	$19.99 US/$27.99 CAN
Desktop Publishing and Design For Dummies®	Roger C. Parker	1-56884-234-1	$19.99 US/$27.99 CAN
Digital Photography For Dummies®, 3rd Edition	Julie Adair King	0-7645-0646-3	$24.99 US/$37.99 CAN
Microsoft® Publisher 98 For Dummies®	Jim McCarter	0-7645-0395-2	$19.99 US/$27.99 CAN
Visio 2000 For Dummies®	Debbie Walkowski	0-7645-0635-8	$19.99 US/$27.99 CAN
Microsoft® Publisher 2000 For Dummies®	Jim McCarter	0-7645-0525-4	$19.99 US/$27.99 CAN
Windows® Movie Maker For Dummies®	Keith Underdahl	0-7645-0749-1	$19.99 US/$27.99 CAN

Dummies Books™
Bestsellers on Every Topic!

GENERAL INTEREST TITLES

EDUCATION & TEST PREPARATION

Title	Author	ISBN	Price
The ACT For Dummies®	Suzee Vlk	1-56884-387-9	$14.99 US/$21.99 CAN
College Financial Aid For Dummies®	Dr. Herm Davis & Joyce Lain Kennedy	0-7645-5049-7	$19.99 US/$27.99 CAN
College Planning For Dummies®, 2nd Edition	Pat Ordovensky	0-7645-5048-9	$19.99 US/$27.99 CAN
Everyday Math For Dummies®	Charles Seiter, Ph.D.	1-56884-248-1	$14.99 US/$21.99 CAN
The GMAT® For Dummies®, 3rd Edition	Suzee Vlk	0-7645-5082-9	$16.99 US/$24.99 CAN
The GRE® For Dummies®, 3rd Edition	Suzee Vlk	0-7645-5083-7	$16.99 US/$24.99 CAN
Politics For Dummies®	Ann DeLaney	1-56884-381-X	$19.99 US/$27.99 CAN
The SAT I For Dummies®, 3rd Edition	Suzee Vlk	0-7645-5044-6	$14.99 US/$21.99 CAN

AUTOMOTIVE

Title	Author	ISBN	Price
Auto Repair For Dummies®	Deanna Sclar	0-7645-5089-6	$19.99 US/$27.99 CAN
Buying A Car For Dummies®	Deanna Sclar	0-7645-5091-8	$16.99 US/$24.99 CAN

LIFESTYLE/SELF-HELP

Title	Author	ISBN	Price
Dating For Dummies®	Dr. Joy Browne	0-7645-5072-1	$19.99 US/$27.99 CAN
Making Marriage Work For Dummies®	Steven Simring, M.D. & Sue Klavans Simring, D.S.W	0-7645-5173-6	$19.99 US/$27.99 CAN
Parenting For Dummies®	Sandra H. Gookin	1-56884-383-6	$16.99 US/$24.99 CAN
Success For Dummies®	Zig Ziglar	0-7645-5061-6	$19.99 US/$27.99 CAN
Weddings For Dummies®	Marcy Blum & Laura Fisher Kaiser	0-7645-5055-1	$19.99 US/$27.99 CAN

TECHNOLOGY TITLES

SUITES

Title	Author	ISBN	Price
Microsoft® Office 2000 For Windows® For Dummies®	Wallace Wang & Roger C. Parker	0-7645-0452-5	$19.99 US/$27.99 CAN
Microsoft® Office 2000 For Windows® For Dummies® Quick Reference	Doug Lowe & Bjoern Hartsfvang	0-7645-0453-3	$12.99 US/$17.99 CAN
Microsoft® Office 97 For Windows® For Dummies®	Wallace Wang & Roger C. Parker	0-7645-0050-3	$19.99 US/$27.99 CAN
Microsoft® Office 97 For Windows® For Dummies® Quick Reference	Doug Lowe	0-7645-0062-7	$12.99 US/$17.99 CAN
Microsoft® Office 98 For Macs® For Dummies®	Tom Negrino	0-7645-0229-8	$19.99 US/$27.99 CAN
Microsoft® Office X For Macs For Dummies®	Tom Negrino	0-7645-0702-8	$19.95 US/$27.99 CAN

WORD PROCESSING

Title	Author	ISBN	Price
Word 2000 For Windows® For Dummies® Quick Reference	Peter Weverka	0-7645-0449-5	$12.99 US/$19.99 CAN
Corel® WordPerfect® 8 For Windows® For Dummies®	Margaret Levine Young, David Kay & Jordan Young	0-7645-0186-0	$19.99 US/$27.99 CAN
Word 2000 For Windows® For Dummies®	Dan Gookin	0-7645-0448-7	$19.99 US/$27.99 CAN
Word For Windows® 95 For Dummies®	Dan Gookin	1-56884-932-X	$19.99 US/$27.99 CAN
Word 97 For Windows® For Dummies®	Dan Gookin	0-7645-0052-X	$19.99 US/$27.99 CAN
WordPerfect® 9 For Windows® For Dummies®	Margaret Levine Young	0-7645-0427-4	$19.99 US/$27.99 CAN
WordPerfect® 7 For Windows® 95 For Dummies®	Margaret Levine Young & David Kay	1-56884-949-4	$19.99 US/$27.99 CAN

SPREADSHEET/FINANCE/PROJECT MANAGEMENT

Title	Author	ISBN	Price
Excel For Windows® 95 For Dummies®	Greg Harvey	1-56884-930-3	$19.99 US/$27.99 CAN
Excel 2000 For Windows® For Dummies®	Greg Harvey	0-7645-0446-0	$19.99 US/$27.99 CAN
Excel 2000 For Windows® For Dummies® Quick Reference	John Walkenbach	0-7645-0447-9	$12.99 US/$17.99 CAN
Microsoft® Money 99 For Dummies®	Peter Weverka	0-7645-0433-9	$19.99 US/$27.99 CAN
Microsoft® Project 98 For Dummies®	Martin Doucette	0-7645-0321-9	$24.99 US/$34.99 CAN
Microsoft® Project 2000 For Dummies®	Martin Doucette	0-7645-0517-3	$24.99 US/$37.99 CAN
Microsoft® Money 2000 For Dummies®	Peter Weverka	0-7645-0579-3	$19.99 US/$27.99 CAN
MORE Excel 97 For Windows® For Dummies®	Greg Harvey	0-7645-0138-0	$22.99 US/$32.99 CAN
Quicken® 2000 For Dummies®	Stephen L. Nelson	0-7645-0607-2	$19.99 US/$27.99 CAN
Quicken® 2001 For Dummies®	Stephen L. Nelson	0-7645-0759-1	$19.99 US/$27.99 CAN
Quickbooks® 2000 For Dummies®	Stephen L. Nelson	0-7645-0665-x	$19.99 US/$27.99 CAN

Dummies Books™
Bestsellers on Every Topic!

GENERAL INTEREST TITLES

CAREERS

Cover Letters For Dummies®, 2nd Edition	Joyce Lain Kennedy	0-7645-5224-4	$12.99 US/$17.99 CAN
Cool Careers For Dummies®	Marty Nemko, Paul Edwards, & Sarah Edwards	0-7645-5095-0	$16.99 US/$24.99 CAN
Job Hunting For Dummies®, 2nd Edition	Max Messmer	0-7645-5163-9	$19.99 US/$26.99 CAN
Job Interviews For Dummies®, 2nd Edition	Joyce Lain Kennedy	0-7645-5225-2	$12.99 US/$17.99 CAN
Resumes For Dummies®, 2nd Edition	Joyce Lain Kennedy	0-7645-5113-2	$12.99 US/$17.99 CAN

FITNESS

Fitness Walking For Dummies®	Liz Neporent	0-7645-5192-2	$19.99 US/$27.99 CAN
Fitness For Dummies®, 2nd Edition	Suzanne Schlosberg & Liz Neporent	0-7645-5167-1	$19.99 US/$27.99 CAN
Nutrition For Dummies®, 2nd Edition	Carol Ann Rinzler	0-7645-5180-9	$19.99 US/$27.99 CAN
Running For Dummies®	Florence "Flo-Jo" Griffith Joyner & John Hanc	0-7645-5096-9	$19.99 US/$27.99 CAN

FOREIGN LANGUAGE

Spanish For Dummies®	Susana Wald	0-7645-5194-9	$24.99 US/$34.99 CAN
French For Dummies®	Dodi-Kartrin Schmidt & Michelle W. Willams	0-7645-5193-0	$24.99 US/$34.99 CAN

TECHNOLOGY TITLES

DATABASE

Access 2000 For Windows® For Dummies®	John Kaufeld	0-7645-0444-4	$19.99 US/$27.99 CAN
Access 97 For Windows® For Dummies®	John Kaufeld	0-7645-0048-1	$19.99 US/$27.99 CAN
Access 2000 For Windows For Dummies® Quick Reference	Alison Barrons	0-7645-0445-2	$12.99 US/$17.99 CAN
Approach® 97 For Windows® For Dummies®	Deborah S. Ray & Eric J. Ray	0-7645-0001-5	$19.99 US/$27.99 CAN
Crystal Reports 8 For Dummies®	Douglas J. Wolf	0-7645-0642-0	$24.99 US/$34.99 CAN
Data Warehousing For Dummies®	Alan R. Simon	0-7645-0170-4	$24.99 US/$34.99 CAN
FileMaker® Pro 4 For Dummies®	Tom Maremaa	0-7645-0210-7	$19.99 US/$27.99 CAN

NETWORKING/GROUPWARE

ATM For Dummies®	Cathy Gadecki & Christine Heckart	0-7645-0065-1	$24.99 US/$34.99 CAN
Client/Server Computing For Dummies®, 3rd Edition	Doug Lowe	0-7645-0476-2	$24.99 US/$34.99 CAN
DSL For Dummies®, 2nd Edition	David Angell	0-7645-0715-X	$24.99 US/$35.99 CAN
Lotus Notes® Release 4 For Dummies®	Stephen Londergan & Pat Freeland	1-56884-934-6	$19.99 US/$27.99 CAN
Microsoft® Outlook® 98 For Windows® For Dummies®	Bill Dyszel	0-7645-0393-6	$19.99 US/$28.99 CAN
Microsoft® Outlook® 2000 For Windows® For Dummies®	Bill Dyszel	0-7645-0471-1	$19.99 US/$27.99 CAN
Migrating to Windows® 2000 For Dummies®	Leonard Sterns	0-7645-0459-2	$24.99 US/$37.99 CAN
Networking For Dummies®, 4th Edition	Doug Lowe	0-7645-0498-3	$19.99 US/$27.99 CAN
Networking Home PCs For Dummies®	Kathy Ivens	0-7645-0491-6	$24.99 US/$35.99 CAN
Upgrading & Fixing Networks For Dummies®, 2nd Edition	Bill Camarda	0-7645-0542-4	$29.99 US/$42.99 CAN
TCP/IP For Dummies®, 4th Edition	Candace Leiden & Marshall Wilensky	0-7645-0726-5	$24.99 US/$35.99 CAN
Windows NT® Networking For Dummies®	Ed Tittel, Mary Madden, & Earl Follis	0-7645-0015-5	$24.99 US/$34.99 CAN

PROGRAMMING

Active Server Pages For Dummies®, 2nd Edition	Bill Hatfield	0-7645-0065-1	$24.99 US/$34.99 CAN
Beginning Programming For Dummies®	Wally Wang	0-7645-0596-0	$19.99 US/$29.99 CAN
C++ For Dummies® Quick Reference, 2nd Edition	Namir Shammas	0-7645-0390-1	$14.99 US/$21.99 CAN
Java™ Programming For Dummies®, 3rd Edition	David & Donald Koosis	0-7645-0388-X	$29.99 US/$42.99 CAN
JBuilder™ For Dummies®	Barry A. Burd	0-7645-0567-X	$24.99 US/$34.99 CAN
VBA For Dummies®, 2nd Edition	Steve Cummings	0-7645-0078-3	$24.99 US/$37.99 CAN
Windows® 2000 Programming For Dummies®	Richard Simon	0-7645-0469-X	$24.99 US/$37.99 CAN
XML For Dummies®, 2nd Edition	Ed Tittel	0-7645-0692-7	$24.99 US/$37.99 CAN

Hungry Minds, Inc., End-User License Agreement

READ THIS. You should carefully read these terms and conditions before opening the software packet(s) included with this book ("Book"). This is a license agreement ("Agreement") between you and Hungry Minds, Inc. ("HMI"). By opening the accompanying software packet(s), you acknowledge that you have read and accept the following terms and conditions. If you do not agree and do not want to be bound by such terms and conditions, promptly return the Book and the unopened software packet(s) to the place you obtained them for a full refund.

1. **License Grant.** HMI grants to you (either an individual or entity) a nonexclusive license to use one copy of the enclosed software program(s) (collectively, the "Software") solely for your own personal or business purposes on a single computer (whether a standard computer or a workstation component of a multi-user network). The Software is in use on a computer when it is loaded into temporary memory (RAM) or installed into permanent memory (hard disk, CD-ROM, or other storage device). HMI reserves all rights not expressly granted herein.

2. **Ownership.** HMI is the owner of all right, title, and interest, including copyright, in and to the compilation of the Software recorded on the disk(s) or CD-ROM ("Software Media"). Copyright to the individual programs recorded on the Software Media is owned by the author or other authorized copyright owner of each program. Ownership of the Software and all proprietary rights relating thereto remain with HMI and its licensers.

3. **Restrictions On Use and Transfer.**

   (a) You may only (i) make one copy of the Software for backup or archival purposes, or (ii) transfer the Software to a single hard disk, provided that you keep the original for backup or archival purposes. You may not (i) rent or lease the Software, (ii) copy or reproduce the Software through a LAN or other network system or through any computer subscriber system or bulletin-board system, or (iii) modify, adapt, or create derivative works based on the Software.

   (b) You may not reverse engineer, decompile, or disassemble the Software. You may transfer the Software and user documentation on a permanent basis, provided that the transferee agrees to accept the terms and conditions of this Agreement and you retain no copies. If the Software is an update or has been updated, any transfer must include the most recent update and all prior versions.

4. **Restrictions on Use of Individual Programs.** You must follow the individual requirements and restrictions detailed for each individual program in Appendix B of this Book. These limitations are also contained in the individual license agreements recorded on the Software Media. These limitations may include a requirement that after using the program for a specified period of time, the user must pay a registration fee or discontinue use. By opening the Software packet(s), you will be agreeing to abide by the licenses and restrictions for these individual programs that are detailed in Appendix B and on the Software Media. None of the material on this Software Media or listed in this Book may ever be redistributed, in original or modified form, for commercial purposes.

5. **Limited Warranty.**

(a) HMI warrants that the Software and Software Media are free from defects in materials and workmanship under normal use for a period of sixty (60) days from the date of purchase of this Book. If HMI receives notification within the warranty period of defects in materials or workmanship, HMI will replace the defective Software Media.

(b) **HMI AND THE AUTHOR OF THE BOOK DISCLAIM ALL OTHER WARRANTIES, EXPRESS OR IMPLIED, INCLUDING WITHOUT LIMITATION IMPLIED WARRANTIES OF MERCHANTABILITY AND FITNESS FOR A PARTICULAR PURPOSE, WITH RESPECT TO THE SOFTWARE, THE PROGRAMS, THE SOURCE CODE CONTAINED THEREIN, AND/OR THE TECHNIQUES DESCRIBED IN THIS BOOK. HMI DOES NOT WARRANT THAT THE FUNCTIONS CONTAINED IN THE SOFTWARE WILL MEET YOUR REQUIRE-MENTS OR THAT THE OPERATION OF THE SOFTWARE WILL BE ERROR FREE.**

(c) This limited warranty gives you specific legal rights, and you may have other rights that vary from jurisdiction to jurisdiction.

6. **Remedies.**

(a) HMI's entire liability and your exclusive remedy for defects in materials and workman-ship shall be limited to replacement of the Software Media, which may be returned to HMI with a copy of your receipt at the following address: Software Media Fulfillment Department, Attn.: *CCNA For Dummies,* Hungry Minds, Inc., 10475 Crosspoint Blvd., Indianapolis, IN 46256, or call 1-800-762-2974. Please allow four to six weeks for delivery. This Limited Warranty is void if failure of the Software Media has resulted from accident, abuse, or misapplication. Any replacement Software Media will be warranted for the remainder of the original warranty period or thirty (30) days, whichever is longer.

(b) In no event shall HMI or the author be liable for any damages whatsoever (including without limitation damages for loss of business profits, business interruption, loss of business information, or any other pecuniary loss) arising from the use of or inability to use the Book or the Software, even if HMI has been advised of the possibility of such damages.

(c) Because some jurisdictions do not allow the exclusion or limitation of liability for conse-quential or incidental damages, the above limitation or exclusion may not apply to you.

7. **U.S. Government Restricted Rights.** Use, duplication, or disclosure of the Software for or on behalf of the United States of America, its agencies and/or instrumentalities (the "U.S. Government") is subject to restrictions as stated in paragraph (c)(1)(ii) of the Rights in Technical Data and Computer Software clause of DFARS 252.227-7013, and in subparagraphs (a) through (d) of the Commercial Computer—Restricted Rights clause at FAR 52.227-19, and in similar clauses in the NASA FAR supplement, as applicable.

8. **General.** This Agreement constitutes the entire understanding of the parties and revokes and supersedes all prior agreements, oral or written, between them and may not be modified or amended except in a writing signed by both parties hereto that specifically refers to this Agreement. This Agreement shall take precedence over any other documents that may be in conflict herewith. If any one or more provisions contained in this Agreement are held by any court or tribunal to be invalid, illegal, or otherwise unenforceable, each and every other pro-vision shall remain in full force and effect.

Installation Instructions

For complete details about the contents of the CD, see Appendix B. To install the items from the CD to your hard drive using Microsoft Windows, follow these steps:

1. **Insert the CD into your computer's CD-ROM drive.**

2. **Click Start⇨Run.**

3. **In the dialog box that appears, type** D:/setup.exe **and then click OK.**

   If your CD-ROM drive uses a different letter, type the appropriate letter in the Run dialog box.

4. **Read through the license agreement that appears, and then click the Accept button if you want to use the CD.**

5. **Click anywhere on the Welcome screen that appears to enter the interface.**

   The next screen lists categories for the software on the CD.

6. **To view the items within a category, just click the category's name.**

7. **For more information about a program, click the program's name.**

8. **If you don't want to install the program, click the Go Back button to return to the previous screen.**

   You can always return to the previous screen by clicking the Go Back button. This feature enables you to browse the different categories and products and decide what you want to install.

9. **To install a program, click the appropriate Install button.**

10. **To install other items, repeat Steps 7 through 10.**

11. **When you finish installing programs, click the Quit button to close the interface.**

    You can eject the CD now. Carefully place it back in the plastic jacket of the book for safekeeping.

To run some of the programs on the CD, you need to leave the CD in the CD-ROM drive.

FOR DUMMIES
BOOK REGISTRATION

Register This Book and Win!

We want to hear from you!

Visit **dummies.com** to register this book and tell us how you liked it!

- ✔ Get entered in our monthly prize giveaway.

- ✔ Give us feedback about this book — tell us what you like best, what you like least, or maybe what you'd like to ask the author and us to change!

- ✔ Let us know any other *For Dummies* topics that interest you.

Your feedback helps us determine what books to publish, tells us what coverage to add as we revise our books, and lets us know whether we're meeting your needs as a *For Dummies* reader. You're our most valuable resource, and what you have to say is important to us!

Not on the Web yet? It's easy to get started with *Dummies 101: The Internet For Windows 98* or *The Internet For Dummies* at local retailers everywhere.

Or let us know what you think by sending us a letter at the following address:

For Dummies Book Registration
Dummies Press
10475 Crosspoint Blvd.
Indianapolis, IN 46256

…FOR DUMMIES ™

BESTSELLING BOOK SERIES